A WORLD BANK COUNTRY STUDY

Decentralization, Democracy, and Development

Recent Experience from Sierra Leone

Edited by Yongmei Zhou

THE WORLD BANK
Washington, D.C.

ISBN-13: 978-0-8213-7999-8
eISBN: 978-0-8213-8001-7
ISSN: 0253-2123   DOI: 10.1596/978-0-8213-7999-8

Library of Congress Cataloging-in-Publication Data has been requested.

Contents

3. Administrative Decentralization: Building the Non-Financial Capacity of Local Governments 28

Alhassan Kanu

4. Decentralization in Practice... 60

Katherine Whiteside Casey

Tables

Figures

Boxes

Foreword

In 2004, the government of Sierra Leone opted for a rethink of its national governance arrangement by embarking on the resuscitation of democratically elected local government after 32 years experimenting with central government appointed district and municipal governments. The decision by the government and the people of Sierra Leone was driven by a primary consideration to address the country's seeming non-performance in the areas of citizens' participation in governance and responding to the needs of citizens as it relates to attainment of the Millennium Development Goals (MDGs) as well as ensuring poverty reduction in the country.

The process of reintroducing the current and ongoing National Decentralization Program in the country assumed a partnership model involving the government of Sierra Leone, development partners and a host of national nonstate actors, especially civil society organizations. The path that was taken involved consultations and consensus building among the stakeholders on the design, structures and systems which culminated in the development of a comprehensive legislation—the Local Government Act (2004).

Since the commencement of the implementation of the "big bang" approach to the Decentralization Program in Sierra Leone, there has been a well planned mechanism for advancing the process in the political, administrative, functional, and fiscal areas. There has been a record of marked results, in particular, establishment of 19 local government entities in the country; two consecutive local government elections conducted in 2004 and 2008; and facilitation of a comprehensive national devolution program leading to core functions and responsibilities in health, education and agriculture being devolved to the local authorities with the attendant fiscal resources to assume and execute such responsibilities.

There are successes associated with the reintroduction of the National Decentralization Program but the reform has also had to contend with a number of critical challenges such as weak human resource base at the level of the local authorities, ineffective revenue mobilization efforts by local councils, and the existence of conflicting legislations which tend to impede smooth implementation of the decentralization program.

The National Decentralization Program is now in phase two of implementation (2008–2012). This phase will pose a number of critical paths for the government and people of Sierra Leone. There is the critical and urgent need for the legal and regulatory environment to be enhanced by the government. The ongoing public sector reform process will therefore focus on the human resource requirements of local councils, capacity building for local councils in revenue mobilization, and strengthening financial management. In order to achieve these objectives in the second phase, the government of Sierra Leone will need to demonstrate even greater support for the process through increased commitment in the governance and fiscal areas of the program. The government remains committed to ensuring that the National Decentralization Program is accorded the necessary attention. There is strong conviction in the reform's capacity to deliver positive dividends leading to improvement in citizens' lives across the country while accelerating the government's attainment of its overarching objectives of poverty reduction and inevitably attaining the MDGs, and promoting overall national development.

This publication is the sum total of efforts from the country's development partners and the corps of Sierra Leonean professionals who have worked on program design, implementation, monitoring and evaluation. I will be amiss in my duty if I fail to extend my government's thanks and appreciation to all the partners and our Sierra Leonean compatriots for all the good work done to date. I once more reaffirm that the government of Sierra Leone remains firmly committed to ensuring that the Decentralization Program as a flagship reform is supported and sustained so that it will continue to serve as our major engine for all inclusive national growth and development.

Dr. Samura M.W. Kamara
Minister of Finance and Economic Development
Sierra Leone

Editor and Contributors

YONGMEI ZHOU is Senior Institutional Development Specialist in the Sustainable Development Department at the South Asia Region of the World Bank. After receiving her Ph.D. from the University of California at Berkeley in 1999, she has been working in the World Bank on governance and public sector reform issues in Ghana, Nigeria, Sierra Leone, Bangladesh, and India. She was the World Bank Team Leader for the Institutional Reform and Capacity Building Project that supported Government of Sierra Leone's decentralization reform.

KATHERINE WHITESIDE CASEY has been working on a variety of research projects in Sierra Leone in collaboration with the Institutional Reform and Capacity Building Project and the Jameel Poverty Action Lab at the Massachusetts Institute of Technology since 2004. Prior to that, she worked as a consultant to the World Bank on research projects in Madagascar, Indonesia, and the Comoros. She holds an M.A. in Public Policy from Harvard University and expects to complete a Ph.D. in Economics at Brown University in 2010.

ELIZABETH FOSTER is Evaluation Officer for the Institutional Reform and Capacity Building Project since 2006. She coordinated design and implementation of surveys for tracking and evaluation program impact. After completing an undergraduate degree in math from Harvard University, Ms. Foster worked as a Peace Corps volunteer in Burkina Faso and gained an M.A. in Public Administration from the Woodrow Wilson School at Princeton University.

EMMANUEL A.R. GAIMA is Director of the Decentralization Secretariat in the Ministry of Internal Affairs, Local Government, and Rural Development of the Government of Sierra Leone. A political scientist by training, he started his career as a Lecturer in the Faculty of Social Studies and Law at Fourah Bay College, University of Sierra Leone. He subsequently worked for the United Nations Development Program as Program Manager of its Peace and Development Initiative (PDI) and a Governance Program Specialist.

RACHEL GLENNERSTER is Executive Director of the Abdul Latif Jameel Poverty Action Lab (J-PAL), a center in the economics department at the Massachusetts Institute of Technology devoted to fighting poverty by ensuring that poverty policy is based on scientific evidence. Her research includes randomized evaluations of health and education in India, girls' empowerment in Bangladesh, and community-driven development in Sierra Leone. She oversees J-PAL's work to translate research findings into policy action and helped establish Deworm the World of which she is a board member. She sits on the UK government's Department for International Development's Independent Advisory Committee on Development Impact. Before joining J-PAL, Rachel Glennerster worked on debt relief and the reform of the international monetary system at the International Monetary Fund, and financial regulation at the Harvard Institute for International Development and the UK Treasury. In the mid 1990s she was part of the UK delegation to the IMF and World Bank. She has a Ph.D. in economics from Birkbeck College, University of London.

ALHASSAN KANU is Program Manager at the Decentralization Secretariat in the Ministry of Internal Affairs, Local Government, and Rural Development of the Government of Sierra Leone. A development planning and management specialist by training, he has worked on decentralization and local government development issues in Ghana and Sierra Leone. Previously, he was the Capacity Building Manager at the Decentralization Secretariat. He holds an M.Sc. in Agriculture, Njala University College, University of Sierra Leone, and an M.Sc. in Development Planning and Management, jointly awarded by Kwame Nkrumah University of Science and Technology, Kumasi, Ghana, and the University of Dortmund, Germany.

ADAMS KARGBO is Senior Economist in the Local Government Finance Department, Ministry of Finance and Economic Development of the Government of Sierra Leone. His responsibilities cover interministerial and intergovernmental relations, budgeting and resource distribution. Prior to this, he was an economist in the Economic Policy and Research Unit in the Ministry of Finance. He holds a M.Sc. in Economics from Njala University College, University of Sierra Leone.

RYANN ELIZABETH MANNING moved to Sierra Leone in March 2006 to manage the World Bank's Justice for the Poor program, and is now the Coordinator of the Welbodi Partnership, which supports pediatric healthcare in Sierra Leone. She previously served as the Associate Director of the Center for Universal Education at the Council on Foreign Relations, and worked on HIV/AIDS issues for the University of Natal in Durban, South Africa. She has an M.A. in Public Policy from the Kennedy School of Government at Harvard University, and an A.B. from the Woodrow Wilson School of Public and International Affairs at Princeton University.

YE ZHANG is Assistant Professor of Economics at the Indiana University-Purdue University Indianapolis since 2007. From 2005–2008, he was consultant for the World Bank. He received his Ph.D. in Economics from University of Maryland in 2007.

Acknowledgments

This volume documents four years of reform efforts by a large number of people in Sierra Leone. It is their dedication and commitment to a better future for Sierra Leone that inspired our work. Special thanks go to Osho Coker, who was instrumental in bringing the project preparation to fruition and has continued to support the reform process in his various capacities. Minister J.B. Dauda, Finance Minister between 2003–06, and Dr. Samura Kamara, Finance Secretary until 2007, were critical in driving the fiscal decentralization process. Peter Kaindaneh, IRCBP Project Coordinator during 2004–08, was the glue who kept the project team together and made sure the team members were empowered to achieve their goals. Winston Cole, Head of the Public Financial Management Reform Unit in the Ministry of Finance, was an outstanding manager and professional and led a team who relentlessly monitored and trained national and local government officials in financial management. Ousman Barrie, Sheku Bangura, and Mike Dauda successively shouldered the responsibility of leading the Local Government Finance Department staff, without whose hard work fiscal decentralization would have remained merely policy intentions. So many people have spent the last few years of their careers working in the rural districts and in the Decentralization House at 38 Wellington Street, Freetown. We benefited tremendously from their collaboration and friendship.

The IRCBP team also benefited from technical assistance and advice from a number of select consultants. Some became part of the extended IRCBP family. Robert Searle, former CEO of the Australia Commonwealth Grants Commission, is one of them. His wisdom and love of sharing made him not only a valued advisor to the Local Government Finance Department but also "Uncle Bob" for the young economists there.

The World Bank team has received strong support and guidance from the management, especially three successive Country Directors, Peter Harrold, Mats Karlsson, and Ishac Diwan. Jim Sackey, Engilbert Gudmundsson, Doug Addison, Laura Rose, Vivek Srivastava, Nicola Smithers, Anand Rajaram, Helga Muller, Brian Levy, Vijayendra Rao, Robert Chase, Scott Guggenheim, and Mark Goldstein have generously provided critiques and advice. Alicia Hetzner was the language editor. Sujata Pradhan and Madeleine Chungkong provided valuable assistance in this process.

Abbreviations and Acronyms

CURRENCY EQUIVALENTS
(Exchange Rate Effective February 28, 2004)
Leone 2,998 = US$1

FISCAL YEAR
January 1–December 31

APC	All People's Congress
AWP	Annual Work Plan
BBC	British Broadcasting Co.
CA	Chief Administrator
CAS	Country Assessment Strategy
CGG	Campaign for Good Governance
CLoGPAS	Comprehensive Local Government Performance Assessment System
CSO	Civil society organization
DecSec	Decentralization Secretariat
DO	District Office
DP	Development partner
ECOMOG	Economic Community of West African States Monitoring Group
ENCISS	Enhancing the Interaction and Interface between Civil Society and the State to Enhance Poor People's Lives
EPRU	Economic Policy and Research Unit
EU	European Union
FCC	Freetown City Council
GRS	Governance Reform Secretariat
HDI	Human Development Index (UN)
HPP	Health and Population Project
HRM	Human resource management
IDA	International Development Agency
IMC	Inter-Ministerial Committee on Local Government and Decentralization
INGO	International nongovernmental organization
IPAM	Institute of Public Administration and Management
IRCBP	Institutional Reform and Capacity Building Project
ISM	Implementation Support Mission
IVS	Inland valley swamp
JP4/LG	Justice for the Poor and Understanding Processes of Change in Local Governance projects
JSDF	Japan Social Development Fund
JSDP	Justice Sector Development Program
LC	Local council
LG	Local government
LGA	Local Government Act
LGDG	Local Government Development Grant
LGDGP	Local Government Development Grant Program
LGFC	Local Government Finance Committee
LGFD	Local Government Finance Department
LGSC	Local Government Service Commission

LoCASL	Local Council Association of Sierra Leone
LoCoSA	Local Council Staff Association
M&E	Monitoring and evaluation
MAFS	Ministry of Agriculture and Food Security
MC	Minimum condition
MDAs	Ministries, departments, and agencies
MDG	Millennium Development Goal
MEST	Ministry of Education, Science and Technology
MEYS	Ministry of Education, Youth and Sports
MIALGRD	Ministry of Internal Affairs, Local Government, and Rural Development
MIS	Management information systems
MLGCD	Ministry of Local Government and Community Development
MoF	Ministry of Finance
MoFED	Ministry of Finance and Economic Development
MTEF	Medium-Term Expenditure Framework
NA	Native administration (courts)
NaCSA	National Commission for Social Action
NEC	National Electoral Commission
NGO	Nongovernmental organization
NHS	National Household Survey
NPS	National Public Services (survey)
NPRC	National Provisional Ruling Council
O&M	Operations and maintenance
PETS	Public Expenditure Tracking Study
PFMRU	Public Financial Management Reform Unit (IRCBP, MoF)
PHU	Peripheral health unit
PIU	Project implementation unit
PM	Performance measure
PMC	Project management committee
PMDC	People's Movement for Democratic Change
PPF	Project Preparation Facility
PRS	Poverty reduction strategy
PSMS	Public Sector Management Support Project
QPR	Quarterly Progress Report
RCBSC	Regional Capacity Building Support Coordinators
RRA	Rapid Results Approach
RRI	Rapid Result Initiative
SALWACO	Sierra Leone Water Company
SLPP	Sierra Leone People's Party
SSL	Statistics Sierra Leone
TLM	Teaching and learning materials
TOT	Training of trainers
TSC	Technical Steering Committee
TSP	Training Service Providers
UNDP	United Nations Development Program
VDC	Village Development Committee
WC	Ward committee

Introduction

Yongmei Zhou

This book is a retrospective of the decentralization reform process in Sierra Leone from 2003–07. During this period, the Government of Sierra Leone (GoSL) re-established elected district and urban councils across the country, transferred certain responsibilities for primary services and local investment and some financial resources to the new councils, and invested heavily in building the administrative infrastructure and capacity of the local councils. The authors are partners who were intimately involved in the reform. Through recording various aspects of the process and reflecting on our observations and learning during that time, we hope to contribute to the debates on the merits and risks of decentralization in general and its desirability and viability in post-conflict countries.

Literature on Decentralization and Post-Conflict State-Building

This book contributes to two strands of literature. The first concerns the impact of decentralization on government effectiveness. The second debates whether decentralization is a desirable and viable component of the state-building efforts of a post-conflict country.

The literature on the impact of decentralization on government effectiveness is strong in theory and weak in empirics. Bardhan (2002) provides an excellent review of theoretical arguments for and against decentralization. The primary argument for local government (rather than a higher-level government) to perform a certain function is efficiency, that is, local governments are closer to citizens, hence are more informed of local preferences and can more efficiently respond to them. A second efficiency argument derives from the assumption that mobile citizens and businesses in search of better public services and infrastructure create competitive pressure among local governments and improve their performance.

The most obvious arguments against local governments performing a certain function are externality and economy of scale. A third contention is that local government may suffer from human resource constraints, especially in poor rural areas and poor countries, so may not be able to execute certain functions.

Which level of government can better perform a function also depends on the relative degree of elite capture and corruption at different levels of government. The theoretical models cannot predict the outcome. It depends on these variables: local inequality, literacy, national and local media strength, and civic activism.[1]

Whether transferring authority to a lower-level government is desirable depends on the strength of these efficiency, externality, capacity, and accountability arguments in the particular context.

In addition, the actual impact of decentralization depends on how it is implemented. High-performance organizations require clear authority; adequate autonomy, financial, and human resources; and unambiguous accountability. Local governments are no exception. Hence, the decentralization of authority without adequate financial and human resources will only set up local governments to fail. Bahl (1999) lays out several best practices.

The question of whether decentralization improves government effectiveness does not lend itself to analysis. All depends on the nature of the decentralization process. Meaningful empirical research must first define what was decentralized and how decentralization was carried out. Meaningful empirical research also needs to define the context within which decentralization took place and identify key factors that made it a success or a failure. Such empirical work is scarce. This book is a contribution to this literature.

A small literature on post-conflict state building examines whether decentralization helps prevent conflict, accelerate reconstruction and recovery, and build state legitimacy. Sharing power and resources among previously warring regional forces may reduce regional tensions and keep the country together. This sharing of power and resources has been the main driving force of decentralization in Bosnia, Ethiopia, Herzegovina, and Sudan. Whether this strategy succeeds depends on whether the sharing arrangement is perceived by all stakeholders as fair and transparent.

In some countries, governmental failure to provide minimum security and well-being was the fundamental cause of armed uprising. In these cases, the rapid recovery of public services after the war can be particularly important to re-establish government legitimacy. Government also may choose to decentralize certain functions if the efficiency argument for local government is particularly strong.

Additional challenges in post-conflict countries make decentralization a riskier proposal. Most post-conflict countries suffer severe shortage of human resources. Decentralization can be seen as a distraction from the core task of consolidating central government control, especially the urgent need to strengthen the police force and to get control of revenue collection and fiscal and monetary policies. Local governments usually have difficulty competing with central government or other private sector and nongovernmental organizations in the labor market. Thus, even if the central government decides to transfer functions and funds to local government, the latter may not have qualified staff to perform these functions.

Skeptics also pointed out that some post-conflict countries' decentralization was not sustainable. The reason was that it sometimes was initiated under pressure from influential external actors in the peace process, who had a preference for political pluralism and popular participation. Cambodia is a case in point. It had committed to decentralization on paper but did not transfer much power or fiscal resource to local government (Blunt and Turner 2005).

Literature on the actual decentralization experience of post-conflict countries and World Bank support is limited. Some internal World Bank analyses of the motivation behind decentralization and design of the decentralization framework exist for

Ethiopia, Sudan, and Uganda. "The World Bank's Experience with Post-Conflict Reconstruction" hardly mentioned decentralization.[2] In 2004 the Africa Region's "Findings" #241 reviewed the World Bank Transition Assistance Strategies approved during 2000–02 for 9 post-conflict countries and found that only in Sierra Leone had the World Bank supported decentralization. The article suggested evaluating various approaches to post-conflict reconstruction and understanding whether it was by design or by default that priorities had not been given to capacity building in strengthening policymaking, promoting administrative decentralization, improving HRM, and making the civil service more responsive to citizens. Four years later, the World Bank Independent Evaluation Group (IEG) Report (2008) reviewed World Bank support for decentralization efforts in 20 client countries during 1990–2007. Only two cases were post-conflict countries: Sierra Leone and Uganda, both of which had received strong support from the World Bank. The present analysis of Sierra Leone's decentralization process and the World Bank support for it will fill a gap in this literature.

Brief Background on Sierra Leone

Sierra Leone is a small country in West Africa with approximately 5 million people and 71,740 square kilometers (sq km) of land area. It is infamous for its brutal civil war from 1991 to 2002 and for "blood diamonds," which are believed to have fueled the conflict.

Sierra Leone has had a tragic history since independence in 1961. After two Sierra Leone People's Party (SLPP) prime ministers in the initial years after Independence, the All People's Congress (APC) ruled the country for 25 years (1967–92). During this period, multiparty democracy was replaced by single-party hegemony that had little tolerance for dissent. In 1972 elected local councils were abolished, and power was centralized in the hands of elites in Freetown. Rampant corruption and collapse of government services led to widespread deprivation and distrust of government (Reno 1995). By the end of the 1980s, Sierra Leone was the second poorest country in the world (UNDP 1993). When a small group of rebels entered from Liberia in 1991, they found easy recruits among angry youth who were hungry and had no education and little voice in a society controlled by thugs in the cities and authoritative chiefs in the countryside (Keen 2005, Richards 1996, Humphreys and Weinstein 2008). It took heavy military interventions by ECOMOG (Economic Community of West African States Monitoring Group) and Britain to end the war 11 years later.

When peace was finally declared in 2002, Sierra Leone once again ranked second worst in the UN Human Development Index (HDI). Infant mortality was 166 (of 1000), under-5 mortality was 284 (of 1000), life expectancy was 37, and adult literacy was 36 percent.[3] Regional inequality was highly visible. The Sierra Leone Integrated Household Survey of 2002–03 showed that, using the absolute poverty line of Le 786,204 (roughly US$260) per year, nearly 80 percent of rural population fell below this poverty line, in contrast to 28 percent in Freetown and 63 percent in other urban areas. The road network was severely damaged in the war, which made it all the more difficult to reach remote areas.

Britain and multilateral agencies under the United Nations UK played a highly visible role in peace-making and peace-keeping (Thompson 2007). Demobilization was accompanied by immediate efforts to professionalize the military and the Ministry of

Defense. The World Bank managed a multi-donor trust fund that financed the demobilization. The Bank also supported immediate recovery and reconstruction through a series of community-driven development (CDD) projects.

Unfolding Sierra Leone's Decentralization in the Context of Post-Conflict State-Building

The post-conflict recovery process was as much about re-establishing state capacity and legitimacy as it is about rebuilding livelihoods and assets. Following the exodus of professionals during the war, Sierra Leone was left with a thin labor market and a public sector inadequate to deal with its overwhelming tasks (World Bank 2003). When Sierra Leone emerged from war in 2002, government effectiveness ranked near bottom in the world (Kaufmann, Kraay, and Mastruzzi 2006).

GoSL prioritized strengthening government economic management capacity, especially in revenue collection and macroeconomic management. Financial and technical assistance to strengthen the Presidency, Ministry of Finance, central bank, and National Revenue Authority was sought from the World Bank, DfID, EC, and AfDB. The World Bank responded with two Public Sector Management Support Projects. More than two dozen senior economic management positions were filled with contract staff, some of whom had returned to the country from abroad. MoF filled nearly entire departments such as the Budget Bureau and the Economic Policy and Research Unit (EPRU) with contract staff. Thus, in effect, the ministry had 2 streams of employees and 2 work cultures.

Significant effort was made to increase spending for primary services, especially education, health, and agriculture. However, MoF and the donor agencies were dismayed by the pervasive leakage of resources, which was documented in the annual Public Expenditure Tracking Studies (PETS) conducted by EPRU of MoF. PETS 2002 found that less than 10 percent of essential drugs said to be delivered at the central government level could be verified by district medical officers (DMOs) and less than 5 percent could be verified by peripheral health units. Only 72 percent of teaching and learning materials had reached the intended schools from District Education Officers, and arrived on average 170 days later than required. Only 8 percent of centrally distributed free seed rice had reached the farmers before planting season. Thirty-five percent had reached them during the planting season, and 57 percent had reached them only after the planting season. It was clear to MoF that something must be done to reduce the leakage of resource between the center and the frontline. Partly out of frustration with the slow progress in reforming a centralized and corrupt public financial management system, MoF became an unusual champion of fiscal decentralization.

Re-establishing elected district and urban councils was part of the Kabbah government's commitment. It also was part of the Framework for Peace, Recovery and Development developed at the Paris Consultative Group meeting in 2002. The key rationale behind the framework was to address two fundamental causes of the war: exclusion and deprivation of the rural masses. Political decentralization was seen as a way to re-energize local leadership across the country and open space for popular participation. The older generation of the SLPP leadership, including President Ahmad Tejan Kabbah, was nostalgic about the days when district councils had managed schools and clinics and maintained roads. Some of these leaders reminisced about the scholarships that they had received from their district councils. After his youth, President Kabbah had served as a district commissioner.

At the same time, the SLPP leadership was protective of the existing chieftancy system. It had been the predominant governance system in the countryside since 1972, when elected local councils had been abolished. Each of the 149 chiefdoms in the country was headed by a paramount chief elected by an electoral college of male taxpayers. Candidacy for a paramount chief post was restricted to members of the "ruling families," a privilege defined by the erstwhile British colonial administration. The paramount chief was aided by a chiefdom council, which consisted of 1 representative for every 20 taxpayers. Below the paramount chief, section chiefs headed section chiefdoms, and village chiefs headed villages. The chiefdom administration dispensed law and order and local justice functions through chiefdom police and local courts as well as informal dispute resolution facilitated by the chiefs. The chiefdom administration had power in raising local revenue, which typically includes head tax, market dues, mining royalty, and fines imposed by the local court.

As in the colonial times, the chieftancy system remained a tool for indirect rule by the state authority in the capital city. In exchange for loyalty and political control in the countryside, the state allowed the chiefdom administration to indulge in arbitrary and unaccountable governance practices. Much of the exploitation of the people by the chiefs had related to their prerogative to identify those who were indigenous to the chiefdom (indigenes) and guarantee their rights to local residence, land use, and political and legal representation (Fanthorpe and others 2002). Local courts operated on the basis of uncodified customary law and often made arbitrary rulings and imposed fines that did not match the crimes. Young people, especially young migrants, in the countryside suffered the most from the authoritarian and abusive rule of some chiefs (Richards and others 2004). During the war, more than 60 paramount chiefs died, either as victims of war or by natural causes. Most other paramount chiefs were in exile in Freetown.

After the war, GoSL requested financial support from DfID to build houses for the chiefs. The rationale behind this Paramount Chief Restoration Project was that facilitating the return of the paramount chiefs to their chiefdoms would encourage the return of refugees and also would restore the lowest tier of government in the interior (Fanthorpe and others 2002). Given that the earlier poor practices of chiefdom governance had caused resentment in the youth, DfID put pressure on GoSL to initiate chiefdom reform. Public consultations were held in dozens of localities. The consultations elicited a strong demand for democratic reform rather than the abolition of the chiefdom system (Fanthorpe 2005b). In fact, average citizens in the countryside saw the chiefs as the single most important authority, even though they criticized the autocracy and abuses of some chiefs. The Paramount Chief Restoration Project was renamed the Chiefdom Reform Project.

Soon after being elected with an overwhelming majority in May 2002, the Kabbah government decided to *re-establish* elected local councils. The Ministry of Local Government and Community Development (MLGCD) organized national consultations to gauge popular opinions on how local council elections should be run. There was an overwhelming preference for nonpartisan elections that reflected deep suspicions of party control of local politics. During the same period, a Task Force on

Decentralization, nominally chaired by the vice president but in reality presided over by the Minister of MLGCD, was working at full steam. A contract legal draftsman recorded the bits and pieces of policy decisions that were reached during these free-flowing but chaotic deliberations. DfID, UNDP, and the World Bank provided some consultants at this stage to facilitate discussions on a number of key policy issues that thus far had been neglected by the task force. These dealt primarily with intergovernmental fiscal relations and accountability arrangements.

The Local Government Act (LGA) enacted in March 2004 mandated a qualitatively different framework of intergovernmental relations from the one that existed during the pre-1972 period (Tangri 1998). Local councils now are required to operate under democratic principles: open about council business, prudent in financial management, and responsive to citizens' needs. The new legislation also sets rules for the central government, especially regarding the timetable for transferring functions to local government, principle of fairness in allocating resources across different levels of government as well as across local councils, and due process in dealing with complaints by local councils or against councils.

LGA specified the first four years as the transition period for implementing the new intergovernmental relations. During this time, authority and corresponding financial resources for a defined set of functions was to be transferred to local councils.

The LGA, however, did not fully address the relationship between the local councils and the chieftancy system. The legislation affirmed that the chieftancy would work in parallel with the local councils. While the authority to fix tax rates and to apportion the share of revenue to go to the local councils and chiefdom administration theoretically belonged to the local councils, actual tax administration remained in the hands of the chiefdom administration. Land management and local courts remained the domains of the chiefdom administration. Thus, the elected councils had to compete with the chiefdoms (whose incumbents also had been elected, but by a different method) for legitimacy and power.[4]

Another demonstration of the ambiguity of the central government toward the two competing authorities in rural areas was the ambivalent role played by the Ministry of Local Government and Community Development (MLGCD) in the decentralization process. As the supervisory ministry for both chiefdoms and local councils, MLGCD had not always been an impartial umpire. It had given ad hoc policy statements and informal advice granting chiefdom councils high shares of local tax and market dues, instead of allowing negotiations between the two parties, as prescribed by the Local Government Act 2004. As a result of the lack of political commitment and poor leadership by MLGCD, the anticipated chiefdom reform process never took off.

While the legislative process and election preparation for local councils proceeded, the World Bank had prepared the Institutional Reform and Capacity Building Project (IRCBP) to provide just-in-time support to decentralization. On May 11, 2004, fewer than two weeks before the historic local council elections, the Executive Directors of the World Bank approved a US$25m grant for the IRCBP. The objectives of this four-year project were to help the GoSL establish a functioning local government system and improve inclusiveness, transparency, and accountability of public resource management at all levels of government. The IRCBP subsequently received an additional $25m grant through an IDA-managed trust fund financed by DfID and EC and extended its project period to the end of 2010. The IRCBP became the primary source of donor funding for the policy reform and local council capacity building process in Sierra Leone.

The Cabinet endorsed establishing several new units in the MoF and MLGCD to provide technical leadership of the decentralization program. A Decentralization Secretariat (DecSec) was established under the MLGCD. It consists of a Legal and Policy Reform Unit, a Capacity Building Unit, and a Monitoring Unit. A Local Government Finance Department was established under the MoF to serve as a technical secretariat for the statutory Local Government Finance Committee, which has responsibility over intergovernmental fiscal issues. A Public Financial Management Reform Unit also was established under the MoF to spearhead the public financial reform in the central government and to help LCs establish a functioning financial management system.

Given the acute shortage of professional staff in government service, it was decided that all managerial and professional staff would be competitively recruited from the open market and be compensated accordingly. These teams, along with an IRCBP Coordinating Unit, were housed in a rental property, which was named the Decentralization House. Co-residence of the teams from MLGCD and MoF had the tremendous benefit of coordinating the political, administrative, and fiscal decentralization agenda. A critical mass of champions of the decentralization program in the same building also helped sustain team morale during the ups and downs of the reform process. At the same time, the distinct work cultures and compensation in the Decentralization House and the parent ministries also led to clashes between the civil servants and the contract staff. In MoF, this problem was somewhat mitigated by the fact that top technocrats (Financial Secretary, Budget Director, Director of EPRU, Accountant General) in the ministry themselves were contract staff. However, in the MLGCD, conflicts between the top civil servants and DecSec were recurring. The ambiguity of the MLGCD policy stance regarding the relationship between LC and chiefdom administration was one reason for the strained relationship.

During 2004–07, the IRCBP made a notable contribution to the country's new intergovernmental fiscal framework and the new local government system. A solid foundation for a fiscal transfer system is in place. The grants system is operational, albeit over-complicated. Funds are allocated across local councils according to transparent formulae, although some formulae need to be revised to reverse unequal distribution of facilities and staff. With intensive training and workplace mentoring provided by the IRCBP, local councils rapidly developed basic capacity in participatory planning, budgeting, financial management, procurement, project implementation, and oversight of public service delivery. Three actors who were deeply involved in this process provide a detailed documentation in the first three chapters.

In chapter 1, Emmanuel Gaima, the Director of the Decentralization Secretariat, Ministry of Local Government and Community Development (MLGCD) during 2004–09, discusses the legislative, political, and administrative framework for decentralization.

In chapter 2, Adams Kargbo, a Senior Economist in the Local Government Finance Department, Ministry of Finance (MoF), discusses the evolution of the intergovernmental fiscal relations and efforts to improve the financial capacity of the local councils. As required by law, a grant system that included a discretionary grant for local development initiatives and tied grants to finance primary health, solid waste management, agriculture services, and rural water was established.

In chapter 3, Alhassan Kanu, Program Manager of the Decentralization Secretariat, discusses the capacity building program that the IRCBP supported and the growth of capacity in local councils.

The MoF's willingness to implement the decentralization law proved instrumental in making decentralization a reality. The Local Government Act 2004 (LGA) mandates that, (1) for each devolved function, local councils should receive no less than what the central government spent in the year prior to devolution; and (2) the sharing of resources among councils should be on the basis of a transparent formula. Formulae for various grants were quickly developed and were not controversial. For the sectors whose pre-devolution budget allocation between central and local cost centers had been relatively transparent, as with primary health, MoF quickly negotiated a vertical share with the health ministry on behalf of the local councils. The pre-devolution budget allocation and execution for devolved functions of almost all other ministries was not transparent. In these cases MoF and the line ministries negotiated ad hoc vertical shares. At that time, MoF gave clear instruction that these grants were to be *directly* transferred from the central treasury to the local council bank accounts without passing through the line ministries.

The first goal of IRCBP was that newly elected local councils should be supported to achieve and demonstrate quick results to their constituents so as to stimulate citizens' interest and build their confidence in their local councils. The underlying rationale was that the initial success would be critical to generate a virtuous cycle of local governance improvement (figure 1).

Figure 1. Initial Phase of IRCBP: Generating a Virtuous Cycle of Local Government Improvement

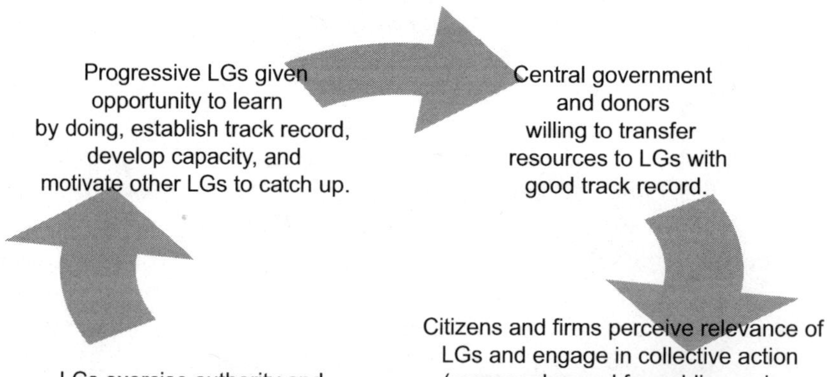

Progressive LGs given opportunity to learn by doing, establish track record, develop capacity, and motivate other LGs to catch up.

Central government and donors willing to transfer resources to LGs with good track record.

Citizens and firms perceive relevance of LGs and engage in collective action (express demand for public service, participate in co-production, hold LGs accountable, pay taxes).

LGs exercise authority and accumulate capacity. LGs adopt inclusive accountable practices.

In June 2004, the IRCBP held a launch workshop to meet representatives from the newly elected councils and introduce them to the immediate capacity building support that the project intended to provide. During this first interaction, the IRCBP team announced that a small untied block grant called the Local Government Development Grant (LGDG) would be provided immediately to each council. The team challenged each LC to implement local projects that are beneficial and visible within 100 days. The team introduced the Rapid Results Approach. RRA emphasizes empowering stakeholders to identify creative solutions that will achieve bottom-line results quickly and promote participatory implementation and monitoring. Follow-up training on the approach and resident RRA coaches was provided to the councils.

The first wave of Rapid Results Initiatives (RRI) brought visibility and credibility to the decentralization program. Councils embraced the opportunity. Although each council received on average only $30,000, it used the LGDG to rehabilitate roads, bridges, and small water systems; build markets and toilets; and upgrade sanitation standards of slaughtering. These initial successes strengthened the position of decentralization advocates. Local councils and their supporters pointed to RRI's success and argued for timely transfer of responsibilities and resources from reluctant sector ministries (Education, in particular) in compliance with the LGA.

In the 2005 budget, in addition to a general administrative grant and the Local Government Development Grant, tied grants for primary health and solid waste management were given. The 2005 LGDG was increased 300 percent over the 2004 allocation. The 2005 grant was distributed to councils by a formula comprising indicators of population, infrastructure endowment, and infrastructure damage caused by the war.

To support the devolution process related to service delivery areas, the IRCBP brought together local councils and district staff of line ministries (Health, Agriculture, and Education) to map out the transition, and their respective roles and responsibilities in local council planning, budgeting, and execution. RRA was introduced to this joint team, and team members were encouraged to carry out RRIs using a tied grant for the specific function. This collaborative approach plus the fact that the council and the district line department are joint signatories of the tied grant account facilitated a mutually dependent and collegial relationship between council administrations and the line departments. The district health management teams, in particular, embraced the approach. They had had some experience under the deconcentration model with which the ministry had been experimenting. The new increased financial autonomy and close contact with local administration made it easier for them to implement their annual plans. When the authors asked them what the decentralization process had meant for them, three district health management team members answered as follows:

1. "Decentralization has stopped the tide of brain drain among medical professionals because we now have interesting work to do."
2. "Decentralization allows us to quickly respond to disease outbreaks. We don't have to wait for the ministry."
3. "Decentralization means if I have a problem, I can knock on the doors of our council rather than sitting on a long bench in Youyi Building for a week and waiting for an audience with a ministry official."

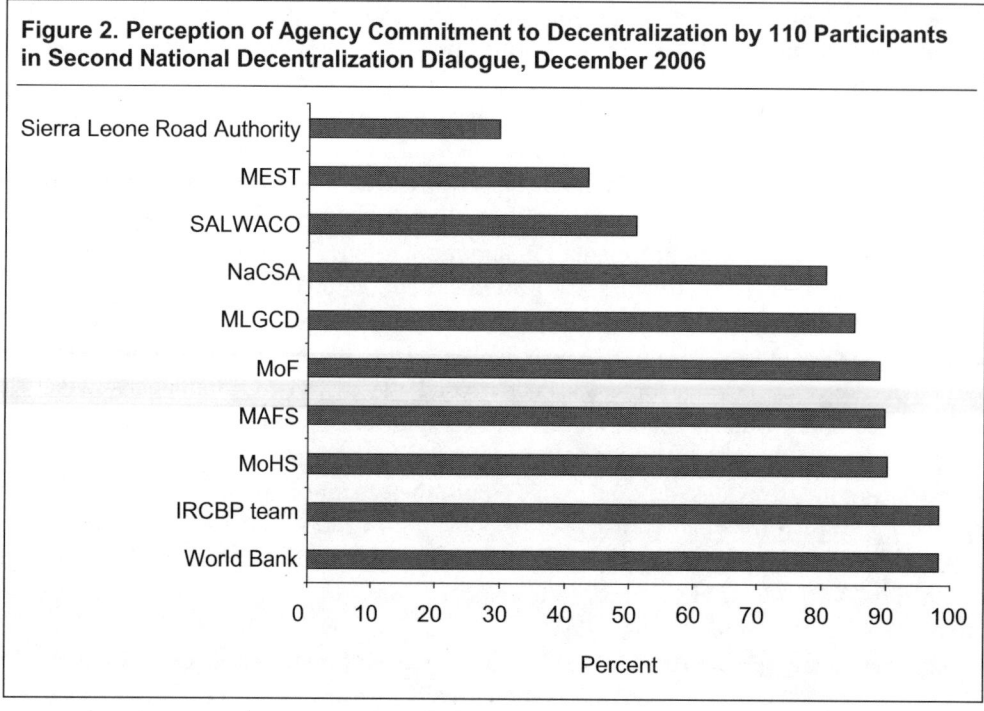

Figure 2. Perception of Agency Commitment to Decentralization by 110 Participants in Second National Decentralization Dialogue, December 2006

The commitment to decentralization varied by ministries. During the Second National Decentralization Dialogue in December 2006, a survey was carried out to gauge perception by participants of various agencies' commitment to decentralization. Respondents to the survey numbered 110 (including national and local government officials as well as civil society representatives). Figure 2 indicates the percentage of respondents who considered an agency to be committed to decentralization. Clearly, there was no illusion of universal commitment to decentralization across government.

Devolution of responsibilities and resources was accompanied by intensive training and mentoring. Chapter 3 by Alhassan Kanu documents the overall approach and achievement of the capacity building program. The capacity building program under the IRCBP promoted inclusive and transparent governance practices, including participatory planning, Public Budget Day, publication of council budget, procurement notices and contract awards, and annual financial audits. In many ways, local councils were ahead of ministries in adopting participatory and open management practices. Despite very weak human resources bases, with intensive training and mentoring, all councils developed basic budgeting, procurement, and accounting capacity.

The capacity building effort during 2003–07 contributed significantly to establish a functioning local council system. Kanu's chapter details how capacity was assessed and the growth of local council capacity in the past few years. The first annual Comprehensive Local Government Performance Assessment (CLoGPAS) was undertaken in October 2006. As expected, the assessment revealed variation of capacity and management practice across councils. Only 3 councils met 5 of 7 minimum conditions.[5] Average level of competency and legal and regulatory compliance was high in the areas of development planning and procurement. Capacity in records management, financial management, and revenue mobilization is generally poor.

The second comprehensive assessment in 2008 showed general improvement in LCs' performance. Especially improved were the regularity of conducting local council meetings and preparation of minutes; citizen participation in council meetings; a basic filing system in some councils; a participatory development planning process; the Rapid Results Approach to project management, procurement, reconciliation between accounts and bank statements, and disclosure of financial information (see chapter 3).

The IRCBP actively advocated for policy and administrative reform to facilitate decentralization. Although MoF supported the fiscal decentralization process, the Accountant General's (AG) Department had extremely cumbersome procedures for disbursing funds to councils. Its tight control measures reflected MoF's distrust in ministries' abilities to properly manage their budgets. These procedures clearly were inconsistent with the philosophy behind the local council grant system. A detailed review of the disbursement process revealed that, in 2006, for every quarterly payment of each of the 14 grants to 19 councils, 237 signatures were required before a payment could be made! Altogether, 13,272 signatures were required to disburse 14 grants on a quarterly basis to 19 councils. Once these numbers were acknowledged, the AG's Department and the Local Government Finance Department worked out a simpler procedure and expenditure authorization forms for grants to local councils.

IRCBP recognized that predictable and adequate funding was a key ingredient of an enabling environment to develop local council capacity. The program advocated that, as more and more functions were devolved to LCs, GoSL should gradually increase transfers to them and meet the full budget commitment to them. Unconditional grants in the form of LGDGs slowly but steadily increased during 2004–06. In these years, LGDG per capita was $0.10, $0.34, and $0.52, respectively. However, in 2007 it declined to $0.20. Since 2004, budgeted tied grants to local councils have steadily increased, both in volume and as a share of government nonsalary, noninterest recurrent expenditure—although actual execution has always fallen short. Actual disbursement of tied grants as a share of government nonsalary, noninterest, recurrent expenditure increased from 4.4 percent in 2005 to 8.7 percent in 2006, but declined to 4 percent in 2007. The execution ratio of *total* transfers (including all grants) to local councils improved from 56.4 percent in 2005 to 72.2 percent in 2006, but declined sharply to 41.0 percent in 2007.

FY2007 was the year of the most recent national elections. Decline in revenue performance is a common phenomenon in election years, and FY2007 was no exception. As a result, there was drastic budget cut during the fiscal year. With the exception of personnel expenditure, there was a significant budget cut across the board. Nevertheless, the local councils bore disproportionate burden (table 1). Clearly, transfers to local councils have not received priority in government spending.

Table 1. Deviations of Actual Spending from Budget Allocations, 2003–07 (%)

	Deviations from budget allocations (%)					Count of years that meet criteria		
	2003	2004	2005	2006	2007	D<−5%	Mini-mal	D>+5%
Total budgetary spending	−3.1	−9.1	−0.5	0.9	−22.3	2	3	0
A. Personnel	3.7	−5.2	2.9	2.4	−3.4	1	4	0
B. Other recurrent	−6.4	−9.8	2.5	3.4	−28.1	3	2	0
C. Domestic development [a]	−9.1	−23.5	−21.3	0.6	−49.4	4	1	0
D. Transfers local councils [b]	na	na	−43.6	−27.8	−59.0	3	0	0

Source: World Bank country economist calculation based on national budget, November 2008.
Notes:
a. Excludes externally financed development spending.
b. Excludes personnel and other administrative expenses as well as development grants.

Has Decentralization Improved Coverage and Quality of Primary Health, Agriculture, and Primary Education Services?

The three largest sectors—education, health, and agriculture—underwent varying degrees of decentralization and devolution of funds, but all were limited to nonsalary recurrent expenditures. In 2005, 2006, and 2007, 2.66 percent, 2.95 percent, and 2.99 percent, respectively, of total GoSL nonsalary, noninterest spending was devolved to local councils for primary health. In 2006 and 2007, only 0.79 percent and 0.68 percent, respectively, of total GoSL nonsalary, noninterest spending was devolved to LCs for agriculture. In 2007 only 1.12 percent of total GoSL nonsalary, noninterest spending was devolved to LCs for education.

According to the analysis by Katherine Whiteside Casey (chapter 4) that focused on noncapital nonsalary expenditures *financed by GoSL,* local councils control:

- 23 percent of health expenditures
- 62 percent of primary healthcare expenditures
- 16 percent of agriculture expenditures
- 67 percent of Crops Division funds
- 55 percent Livestock Division funds
- 21 percent of Land and Water Division funds.

In the education sector, the only monies from the education sector that LCs control directly come from a Le 4 billion overestimate of the 2007 schools fees subsidies budget. The LGFD reallocated these savings to school supervision and government libraries (which were unfunded) and two discretionary line items: education administration and development.

However, it is important to point out that donor-funded projects finance over 50 percent of total health expenditures, 75 percent of total agriculture expenditures and 76 percent of the total education budget in Sierra Leone. Very little donor funding is managed directly by the councils. Thus, in FY2007, only 11 percent of national health budget, 4 percent of national agriculture and 5 percent of national education budget was allocated for transfers to local councils. It is clear that, unless donors embrace, the decentralization agenda, local councils will only control a minority share of the national spending on education, health, and agriculture.

The overwhelming importance of donor funding in these three sectors makes it difficult to separate out decentralization's direct impact upon them. The IRCBP Evaluation Unit tracked indicators of access to services and citizen satisfaction over the years through national household surveys in 2005 and 2007. The unit also conducted focus group discussions and interviews to understand the qualitative changes that decentralization had introduced.

In chapter 4, Katherine Whiteside Casey identifies several areas in which decentralization likely would have affected the quality and reach of public services. First, given the early and sustained transfers of tied funding for health, if the original hypotheses about decentralization are correct, it seems reasonable to expect some positive change in healthcare provision. Since the health sector already had been heavily de-concentrated with significant autonomy at the district level, we expect decentralization not so much to change *what* is being done in primary health but to improve the *efficiency* with which work plans are executed and the *reach* of services and resources. In interviews with district-level health employees, they repeatedly emphasized the elimination of bureaucratic delays in accessing resources from Freetown as the most significant contribution of decentralization. Moving budgetary and activity approval to the district level closes the gap between planning and implementation, enabling district teams to spend more time and energy doing their jobs. Furthermore, delivering and storing drugs and supplies at district-level facilities may have reduced supply chain leakages and thus increased the availability of resources. Finally, district and clinic staff suggested that the provision of outreach incentives has expanded the catchment area of clinics and the number of clients who benefit from their services. Summing up these operational improvements, the director of primary healthcare reported that, in 3 recent supervisory visits, he was impressed to see that clinics are now implementing approximately 80 percent of their planned activities—a notable increase over previous years. Similarly, the district medical officer from Kenema remarked, "Decentralization makes you more effective and less expensive."

Foster and Glennester (chapter 5) report findings from the analyses of the national household surveys conducted by IRCBP in 2005 and 2007 and the annual health facility surveys conducted by IRCBP since 2005. The annual health facility surveys show steady improvement in quality of clinics (figure 5.1) over the 3 years. The household surveys show that access to schools, clinics, shared storage space, drying floor, drivable roads, market, and water source improved during these two years. Only access to agriculture extension workers declined. Public satisfaction with health clinics and primary schools also has improved. In addition, Foster and Glennester find that areas with initially low levels of service have caught up in some sectors. In particular, satisfaction with health, registration of births, and access to roads saw their largest gains among those who previously had been in the bottom third of the distribution, although this change could have been due to reversion to the mean in data.

Foster and Glennester recognize the methodological difficulties of separating the effect of decentralization on service coverage and quality. They conclude: "It is impossible to know what Sierra Leone would have looked like in the absence of decentralization. It is therefore impossible to say precisely how much of the general improvement in public services observed over the past few years is due to decentralization. At the very least, we can say that decentralization has been compatible with consistent improvements in public service delivery."

Has Decentralization Energized Civic Participation in Local Governance?

A key hypothesis about the merits of decentralization is that it brings government closer to people and make it easier for people to express demand for public services and hold government accountable. To examine the empirical validity of this hypothesis in a young democracy such as Sierra Leone, in which a majority of the rural population is poor and illiterate, Zhou and Zhang analyzed the national household surveys conducted by IRCBP in 2005 and 2007 and reported the findings in Chapter 6.

Zhou and Zhang find that election of the local councils in 2004 has brought government closer to people, especially to some of the communities who are cut off from transport, telecommunication, market, or contact with the state. Local councils provided rare opportunities for rural citizens to interact with authorities and have their voices heard. Their presence is particularly valuable in rural areas off the beaten track that hitherto have been neglected by central government authorities. On the other hand, in remote areas, the benefits of decentralization have accrued disproportionately to the home villages, or, rather, towns, of elected councilors. Rural villages represented by someone living in a different town or village within the constituency still require effective representation. However, presently, since they see less of their councilors, they also are less likely to benefit from council projects.

Where there is more outreach or development initiative on the part of councilors, citizens are more likely to perceive their councils as responsive and trustworthy and have more confidence in their own influence over council decisions. People also are more likely to express support for these councilors' re-election. Across the country, citizens' trust in local councils was low and followed a declining trend between 2005 and 2007. However, people who knew about council projects had a positive and improving view of local government's performance, both in absolute terms and in comparison to central government.

There are two interpretations of this finding. One is that council initiatives generate a legitimacy dividend and that deepening fiscal decentralization will enable councils to undertake more development initiatives and improve legitimacy.

On the other hand, the correlation between council initiatives and perceived legitimacy could be spurious if both popular awareness and trust in local councils correlate positively with a third variable. For example, home communities of the councilors are more likely to benefit from local council projects and are more aware of council initiatives. Given Salone people's general inclination to trust community insiders far more than outsiders, the correlation between high level of trust in the councilors and higher level of awareness may not be evidence for causality. Further investigation is required.

Participation in local elections is widespread. Nevertheless, citizens are not yet actively monitoring council operations even though much information about local council operations is public. Citizens also are not very confident in engaging the authorities and changing the status quo. Younger people are less confident than older people. Women are less confident than men. Similar gender and generational gaps are reflected in individuals' voices in public fora.

Zhou and Zhang caution that these observations are only a snapshot of a long-term social evolution. The attitudinal survey reveals a rather liberal political attitude among the population relating to women's participation in politics and youth leadership as well as intolerance for corruption and a more questioning civil society. Recent increases in the number of females and youth winning national and local elections seem consistent with people's liberal attitude. The huge turnover in the 2008 elections is quite consistent with what the local opinion leaders predicted a year ahead of the elections. Whatever the citizens know about their councilors' performance, they do seem to give the most consideration to whether the councilors have brought development to their communities. Such widespread acceptance of democratic values gives hope that Sierra Leone is heading in the direction of a more inclusive and accountable polity.

Sustainability Challenges in Sierra Leone

Measured by the budget figures, the degree of power that has been transferred to local councils appears quite small. However, from local councils having no autonomy to having autonomy over 6 percent of government primary spending is a significant qualitative change of the intergovernmental relationship. As the previous section documented, the progress was hard fought. Compared to most other SSA countries that have embarked on decentralization, Sierra Leone's progress in building local government capacity and restructuring the fiscal system is enviable. As Sierra Leone moves forward to the second phase of the decentralization program, many sustainability challenges remain that the government must address.

The first sustainability challenge is local councils' ability to attract and retain qualified staff. In 2007 the Local Government Service Commission (LGSC) issued the Local Council Human Resource Management Guidelines and allowed councils to recruit their own staff. The central government civil servants who had been seconded to the councils on a temporary basis were given the option to return to the civil service or to apply for the local positions that they had been occupying. The only change was that, in the latter case, the staff would be fully accountable to the councils. Almost all opted to return to the civil service positions in Freetown. These civil servants cited rural hardship, lack of job security and upward mobility, and uncompetitive compensation policy for local council positions as the reasons.

New officers were recruited by the local councils but generally do not have experience or the requisite qualifications for their positions. The IRCBP is organizing a new round of training for the new staff. Despite this, without a new human resource management (HRM) policy, there is no guarantee that the trained staff will stay.

In a small country such as Sierra Leone, segregating the public sector job market into a central government service and a local government service did not seem a good idea. On the contrary, mobility between local government and central government not only would make a local government job more attractive but also would systematically integrate local government perspectives in central government employees. So far, this option is not feasible because central government civil service is a closed service, that is, all nonentry positions are filled by promotion. Lateral recruitment from outside the service is not allowed. This rigidity needs to change.

The second sustainability challenge is councils' high dependence on government transfers. Local revenue mobilization performance has been very poor across councils. Local councils remain heavily dependent on central government for financing. In 2005 a study was conducted to review revenue administrative practice and performance in all councils. Local revenue mobilization had been weak across the board. Per capita own revenue generation was negligible in most rural councils. However, even in cities and diamond-rich areas, per capita own revenue was rather low. In 2005 it ranged from almost nonexistent (Port Loko) to $1.70 (Koidu). In 2006 the situation improved marginally: Koidu and Kono collected about $1.80 per capita, but Port Loko still collected almost nothing. Total local revenue increased by 24 percent to Le 5.80 billion in 2006. However, the progress made in 2006 was lost in 2007 when total local revenue declined by 28 percent to Le 1.6 billion. The main reason for the poor performance related to the central government elections that year. Many people were busy with politics, and some politicians and others sent out campaign messages that negatively affected revenue mobilization.

The third sustainability challenge is lack of commitment to chiefdom governance reform. Conflict between local councils and chiefdom councils regarding revenue sharing contributed to lackluster revenue performance. Merely clarifying the relationship between local council and chiefdom administration will not be sufficient. If the chieftancy and the local councils are to co-exist effectively as institutions of good governance, in addition to a viable and transparent local council finance system, there must be a viable and transparent chiefdom finance system.

The fourth sustainability challenge is the reform process itself. The first phase of the decentralization program was driven largely by the IRCBP team and was supported by some leaders of MoF and donors. When MLGCD policy reform activism was needed to deal with bottlenecks related to chiefdom administration and local council human resource shortage, the ministry stopped short. As the reform moves forward to address binding policy constraints, ownership and leadership by the new MIALGRD are critical.

The lack of institutionalized training for local councils poses another sustainability challenge. The IRCBP team needs to move away from designing and delivering training directly to facilitating the emergence of a competitive market of capacity building service providers, including tertiary training institutions, firms, and NGOs.

Conclusions: What Have We Learned from Sierra Leone's Experience?

Sierra Leone's experience shows that political and fiscal decentralization can be consistent with improved security and service delivery in a post-conflict country. The solid foundation of a fiscal transfer system is in place. The grants system is operational, albeit over-complicated. Funds are allocated across local councils according to transparent formulae, although equalization features of the formulae can be improved. At least in a small country such as Sierra Leone, an intensive capacity building program for local councils is doable and indispensable. Benefiting from intensive training and workplace mentoring, local councils rapidly developed basic capacity in participatory planning, budgeting, financial management, procurement, project implementation, and oversight of public service delivery. Decentralization has energized frontline public service managers and delivery staff. Statistically, we cannot attribute the improvement in coverage and quality of public services to local councils' effort. Nevertheless, at least data shows that improvement in public services is possible under a decentralized (or, rather, decentralizing) framework. The second round of elections in 2008 attracted more candidates, an indication of more interest in the local councils.

Sierra Leone's experience highlights the importance of fiscal decentralization as the driving force of decentralization. Decentralization liberated suppressed capacity and was most enthusiastically embraced by local officials and staff. The most consistent decentralization efforts were made in the primary health sector. There, client-readiness of peripheral health units (PHUs) improved, and client satisfaction rose. Untied grants (LGDG) also gave LCs the freedom to undertake initiatives in response to constituent needs. Central government commitment to the decentralization agenda can be gauged by the adequacy and predictability of ministries, departments, and agencies' (MDAs) fiscal transfers to local councils.

Sierra Leone's experience demonstrates the importance of sequencing interventions to generate early results and to continuously expand constituency for reform. The initial decentralization process in Sierra Leone was energized by the Rapid Results Approach. RRA provided a methodology of timely and participatory project implementation that was welcomed by people who saw RRIs as a refreshing change of how government works. Early results on the ground also sustained the energy and commitment of the champions of decentralization.

The Sierra Leone experience also confirms the power of transparency, participation, and internal checks and balance. Elite capture and corruption at the local level certainly exists, but they are mitigated by transparent processes of funds transfer and project implementation. Liberal disclosure policies also enabled close monitoring by stakeholders. An example was an active NGO in Makeni, which blew the whistle on corrupt practice in the town council and forced the departure of the first mayor.

It is hard to imagine the same achievements if the decentralization program were to be implemented by the existing civil servants in government. With extremely limited human resources in the labor market, let alone the public sector, a poor post-conflict country will face major difficulty in assembling a team to lead the reform that has the requisite commitment, professionalism, and dynamism. Investing in building a cohesive team, especially one that integrates key actors in the ministries of finance and local government, is a must.

A professional team can make only limited achievements if political commitment is lacking. On issues such as chiefdom reform and public service reform, for which political commitment was not strong, the IRCBP did not make much headway despite active advocacy.

Perhaps the most important lesson from the Sierra Leone experience is that reforms of this nature cannot be fully planned. Hence, it is extremely important to cultivate a learning culture in the implementation team and maintain the flexibility to adjust course based on learning. It is in this spirit that this book has been written, both as a pause to reflect and a moment to share.

Notes

[1] Bardhan and Mookherjee 2000, 2006.

[2] World Bank 1998.

[3] To put these indicators in perspective, Sub-Saharan Africa's (SSA) averages for the same indicators were 101, 171, 46, and 71%, respectively. World averages of these indicators were 57, 86, 67, and 80%, respectively.

[4] Manning, chapter 7 of this volume.

[5] No councils met these two conditions: (1) timely completion of audit, although the fault was not entirely of the councils. The Auditor General's team was unable to complete audit. (2) Submission of local council budget to LGFD by September 30. Because central government did not announce ceilings for grants, which constitute the bulk of council budget, it was not fair for GoSL to require local councils to submit budgets by that date.

CHAPTER 1

Establishing the Legislative, Political, and Administrative Framework for Local Government and Decentralization in Sierra Leone

Emmanuel Gaima

How the Decentralization Policy and Local Government Act 2004 Were Developed

In 1996, after a four-year military interregnum by the National Provisional Ruling Council (NPRC), Sierra Leone conducted its first democratic elections. These ushered in a new Parliament and a new President. The election of the new Government of Sierra Leone (GoSL) galvanized the initiation of a host of priority reform programs in the country. To coordinate and harmonize the reform programs, a national strategy document, "Good Governance and Public Sector Reform Strategy," was prepared by the government. This strategy identified *local governance and decentralization* as a major reform target that would accelerate post-conflict rebuilding and promote development, especially rural, in the country.

Sierra Leone had experienced a 10-year war from 1991–2002. In 2002 the end of war was peacefully negotiated with the assistance of international, continental, and subregional organizations and led to the signing of the famous Lome Accord. On several occasions, the war was justified by the leader of the Revolutionary United Front (RUF) on the grounds that there were high levels of exclusion, marginalization, deprivation, and poor service provision and delivery in the country; and that these had culminated in extreme poverty, especially in rural Sierra Leone. The national Decentralization Program was designed to respond to the antecedents of the war by embarking on a local governance and decentralization reform program. The objective was to reverse the negative trends that were widely believed to have necessitated the war and its attendant massive destruction of lives, properties, and the already deteriorated national infrastructure.

GoSL piloted the local Governance and Decentralization Reform Program through the Ministry of Local Government and Rural Development.[1] The process was managed via a National Taskforce, which was constituted by the government under the Chairmanship of the Hon. Vice President of the Republic of Sierra Leone.[2] The terms of reference (TOR) of the taskforce (TF) were to "review consolidated laws supporting local government and decentralization in Sierra Leone" and make recommendations for the preparation of a draft bill for the government's consideration and enactment into law.[3] The TF members were inaugurated and oriented on the TOR. A schedule of meetings to guide and regulate their operations was prepared, discussed, and endorsed by the members. To guide the deliberations, the TF chair ensured that the key issues in the consolidated legislation were identified and categorized.

To facilitate the work of the taskforce, development partners (DPs) provided technical assistance (TA) to backstop the process. The TA was in the form of international consultant support to provide advice, policy direction, and experience-sharing to the TF by contracting out short-term assignments to international consultants required to bring to the process international experiences and best practices.[4]

In addition to the revision and review of the consolidated laws, the taskforce also divided the country into 14 districts and designed and conducted national district-based consultations. These consultations considered primarily issues that required consensus and were open to controversies.[5] The report recommended the subcategorization of the taskforce into thematic groups to address recommendations and provide input for preparation of the draft bill on local government and decentralization.[6]

The Ministry of Local Government and Community Development provided GoSL political leadership in preparing and drafting the Local Government Act 2004. The actual drafting was undertaken by a consultant attached to the Law Officers Department in the Office of the Attorney General and Minister of Justice of Sierra Leone. The design of the national decentralization program in Sierra Leone experienced a major flaw at conceptualization. The Ministry of Local Government and Rural Development at the time emphasized the preparation of the Local Government Act without due regard to the fact that *there was no policy framework in place to inform the preparation of the legislation*. Thus, the taskforce proceeded to review consolidated legislation and commenced piecemeal drafting of the LGA in the absence of an overarching policy.

Since the inception of the process to resuscitate decentralization, the design and formulation of the country's decentralization program were a partnership between GoSL and its major DPs. Realizing the potential implementation bottlenecks if the LGA were developed and piloted through Parliament without a policy framework, the DPs advised the Ministry of Local Government and Community Development to ensure that a policy document was developed.

The policy development was led by a Sierra Leonean consultant working closely with international consultants fielded from time to time by the various DPs as technical backstoppers and to introduce international experiences and best practice. Nevertheless, the policy development was fraught with serious shortcomings:

- The timeline given to the consultants to develop the draft policy was tight.
- Instead of preceding the LGA, the policy development ran parallel to drafting the LGA.
- There was an abundance of information but not enough time for analysis and inclusion to ensure that all issues of relevance to the taskforce were captured.

Since the "process" was so constrained, it was anticipated that the product would definitely have major deficiencies. To all intents and purposes, the drafting of the policy was closely aligned to the structure and content of the draft bill in preparation. The policy document was more descriptive and not quite adequate in prescribing *how* to address issues relating to structures, institutions, regulations, and sectors. More importantly, the draft policy failed to address definitively the thorny issues of functional relationships and interrelationships between and among the various entities and stakeholders in the decentralization process. With these identified weaknesses, the document never went full cycle (going through the processes) of government approval and at best could be described as "working draft" policy document.

Statutory Instrument and Timetable for Decentralization

The 2004 LGA was drafted to serve as comprehensive legislation that would encapsulate the major thematic focus of a well-functioning local government and decentralization program. It focused on the political, administrative, functional, and fiscal components of decentralization. To facilitate the devolution of functions, in its third schedule the LGA provided (a comprehensive listing by ministries, departments, and agencies (MDAs) of key functions that were to be broadly devolved to local councils. It should be noted that merely listing these functions was not adequate to ensure a roll-out of such functions. It also later was to be realized that there were a number of core and supplementary activities that could be embedded within functions. These activities were not detailed in the legislation. Finally, there was no indication of timing (timeline/timeframe) as to when the MDAs were to roll out the identified functions.

The inadequacy of the legislation that merely listed broad functions to be devolved necessitated the preparation of the Statutory Instrument Assumption of Functions No. 13 (SI) (2004) by the Decentralization Secretariat (DecSec).[7] The SI is a legal document structured as follows:

- It provided a broad listing of identified functions slated for devolution by 16 MDAs.
- Each function to be devolved by MDAs was disaggregated into activities and subactivities.
- Each activity and subactivity was assigned a timeline by which it was to be devolved from the sectoral MDAs to local councils.

Experiences world-wide associate devolution of authority, functions, and resources with resistance and bureaucratic hurdles. The Sierra Leone Local Government and Decentralization Program is no exception to experiencing resistance to reform, perceived or real. To ensure that the devolution of functions was given meaning and effect and to ensure compliance by MDAs, the SI was prepared by DecSec, reviewed with the four-year transitional timeframe (2004–08) by the Law Officers Department, and finally taken to Parliament. In accordance with the country's legislative procedures and processes, the minister responsible for local government formally read the SI in the Chamber of Parliament and formally laid the document in Parliament for a statutory period of 21 working days. After that time, it became an instrument of law that could be enforced for compliance.[8]

Local Government Act 2004 and the Political Framework

LGA 2004 comprehensively supports the political framework for local government and decentralization in Sierra Leone. It defines what is meant by "local government" and "local council" in this country as a unit of governance that should be considered "the highest political authority in the designated locality."[9] In laying out the political framework, the LGA addresses:

- Election and composition of local councils as well as term of each local council (four years)
- Qualifications for becoming a councilor, which focus on being a resident of the locality
- Procedures for electing a mayor and chair as well as removal from office
- Procedures and processes to conduct the first Business of Councils after it was constituted (post elections)
- Convening and conduct of meetings with regard to the relevance and use of Standing Orders
- Operations of councils through council committees
- Powers of local councils to make and execute byelaws
- Facilitation, mediation, and coordinating roles and responsibilities of the Ministry of Local Government and Rural Development and of the Ministry of Finance, which must be consulted on all fiscal decentralization matters.

LGA 2004 recognizes the importance and role of chiefdom authority and chiefdom administration. The Paramount Chiefs are both the natural and elected leaders and the heads of chiefdoms in Sierra Leone. They also run the chiefdom administration, which has set laws and regulations.[10] The laws and supporting regulations in force to support chiefdom governance were not repealed at the time that LGA 2004 was prepared. This omission has contributed to a number of conflicts in roles and responsibilities. It is important to note that chiefdoms are the lowest units of administration in Sierra Leone. Nevertheless, they have many cultural and traditional powers vested in them, and, by extension, in the Paramount Chiefs.

LGA 2004 failed to recognize the strategic role of Paramount Chiefs in chiefdom governance and to make for them a more meaningful role in the overall decentralization program. The focus of the legislation was primarily on creating the local councils and defining their powers and functions. The role of Paramount Chiefs was limited to "token representation"[11] in local councils as well as to "sitting members"[12] of ward committees (WCs), which are required to discuss and set development priorities for local councils.

The seeming nonrecognition of the "dominant" and "strategic" roles of Paramount Chiefs in the decentralization program, and in local council administrations in particular, very well may be responsible for the lack of enthusiasm as well as poor cooperation demonstrated in critical areas such as revenue mobilization (raising and sharing), particularly of local tax revenue and market dues. This poor revenue mobilization performance has constrained the abilities of local councils to mobilize any meaningful own/domestic resources with the resulting negative implications for local councils to operate effectively in the absence of central government fiscal transfers.

At conceptualization, the decentralization program in Sierra Leone envisaged and identified mechanisms to ensure the integration of citizens in the processes and programs. The legislation provides for local councils to send out notices for meetings at least seven days in advance as well as to make them "open/public" meetings, and even further stipulated that Council meetings could be conducted in the "local language" of the area. These provisions were to ensure greater citizen participation in local council agenda-setting and opportunity to witness the policy deliberations. The various mechanisms proposed in the legislation did not yield the much required dividend of increasing the interface and participation of citizens in local council meetings. Citizens complained that the law makes them "mere/ passive" observers because they were not permitted intervene in or contributes to the debates at Council meetings. Over time, this perception of controlled participation undermined the interest of citizens in the meetings.

The need for more and active downward citizen engagement in the decentralization process had been envisaged by GoSL and led to the establishment of ward committees in each ward in the country. Each ward was to elect 10 people to serve as ward committee members, with the strict provision that no fewer than 5 of 10 members be women. The broad mandate of the ward committees was to "mobilise residents of the ward for implementation of self help and development projects, as well as providing a focal point for the discussion of local problems…."

The ward committees were not able to fully and effectively play the required roles. Funded by IRCBP and in most cases working with partners (INGOs), GoSL designed and conducted comprehensive capacity building for ward committee members throughout the country. The trainings were aimed at increasing the functionality and effectiveness of the ward committees. To a great extent, this was achieved. However, it was equally constrained by the lack of inputs (logistics and working tools), as well as absence of any incentive (transportation allowances and even refreshments) for attending meetings.

The involvement of women—who are considered to make up over 50 percent of the population of Sierra Leone yet are still marginalized and disempowered—remains a huge challenge. The requirement of having 5 of every 10 women in ward committees was difficult to meet in many local council areas because of lack of interest by women. In a poor country in which great demands are placed on women's time to secure their families' livelihoods, it is a herculean task to persuade women to free up time that otherwise could be spent on the farm or in petty trading to attend community/communal meetings, irrespective of whatever empowerment notion may be associated with their participation.

Part XV (15) of LGA 2004 makes elaborate provisions to support and promote transparency, accountability, and participation. It provides for disclosures wherein councilors are required to undertake declaration of assets (entry and exit) declaration. The legislation also prescribes the standard practices that all local councils should maintain an inventory of assets and undertake security printing of receipts as well as and other financial and accounting documents.

The legislation also adamantly requires that notice boards be kept in all wards within each and every local council area. The purpose is to display financial and other strategic documents such as development plans, tender documents, and contracts. There were varying degrees of compliance with the provision of maintaining notice boards. Most urban and city councils had higher degrees of compliance than did many district/rural councils, in which the compliance rate was lower. Explanations varied. It often is stated that urban and city councils could use the financial resources accruing from property taxes, markets dues, and other fees to erect Notice Boards in all wards. In contrast, the narrow revenue bases of district/rural councils made it extremely difficult to finance such a notice board scheme, despite its contribution to transparency, accountability, and community-information sharing.

Local Government Act 2004 and Other Laws (Complementarity and Contradictions)

As an overriding national legislation, LGA 2004 should have had several sectoral laws aligned to it. Instead, unfortunately, they are running parallel to it. There is a traditional understanding in Western legal circles that new and emergent laws should normally repeal or supersede old laws. In the case of LGA 2004, however, this understanding does not have validity.

The Third Schedule of LGA 2004 and the Statutory Instrument Assumption of Functions (2004) are legal and regulatory instruments that were prepared with the overarching objective of facilitating the effective and timely devolution of power, authority, functions, and resources from MDAs to local councils in Sierra Leone within the transitional period of 2004–08. Since 2004, the devolution can be credited with significant progress. Nonetheless, it could have achieved even more if the process had not simultaneously suffered legal and regulatory bottlenecks.

Sierra Leone has a general climate of policy and legal inconsistencies in the management of public and—to some extent—private sector programs and activities. There are numerous laws to contend with as well as such laws being outdated and unresponsive to present and current national and international governance realities. In the case of the ongoing national decentralization program, it has been discovered that there are over 30 different laws that are either inconsistent with, parallel to, or conflict with the principal legislation, LGA 2004. This chaotic environment has, to a great degree, undermined meaningful and effective devolution of functions from MDAs to local councils. Furthermore, in the arena of fiscal decentralization, the tangle of laws often has undermined the abilities of local councils to levy, raise, and collect taxes.

Given the multiplicity of laws that have been inventoried as conflicting, parallel, or inconsistent with LGA 2004, the Decentralization Secretariat has identified and analyzed most of these laws. A prioritization scheme has been adopted. The guiding principle is to identify "priority" laws (laws that pose the biggest obstacles to effective devolution, and invariably service delivery, of health and education) as critical social services and human development sectors. These are very vital sectors that necessitated a demand for devolution and frontline service delivery in Sierra Leone. Thus, any perceived or real obstacle should be accorded high priority for response and solution.

To facilitate much more effective devolution as well as improve service delivery to the poor and needy, four key laws[13] have been prioritized for review and rationalization to make them consistent with LGA 2004. Three of these 4 laws have been reviewed to remove impediments and thus accelerate service provision and delivery. These laws place much more control and authority in the Sector Ministers (of Education, Health and Sanitation, Energy and Power) and other institutions, to the disadvantage of the councils. In essence, if not reviewed, these laws will undermine the authority and control of local councils in their bid to take over and provide services in such vital sectors to citizens. The fourth law will be reviewed to enhance legal authority for local councils to expand their tax authority in local tax collection to include women, who now are required to pay such a tax but are not legally bound by the local tax act to pay.

The National Decentralization Taskforce has a subteam made up mostly of legal personnel working with the Policy and Legal Unit of DecSec. Their brief is to study and make recommendations to the government on aspects and/or elements/features of the various laws (both the four prioritized and other identified acts) that require amendment or refinement to be consistent with a revised Local Government Act. Most of the other laws identified for review focus on revenue matters and institutional relationships (for example the Chiefdom and Tribal Administration Act). It has been advised that such review also be based on the content of a reformulated and adopted new National Decentralization Policy document being developed by DecSec.

Administrative Framework to Support Decentralization

The legal framework identifies and defines the institutional and administrative arrangements that will enhance the smooth implementation of decentralization in Sierra Leone.

The internal administrative arrangements are detailed in the legal framework (LGA 04). The LGA is complemented by the prescription of supervisory and regulatory organs required to attain functionality and effectiveness.

The administration of a local council is headed by political leadership in the position of council mayor or chair, with a deputy who is an assistant. The head of general and professional administration is a chief administrator. This person also serves as principal assistant and adviser on all routine administrative and technical matters relating to the effective running and management of the local council to deliver on both mandatory and discretionary mandates in accordance with LGA 2004 and all other policy and regulatory frameworks in existence and operation.

Council administration consists of a section on general administration and finance, with a number of devolving departments in key areas such as agriculture, education, health, social welfare, and services. There also are provisions for specialized departments such as development planning and internal audit. As a complement to the established administrative arrangements, all local councils also are required to constitute and operate sector committees and other relevant committees that undertake more detailed treatment of council business and provide direct oversight over devolving sectors' activities and operations.

Regulatory and supervisory institutions and organs at the project support level (technical steering committee) provide technical oversight over the project development objectives (PDOs) by tracking program design and implementation through participation in the development and review of Annual Work Plans (AWPs), Quarterly Project Reports (QPRs), and Annual Reviews. These institutions also play a direct and active role in the six monthly Joint DPs/GoSL Implementation Support Missions. At the policy supervision and regulatory level, there is the Ministry of Internal Affairs, Local Government, and Rural Development (MIALGRD), the central government's focal point to coordinate and supervise the implementation of the Decentralization Policy and LGA 2004. MIALGRD carries out these responsibilities in concert with MoFED, with which "it must consult" on a variety of issues pertaining to "fiscal matters." The Technical Steering Committee (TSC) is co-chaired by MIALGRD and MoFED. This is a unique arrangement in which the facilitating role is played by MoFED, particularly to accelerate fiscal decentralization. This arrangement reduces the rivalry that normally exists in most African decentralizations between the ministry responsible for local government and the ministry with the finance mandate. Nevertheless, this arrangement is not problem free. MIALGRD often perceives that MoFED has a more dominant role, which motivated MIALGRD to call, for instance, for co-chairmanship because MoFED had been the sole chair at the outset of program implementation.

There are intragovernmental policy, operations, and regulatory organs with very specific and often collaborative mandates and responsibilities. The human resource management (HRM) policy responsibilities reside in a Presidential Commission titled the Local Government Service Commission (LGSC).[14] As of this date, the LGSC has provided local councils with a mix of policy (developing and approving HRM guidelines) and operational roles (playing a lead role in preparing job advertisements for and on behalf of local councils while short-listing and interviewing candidates). There are plans for the Decentralization Secretariat to assist the LGSC in redefining its structure to separate policymaking from operational and administrative roles for greater effectiveness.

The importance attached to matters of fiscal decentralization necessitated the provision in law to create a Local Government Finance Committee (LGFC). The LGFC is provided technical backstopping by a unit in MoFED known as the Local Government Finance Department (LGFD). LGFC performs strategic and policy work such as consideration and review of grants distribution formulae, review of grants releases, consideration of local council plans and budgets and assessing the fiscal performances of local councils. In executing such functions on behalf of local councils, LGFC makes recommendations to the finance minister, who is charged with the responsibility to endorse/approve. To date, LGFC has proved adequate in performing its prescribed functions. However, it has yet to make any meaningful impact in advocating for timely release of funds (predictability), which failure negatively impacts meaningful budgeting by local councils. Similarly, LGFC has no mechanism by which to influence MoFED to ensure an increased volume of grants allocated and released to local councils.

The legal prescription is for devolving MDAs to facilitate devolution of their functions in accordance with schedule (iii) of LGA 04 and SI 04 and to perform post-devolution functions such as responsibilities for sector policies, standards, monitoring, and oversight of the devolved sector. The contribution of 3 of the 5 devolving sectors has not been as supportive as was envisaged in the conceptualization of the program or by the legal framework. Much positive credit can be given to the Health and Agriculture sectors. On the other hand, there is much more to be desired in the present level of engagement and performance by the Education, Water, and Roads MDAs. A strategy for the more meaningful and effective engagement of MDAs is being developed. It would assist them to fully support the roll-out of functions and responsibilities to local councils as well as capacitate MDAs to fully and effectively assume and execute their post-devolution responsibilities.

To facilitate coordination and harmonization between local councils and MDAs at both the district and locality levels as well as nationally, LGA provides for the establishment of 3 Provincial Coordinating Committees[15] at the 3 provincial levels. These committees would be chaired by a central government regional minister, with the regional/provincial secretary serving as secretary. Their mandate is to enhance and coordinate cooperation and collaboration between and among local councils in the regions as well as to promote collaborative projects and address any matters of disagreement. The mandate is laudable, but the lack of budgetary and other logistical support has not made them fully functional beyond hosting occasional meetings.

The highest national organ in the decentralization program in Sierra Leone is the Inter-Ministerial Committee (IMC) on Decentralization.[16] The key, strategic responsibility of the IMC is to "oversee the proper implementation of the Act (LGA 04); oversee the further development and implementation of local government and decentralization; protect and promote local democracy and participatory government; and arbitrate disputes [among] MDAs, provincial administration, and local councils…." The IMC has yet to assume and execute its full responsibilities because, during most of the transition (June 2004–June 2008), the IMC demonstrated that it could hardly meet due principally to the busy schedule and high demands on the time of the chair, the Hon. Vice President. This difficulty has been compounded by the weak Secretariat support to the IMC. The secretariat has failed to take the lead in preparing the agendas and servicing meetings as well as putting in place a structured follow-up mechanism for actions and recommendations emanating from IMC meetings. DecSec has put forward a number of recommendations to improve the functionality and effectiveness of IMC to be able to execute its wide-ranging and critical mandates. These must be performed thoroughly if local government and decentralization are to work in Sierra Leone.

Role of Institutional Reform and Capacity Building Project: World Bank Intervention—Arguments and Process/Actors

In 2003–04 the decentralization and local governance program was in its initial planning stage. World Bank presence in the Sierra Leone Country Office was quite thin and was not quite visible during the preparatory and consensus-building stages.

However, in its in-country engagement, the Bank was quite strong in almost all sectors. These included energy, infrastructure, education, and community development.

The Sierra Leone-World Bank Country Assessment Strategy (CAS) was developed jointly by the World Bank, civil society, GoSL, and other non-state actors. They identified critical areas of underdevelopment that may require substantial donor inflows (technical, financial, and supervisory) as support to the government and people of Sierra Leone.

At the time it considered its intervention, the World Bank weighed various options to make an informed judgment as well as to justify why the anticipated volume of investment should be deployed in Sierra Leone. One major argument advanced was that local government and decentralization should be seen as components of a critical national reform program, which, if undertaken successfully, could produce several dividends with direct as well as outlying/multiplier effects. These could include:

- The near-decay of service provision and delivery will be resuscitated and enhanced with remarkable improvements in coverage at the initial stage. As the program advances, the quality will be equally improved
- Services cannot be delivered in an efficient manner in any state in which major weaknesses in public financial management (PFM) result in mass leakages in funds administration. Mismanagement risks could be minimized when the resources from the center are managed at the levels closest to the service delivery level. This argument asserted that fiscal decentralization leads to more prudent use of national resources if the blend of the having right fiscal regulatory systems and getting the resources to the communities in a devolved system is right.
- Local governance and decentralization, as and when effectively implemented, will facilitate creating a culture and an environment that promote citizens' active engagement in governance. The ultimate product will be to improve voice and accountability, culminating in improved and satisfactory governance
- The involvement of community members in planning and executing community development plans and budgets will promote participation and inclusion, and invariably will reduce marginalization and exclusion, which are symptoms of bad governance and underdevelopment. The principles of community and joint ownership of development programs will be introduced and nurtured resulting in every member of such communities feeling that s/he belongs to the whole and building community trust and social capital

Convinced about the arguments advanced as well as being informed by the CAS, the World Bank committed to engage the GoSL on possible support to resuscitate democratically elected local government in the country. The Bank carefully identified a number of strategic in-country actors for engagement. Some of these were the resident in-country development partners (DfID, EC, and UN system) and civil society organizations (CSOs) engaged in program development dialogue (identifying existing weaknesses in the planning as well as carefully gauging its potential entry point). The consultations with other critical actors further convinced the Bank that arguments advanced for its involvement on a major scale in the country were viable, timely, and likely to produce the desired effects and impacts. Therefore, the Bank committed to engage the GoSL in designing an initial four-year support program for local governance and decentralization (2004–08)

Decentralization Program in Design

The actual design of the program was led by the World Bank. A task team leader (TTL) was appointed to coordinate and supervise the various multistakeholders' engagements and consultations as well as briefings to both GoSL and the Bank.

To support the design of the local government and decentralization program, a grant known as the Project Preparation Facility (PPF) was sourced from the Japanese government. This funding was administered by the GoSL through the Governance Reform Secretariat (GRS). The latter, a unit in the Ministry of Presidential and Public Affairs in the Office of the President of GoSL, was made implementer, and a World-Bank-supported project (Public Sector Management Support 11) was made grants manger on behalf of the Bank.

The PPF was used to identify and recruit the services of experienced and renowned consultants (mostly practitioners and academics) in the field of local governance and decentralization as well as public financial management (PFM). A number of studies and analyses were planned and conducted both in-country and outside to inform the design of the program. The consultants also were targeted because of previous experiences in designing, developing, and implementing decentralization in Africa, Asia, and other parts of the world, to bring experiences and best practice to be built into the process.

The project is known officially as the Institutional Reform and Capacity Building Project, or as its popular acronym, IRCBP. The design of the World Bank's support to decentralization and local governance for Sierra Leone was subjected to the standard and approved World Bank procedures in accordance with World Bank guidelines and processes. A World Bank project appraisal mission conducted meetings and had discussions with the GoSL, development partners (DPs), and non-state actors within the country. The project also went through the World Bank's internal approval processes of review and Board approval.

Ultimately, the IRCBP was approved as a integrated four-component project. It addresses broad and emergent governance issues and challenges in service provision and delivery, budget and financial management, as well as capacity building for public policy work and improvement in personnel efficiency. The four components are:

- *Component One: Decentralization and Capacity Building.* Component is managed by two units of the project—the Decentralization Secretariat and the Local Government Finance Department—with two long-term national consultants as heads.
- *Component Two: Public Financial Management.* Unit is headed by a qualified accountant.
- *Component Three: Development Learning Center.* Unfortunately, unit never became functional because the former government was not able to undertake

its legal obligation as per the DCA to establish the center as a legal entity. Very serious bureaucratic bottlenecks made it impossible for the bill to be passed into law.

■ *Component Four: Project Coordination Unit*. Unit manages all the coordination issues and takes the lead on ensuring effective project management. It is headed by another long-term Sierra Leonean national consultant.

The institutional arrangement of the IRCBP is unique in certain a way. At the outset, the project and the World Bank identified both the Ministry of Finance and Ministry of Local Government and Community Development as champions of the national decentralization program. The unit responsible for overall coordination of the policy, legal, and regulatory as well as capacity building (Decentralization Secretariat) is placed within the Ministry of Local Government and Community Development as a Directorate. The unit that manages all the fiscal decentralization matters (Local Government Finance Department) and the units for Financial Management (Public Financial Management Reform Unit) and Project Coordination (Project Coordination Unit) are within the Ministry of Finance. The uniqueness of this program design is that it has greatly minimized the usual rivalry and bureaucratic competition between Ministries of Finance and Ministries of Local Government in the management of decentralization and local government reform, especially in Sub-Saharan Africa.

In Sierra Leone, there also is a Project Technical Steering Committee (TSC), which provides high-level, upstream policy and technical oversight of the implementation of the program and provides direct in-country support and supervision of the Project Management Team. To promote harmony and joint programming, the technical and administrative head of the Ministry of Finance (Financial Secretary) chairs the TSC. The committee initially had a single Chairperson and two other members: the Permanent Secretary (PS) of the Ministry of Local Government and Community Development and the Establishment Secretary (as the Public Service Human Resource Manager). These high-level managers have the authority and responsibility to facilitate smooth project and program implementation.

In supporting decentralization and local government in Sierra Leone, the project development objective (PDO) of the IRCBP can be summarized as:

"Supporting the efficient functioning of nineteen (19) local councils in Sierra Leone."

This major objective is supported by major outcome and intermediate outcome indicators. These are used by the GoSL and the World Bank to measure progress (or lack of it) in achieving the major objective, which justified the World Bank's initial commitment of $25 million of IDA money over 4 years.

The national decentralization program supported initially by the World Bank and lately by a multi-donor trust fund (MDTF), and managed through the IRCBP, has made major contributions. The Implementation Support Mission was undertaken jointly by DPs and GoSL in June 2008 at the end of the transition period. The mission has registered IRCBPs contributions as:

■ Local counsels (LCs) established after 32 years

- First term of first generation of councilors completed
- Second generation of councilors elected
- Core staff of local councils recruited
- LCs staff salaries introduced as a budget line in the national budget
- Basic infrastructure provided to LCs
- Basic local governance and government systems established in budgeting, planning, and procurement
- Intergovernmental fiscal transfer system established and functioning moderately well
- LCs providing core and basic services at an appreciable level
- Presence and usefulness of LCs felt in the country; interest and enthusiasm for them growing.

Despite these successes and achievements, there are 5 challenges that IRCBP will support GoSL in addressing over the next 3 years:

- Reformulate a comprehensive national decentralization policy to clarify focus and direction for implementation of the reform agenda
- Address the outstanding HR matters relating to attraction and retention of staff (possibly integrating the central and local HR services)
- Build capacity of devolving MDAs to fully assume and execute pre- and post-devolution oversight responsibilities with much more interest and commitment
- Provide capacity building and institutional support to LCs to improve own-source revenue mobilization
- Support the preparation of a Chiefdom Governance Policy and Act to clearly address the functional relationships and interrelationship(s) between and among chiefdom and local council stakeholders in the decentralization process.

Notes

[1] In September 2007, the ministry was redesignated the Ministry of Internal Affairs, Local Government and Rural Development.

[2] Later, the Vice President became the titular head of the taskforce, but the actual chairing was done by the Hon. Minister of Local Government and Rural Development.

[3] Prior to the constitution of the taskforce, a team of 1 international and 1 national consultant was contracted by UNDP on behalf of GoSL to consolidate various laws on local government and decentralization in Sierra Leone.

[4] Consultancy support was provided mainly by World Bank, DfID, and EC. Consultants were primarily from Ghana, Uganda, and United Kingdom, especially the University of Birmingham.

[5] Key issues for the district-based consultations included nature and type of elections; quota system for perceived excluded and marginalized groups (women, youth, and disabled); membership and role of paramount chiefs; and sources of local revenue and sharing mechanisms.

[6] The subgroups were Administrative Decentralization, Fiscal Decentralization, Functional Decentralization, and Capacity Building for Decentralization. Consultancy support was provided

mainly by World Bank, DfID, and EC. Consultants were primarily from Ghana, Uganda, and United Kingdom, especially the University of Birmingham.

[7] Decentralization Secretariat (DecSec) is a Component Unit of IRCBP as well as a Project Unit of MLGCD. DecSec provided technical leadership and coordination of the Local Government and Decentralization Program.

[8] GoSL's decision to authorize the preparation of the statutory instrument as well as to request that it be read and laid before Parliament to gain statutory status manifested political will by the central government to support full and effective devolution. The 21-day period in Parliament was to make room for objection by devolving to MDAs, or local councils, MPs and the public at large. Sierra Leone's SI received no objection within the stipulated 21 days so was passed as an instrument of law.

[9] LGA vests authority in the President of Sierra Leone, acting on the advice of the ministry responsible for local government and in consultation with the National Electoral Commission, to define, name, and upgrade a locality in the country.

[10] The Provinces Act of 1965; Local Courts Act.

[11] LGA provides for 20% of Paramount Chiefs in a district (approximate size of a local council area) to become ex-officio members of local councils and sit side by side with elected councilors as equal members in council with deliberative and voting rights.

[12] The LGA provides for all ward committees to have their meetings chaired by the elected councilors for district-based wards and the four councilors for urban council. This requirement was seen by the Paramount Chiefs as not recognizing their preeminent roles but making the chiefs appear to be "ordinary" members of the ward committees.

[13] The 4 prioritized laws are (1) Hospital Boards Act, (2) Education Act, Sierra Leone Water Company Act (SALWACO Act), and Local Tax Act. The SALWACO Act reorganizes the authority to provide and regulate rural water supply in Sierra Leone.

[14] The LGSC is an 8-person committee appointed by the president. LGA 2004 provides for at least 3 women, and 1 of the non-ex-officio members should be appointed chair. The commissioners are chosen for four-year terms (coinciding with the life of a council). Each of the four regions of the country is represented by a commissioner.

[15] The provincial coordinating committees are constituted as follows: regional minister of central government (chairman), regional (provincial secretary) as secretary, with one representative from each of the local council chairs/mayors in the region. Each committee is required by law to host at least one meeting per quarter.

[16] The Inter-Ministerial Committee (IMC) comprises The Hon. Vice President of the Republic of Sierra Leone (Chairman), Permanent Secretary in the ministry responsible for local government (PS, or Secretary), all central government ministers of devolving sectors (members) and one chair/mayor (from each of the four administrative regions of the country) member to represent the interests of all chairs/mayors in the region.

CHAPTER 2

Fiscal Decentralization: Building the Financial Capacity of Local Governments

Adams Sanpha Kargbo

Legislative Base

Fiscal decentralization in Sierra Leone started in earnest in 2005 after passage of the Local Government Act (LGA) in 2004 and the local government elections held later that year. The LGA supported fiscal decentralization by detailing the councils' expenditure responsibilities and revenue assignments, and supplying the legislative basis for a grants system.

The expenditure assignment is supported by law through Schedule III of the LGA and the Statutory Instrument (SI) of November 2004: the Local Government Assumptions of Functions Regulations. Schedule III of the LGA outlined the functions and related activities to be devolved to local governments over an initial period of four years. The SI then provided more detail on the functions and activities to be devolved to local government and specified when each function was to be devolved during the transition. The overall objective of the expenditure assignment is to make sure that service delivery is improved at the local government level.

The legal basis for the revenue assignment to councils is highlighted in Parts VII and VIII of the LGA, which also mentions issues relating to the expenditure responsibilities of local government. To support their responsibilities, the LGA empowers councils to collect own-source revenue from various sources, including head taxes, property rates, licenses, user fees and charges, and shares of mining revenues. In all of these activities, they are allowed by law to set their own rates and fees.

Although the revenue assignment is supported by LGA 2004, ambiguity in the law constrains the effective implementation of this important pillar of fiscal decentralization. In particular, there is lack of clarity between the LGA and other legal instruments that relate to the fiscal activities of the chiefdom councils—an important lower level of government. Before the reintroduction of decentralization in 2004, most of the revenue sources allocated to councils by the LGA had been collected by chiefdom councils. In some cases, the LGA provides for sharing revenues, but sharing has not worked well.

The failure of the LGA to adequately address the fiscal issues of chiefdom councils, together with actions by some sectors of the central government administration that were based on misinterpretations of the LGA, have created considerable tensions between the chiefdom councils and the local governments. Local administrators were not supportive of the LCs' revenue mobilization drive, which affected the own-source revenue performance of the LCs. These problems are expected to be adequately addressed by the implementation of chiefdom governance reform and a review of the LGA as we end the transition.

Revenue Mobilization

Supporting local governments to maximize their revenue collection is a high priority because this is one way to ensure sustainability of decentralized governance and make councils more accountable to local taxpayers. An initial assessment was done on the revenue-raising effort of urban councils. The results showed that adequate effort had not been made. For instance, it was noted that property rates, usually a major source of revenue for local governments, were either grossly underused or not being used at all. No district councils had credible databases for revenue sources, and, in the urban councils, existing databases were incomplete and outdated. Workshops and seminars were organized to discuss strategies to overcome these inadequacies. Nevertheless, the results remained unsatisfactory. Councils still are not making adequate efforts to mobilize revenue. In part, the explanations are local governments' lack of resources to undertake such assessments and continuing ambiguities in the law.

In 2005 an initial target of Le 2,000 per capita for each council was set to be achieved incrementally over the transition. As we approach the end of the transition, an assessment shows mixed results, with only some councils recently achieving very large increases in collections from some revenue sources.[1] Through the Institutional Reform and Capacity Building Project (IRCBP), central government is funding the establishment of a property cadastre and business licenses database. Initially, this will be done for selected urban councils. In addition, a proposal has been developed to request funding from potential donors so that this important aspect of the fiscal decentralization can be undertaken in all local government areas.

If local councils are to be truly independent, the importance of own-revenue mobilization by them cannot be overemphasized. Councils probably will always have to rely on central government transfers for most of their funding. However, *the more resources that councils are able to generate internally, the more autonomy they will have and the more viable they will be.*

The initial assessment done in 2005 indicated that urban councils that had been operating under management committees were not making adequate efforts to generate own-source revenue. Total revenue generated that year by all the councils amounted to Le 4.7 billion. Approximately Le 3.2 billion, or 68 percent, had been collected from non-tax revenue sources; licenses accounted for the remaining Le 1.5 billion, or 31 percent. Only Le 1.4 billion had been collected from tax revenue, of which Le 1.2 billion, or 82 percent, had come from local tax.

The situation improved in 2006, when total own revenue increased by almost 24 percent to Le 5.80 billion. Again, most of this sum (almost 80 percent, or Le 4.6 billion) had been collected from non-tax revenue sources, of which market dues and licenses accounted for 44 percent and 32 percent, respectively. However, the progress made in 2006 was lost in 2007, when total own-source revenue declined by 28 percent to Le 1.6 billion. Despite the decline, the trend in contributions by revenue source continued as non-tax revenue accounted for over 70 percent of the total; market dues accounted for nearly half of total collections.[2] The main reason for the poor performance was the central government elections held in that year. Many people had been busy with politics, and some politicians and others had sent out campaign messages that negatively affected revenue mobilization.

The performance of the 6 urban councils differs from that of the 13 district councils in revenue strength. The strength of the urban councils lies in non-tax revenue (mostly market dues and licenses). In contrast, district councils rely heavily on revenue from local tax although, in mining areas, revenue from mining activities contributes significantly. The better revenue collection performance by the urban councils is probably due to two reasons: they are relatively more developed, and they do not share their revenues with chiefdoms—a source of tension in the districts.

In 2005 revenue collection in the 6 urban councils was Le 2.5 billion, which represented 54 percent of councils' total collections. Revenue collection in the 13 district councils was Le 2.2 billion, or 46 percent of the total. Non-tax revenue continues to be the greatest source of urban council revenue. In 2006 most of the revenues for these councils came from market dues, whereas in 2005 licenses accounted for a greater share.

The indications for revenue collection by both urban and district councils are encouraging. Significant increases in sums collected were likely in 2008 due to changes in the method of collection. New strategies were adopted that are yielding results. Enforcement of existing regulations also was expected to contribute to increases in 2008. As we move forward, developing efficient collection mechanisms for market dues and the current plan to unfold the property cadastre in all councils are high on the LGFD agenda.

In addition to local governments raising own-source revenue, the LGA provides that:

> ...until and including the financial year ending in 2008, Parliament
> shall appropriate to local governments as a tied grant for each
> devolved service at least that amount necessary to continue the
> operation and maintenance of that service at the standard [at] which
> it was provided in the year prior to its devolution.

This provision was designed to ensure that funds provided to local governments enabled them to provide the pre-devolution level of services that were devolved to them. However, this provision created two problems: (1) determining the standard of service delivery before decentralization and (2) more importantly, measuring the level of transfers necessary for these standards to be continued (or improved).

These issues have resulted in a level of post-devolution vertical fiscal imbalance that the intergovernmental fiscal transfer system has not yet adequately addressed. While the mismatch between available and required resources at the council level has been identified, its true magnitude has yet to be determined and used to adjust the resource allocations between the councils and central government MDAs. The size of the differential will need to be addressed in the post-transition. Determining the true cost of devolved functions is essential if councils are to be adequately funded and service delivery is to be improved to meet Millennium Development Goals (MDGs).

Institutional Framework

The strength behind fiscal decentralization in Sierra Leone is that the Ministry of Finance and Economic Development (MoFED) is a champion of the reintroduction of decentralization. The probable reason is that MoFED sees decentralization as a possible means to promote post-conflict economic development, poverty reduction, fiscal discipline, and administrative efficiency in government operations at both the local and central government levels. It is already clear to the ministry that decentralization has achieved more in these fields than has been achieved by most reform efforts.

To support fiscal decentralization through MoFED, the government created a new department—the Local Government Finance Department (LGFD)—to be the organ to manage local government financing and financial management. LGFD serves as the interface between local governments and central government on all financial matters, including financial planning and budget preparation, financial management, grant distribution, and revenue mobilization. LGFD is charged with the responsibility to design and manage the fiscal decentralization process and serves as the secretariat for the Local Government Finance Committee (LGFC).

The LGFC is the statutory body established under LGA 2004. The committee comprises 7 members: 4 representing the regions and nominated by the chairs of all local governments, and 3 ex-officio members. The four representing local government are persons with considerable knowledge of public finance but no allegiance to any local government. The three ex-officio members are senior representatives of the ministries responsible for finance, local government and development, and economic planning. This ex-officio membership needs to be reconsidered because of the recent merger of the Ministry of Finance and Economic Development (MoFED) and its predecessor, the Ministry of Development and Economic Planning.

The major statutory function of LGFC is to recommend to the finance minister the amounts of the grant allocations to each council for each of the devolved functions. In performing this task, the LGFC also assesses the recommended tied grants for administration for each local government, and indicates the formulae used in arriving at the recommended amounts. This committee also has responsibility for managing the gradual transition to reduce conditionality of grants and the eventual change to grants being untied.

Grants System

The intergovernmental fiscal transfer system was developed in line with the devolution framework. During the transition, the transfer system focused on the recurrent non salary expenditures of the services devolved to local governments. Devolving recurrent salaries and development expenditure will be an issue for discussion soon after transition.

The grants transfer system was developed at two different levels. First, the LGFD assisted the MDAs to determine the vertical allocation: how much should the devolving ministries, departments, and agencies (MDAs) allocate for each of the functions they are devolving? Second, the question of the horizontal distribution of grants was confronted: how much should each local government receive for each of the functions devolved to it?

The Local Government Act of 2004 guided both the determination of the vertical allocation and the horizontal distribution of grants to local governments. As stated above, the law assisted in the determination of the vertical distribution by stipulating that the central government must provide local government with tied grants that were at least equal to the real pre-devolution level of central government expenditure on each function in question. According to the law, funding for the assigned service delivery activities then should fluctuate with the national resource envelope and should move according to the resources allocated to central government budgetary functions. This measure ensured that service delivery did not deteriorate as a result of devolution but was maintained at the pre-devolution level.

Even though the determination of the vertical allocation of grants to local governments was guided in this way, its implementation had been a challenge. As a starting point, it was agreed between the MDAs and MoFED (through the LGFD) that grant funds would be provided at the pre-devolution level for each function that was to be devolved. The actual cost of devolution was to be determined by devolved sector professionals with assistance from the LGFD.

Thus, the first challenge was to determine the cost prior to devolution—how much was being spent on each of the devolved functions by the central government level—so that these amounts could be transferred to local councils. This difficulty arose in part because central government MDA budgets were not activity-based. Thus, LGFD had to negotiate on behalf of local governments to ensure that sufficient funds were transferred as grants. In the absence of activity-based budgets, ad hoc methods were adopted to determine the vertical allocation through annual negotiations with MDAs. As expected, *most functions have been grossly underfunded by MDA budgets, and this underfunding has made it more difficult to rapidly improve service delivery at the local government level.*

Another challenge has been that some of the activities identified for devolution were part of a broader "bundled" function within the MDA. The vertical sharing therefore required careful hiving out and costing these bundled activities. There also was an issue of unfunded mandates—functions that MDAs were to have devolved but whose devolution was not carried out. As a result, there were no associated costs that could be removed from the MDA budgets and given to the councils as grants.

Whether the funding level that has been taken from the MDA budgets was adequate requires further consideration. It is believed by the LGFD that most devolved functions still are underfunded, that is, that the grants allocated to LCs for most of the functions were inadequate for these activities to be effectively implemented. However, the exact amounts of the necessary adjustments are yet to be determined. The upcoming functional reviews of the MDAs will make it easier to decide on a more appropriate vertical sharing. Until this issue is decided, we cannot realistically determine the gap in the funding for devolved functions.

The law provides that the horizontal distribution of grants among councils be done equitably to reflect the differentials in councils' expenditure needs and, in the longer term, revenue-raising ability. The law also provides that, during the transition, grants for devolved functions be tied. In line with these requirements, to reflect relative resource requirements, a grant distribution formula was developed for each devolved function and the councils' administrative grant. As a result, there were some 26 different formulae and grants for Fiscal Year 2008. The development of the formula was impeded by the lack of available data and the difficulties encountered in getting the co-operation of sector professionals, particularly during the first year of the process.

Despite these challenges, the first formulae were developed in 2005, and grants were distributed to local governments for functions devolved in that year. As devolution of functions increased, the number of these formulae also increased. Moreover, over the years, the formulae have been changed, and, as required by the law, devolving sector professionals have played a leading role in determining the allocation criteria. These determinations usually are made through seminars in which MDA representatives and other stakeholders, including local government representatives, donors, NGOs, and civil society organizations (CSOs), discuss the various allocation criteria for each sector with the LGFD staff and LGFC members. Participants bear in mind the availability of the data and the need for simplicity of formula. These negotiations have broadened ownership of the process, helped remove any implied political influence on the distribution, and reduced the scope for councils to protest against the allocation criteria.

The formulae cover grants for devolved functions and for administrative purposes, with councilors' sitting fees and allowances being covered in the administrative grant. This grant is not meant to fully fund councils' administrative expenses but to defray some of their administrative costs. The grant for councilors' sitting fees and expenses is being funded by the central government budget as a grant for salaries. The central government also is funding, through a grant, the salaries of up to six key positions in the local government administration and the administrative support staff transferred from the district offices to the district councils.

At this stage of decentralization, salaries of staff providing devolved functions and working with local governments still are being paid directly by the central government. The payroll still is being held at the central government level, and no definite time has been agreed for its devolution. Devolution of the payroll for staff associated with functions devolved to local government obviously will significantly increase the value of the grants transferred to councils. This is a critical element in the devolution process considering the importance of payroll expenses in the public sector budget. *In the post-transition, payroll devolution must be tackled as a priority.*

A different issue related to salaries for staff exists in urban councils. The salaries for the administrative support staff inherited from the pre–04 Freetown City Council and the urban area management committees are paid by councils from their own resources.

Local Government Development Grants Program

While the development budget has not been devolved, the central government and its donor partners have supported local governments to undertake development projects through a Local Government Development Grant Program (LGDGP). This participatory, demand- and performance-driven program commenced in 2004. Its primary objective was to make sure that all local governments established under LGA 2004 had some capacity to improve the provision of facilities and services for their people. The program was designed so that, in achieving these objectives, councils progressively gain experience in participatory planning, budgeting, financial management, and project implementation.

Initial funding for the program was provided by the World Bank and the GoSL. The Bank-financed component under the Institutional Reform and Capacity Building Project (IRCBP) was to be US$6.0 million over 2004–08. Over the same period, the GoSL targeted a counterpart contribution of US$1.5 million. In addition, DfID later pledged funding of GB £2.5 million, of which £0.950 million was to be provided between June 2006–June 2008, and £1.550 million is to be made available July 2008–December 2010. Over time, additional funding is expected from other donor partners.

Local government's access to funding under the LGDGP is predicated on the fulfillment of a set of minimum conditions. These minimum conditions are based in government statutes, regulations, and guidelines; and are intended to both promote compliance with the legislation and provide safeguards that ensure the efficient and effective use of the grant funds.

In 2005, the first full year of program implementation,[3] local councils were required to meet a set of minimum conditions for access to the LGDG grant:

- Have a duly elected council functioning according to legislation
- Have a bank account into which the grant could be paid
- Have financial management staff operating within the council's office, with capability to manage the funds
- Have a development plan that included the projects it intended to undertake, and on which the council had based its budget
- Have a list of projects that reflected the priorities and needs of the locality as contained in the development plan
- Have a budget that
    - Balanced income and expenditure
    - Was a public document that had been posted on a notice board after being passed by the council
    - Had been submitted to the local government finance committee
- Meet the transparency requirements specified in LGA 04 on matters relating to development plans, financial statements, council assets, and minutes of council meetings.

In subsequent years, based on the experiences noted in the course of program implementation, a number of conditions have been added to the initial set of minimum conditions. Councils must:

- Have a strategic plan that was prepared in a participatory process that involved the community and was debated and approved by the council
- Have accounts prepared, debated by council, and submitted to the auditor-general in accordance with the local government financial regulations

■ Have no substantial adverse comments bordering on dishonesty in the audit report

■ Have a balanced budget that includes the projects that the council intends to undertake and a plan to fund asset maintenance

■ Develop acceptable project proposals with acceptable procurement plans for all projects to be implemented.

Funding under the LGDGP effectively started in 2004 with a challenge grant of Le 1.55 billion. The challenge grant was intended to help local councils to quickly win the confidence of their electorates and kick-start the implementation of development initiatives before devolution of functions commenced in 2005. Projects of up to US$25,000 were supported by the program and implemented through the Rapid Results Initiative (see chapter 5). The objectives were largely met as all but a few of the projects had been successfully completed. Subsequent transfers have been made based on annual formula-based allocations determined prior to the commencement of each financial year, on the condition that the conditions for grant receipt were met.

Since the inception of the program in 2004, over 220 projects have been implemented in various poverty-related sectors such as agriculture, education, roads, and health and sanitation.[4] Roads projects have received the greatest attention, attracting a total of 44 projects (20 percent of all those implemented). Much attention also has been put into the education, health and sanitation, markets, and recreation sectors. These four latter sectors combined attracted 97 projects. Government sees roads as a vital element of the economic development of council areas. To ensure the continuing priority of roads, in 2007 the program was changed so that all eligible councils now receive specific funds that they must spend on roads projects. In total, from 2004–mid-2008, Le 18.27 billion (US$6.19 million) was transferred to councils as development funding under the LGDGP.[5] Of the LGDGP transfers thus far, approximately 85 percent were funded from IRCBP (World Bank) sources. GoSL provided the remaining 15 percent (Le 2.69 billion). The contributions of DfID and other donor partners under the Multi-Donor Trust Fund have been targeted for transfers in 2008 and beyond.

Size of Fiscal Transfers

Budgetary allocations. In 2004 government transferred Le 816.4 million to local governments as start-up administrative grants. In addition to this, each local government received roughly Le 100 million under the LGDGP to develop and implement quick impact-projects using the Rapid Results Initiative described above.

Grants allocated to local governments in the 2005 budget were approximately Le 23.1 billion, roughly 9 percent of total non-salary, non-interest recurrent budgetary allocations. In 2006 it declined to Le 21.6 billion, or approximately 7 percent of total non salary, non-interest recurrent allocation. By 2007, with greater devolution of functions, the grants allocated to local governments more than doubled to over Le 47 billion, or 13 percent of total non-salary, non-interest recurrent central government budgetary allocation for that year. In 2008 total grants allocated to local governments again increased with devolution of functions to Le 56.8 billion, or 20.6 percent of total non-salary, non-interest recurrent budgetary allocation.

While the development budget is yet to be devolved, central government is contributing to local governments' development projects through the contribution it makes to the Local Government Development Grant Program. GoSL allocated Le 1.0 billion each in 2005 and 2006, Le 5.0 billion in 2007, and Le 2.5 billion in 2008.

Actual payments of grants. In most years, actual grants disbursed have fallen short of the allocated amount, mainly as a result of difficulties encountered at the central government level during budget implementation. For example, Le 23 billion was allocated in 2005, but actual transfers in that year were only Le 18.2 billion. In 2006 grant allocations to local governments in the budget were Le 21.6 billion, but actual transfers were only Le 17.2 billion. The situation worsened in 2007 as actual grants transferred were merely 16 percent, or Le 7.5 billion, compared to an allocated amount of Le 47.1 billion. There are indications that the situation might improve in 2008. At end-June 2008, grants transferred to local governments already had exceeded 60 percent of total grants allocated to councils in the FY 2008 budget.

Paying the Grants to Councils

The law provides that grants be paid to local governments on a monthly basis. However, this has not happened. One reason is that the central government makes payments to MDAs on a quarterly basis and therefore finds it much easier to make payments to local governments in like manner. This part of LGA 2004 needs to be revised to make it consistent with what obtains at the central government level.

To reduce administrative bottlenecks and increase the LGFD's capacity to monitor the financial management of the councils, payments are made directly into respective local government bank accounts. A difficulty that this has created is that each council must have a separate bank account for each grant that it receives, thus proliferating the number of accounts. The same degree of financial management scrutiny is possible with fewer accounts, and this change will be considered during the post-transition phase of fiscal decentralization.

The adequacy and timeliness of transfers has been a key challenge in Sierra Leone's fiscal decentralization. In addition to the fact that grants allocated to councils are inadequate for many of the functions, it has been very difficult for local governments to predict the timing of these payments and plan service provision accordingly. Most frequently, payments are made far behind the intended period. For example, first quarter payments are most frequently made in the second quarter of the year and, as described above, have never been equal to full budgetary appropriations. This delay and shortfall seriously affect budget implementation and undermines service delivery by local governments.

There are certain functions which, even though devolved to councils, are funded through transfers to service providers on behalf of local governments. Most of these functions relate to devolved education services and are paid to either service providers or contractors providing goods to schools. Examples are the payment of examination fees and the procurement of textbooks and teaching and learning materials. Issues relating to economies of scale have been the primary consideration for making these payments on behalf of, rather than directly to, councils. However, GoSL may include in the current review of the LGA that local governments eventually will be responsible for making these payments.

Financial Management Capacity of the Councils

Another important element of fiscal decentralization is that local governments have been given responsibility for their own planning, budgeting, and financial management. The law provides that every local government shall prepare, for council approval, a budget for each financial year. The budget should reflect the priorities and needs of the locality as contained in the council's development plan and must balance income and expenditure by way of annual financial estimates of revenue and expenditure. This requirement to balance imposes a hard budget constraint on the councils, which are not allowed to borrow during the transition.

Local governments were supported through the IRCBP by the LGFD and the Public Financial Management Reform Unit (*PFMRU*) of the Ministry of Finance to prepare development plans, which articulate the development aspirations of their various communities. These development plans become the bases for the councils' budgets. The plans are reviewed annually during budget preparation to ensure that they remain in line with local priorities. Local governments were also required to prepare medium-term expenditure framework (MTEF) budgets in line with central government policy. The LGFD provides regular support to local governments in this regard through annual seminars in which key staff of local governments as well as those from the devolving MDAs participate.

Capacity building of local government staff in the first three years of the project has not been as beneficial to local governments as had been anticipated. Many of the staff who received the initial capacity building support had been assigned from central government and had to return there after two years working with local governments. The assignment of these staff to the local governments (and the related sunset clause for their assignment) is perhaps one of the mistakes that was made in the early years of decentralization. Some hold the view that capacity building would have had more effect if new staff had been recruited for local governments at the inception of the program. Nevertheless, capacity building support for budget preparation, implementation, and monitoring is ongoing.

Financial management capacity issues are critical to fiscal decentralization. Even though most of the finance officers and accountants have the basic qualifications in their fields, *they lack experience.* Each local council has a finance officer and an accountant to manage its financial resources. The chief administrator is the vote controller. These officers have acquired a considerable amount of training since their recruitment, and much more is planned for them. Most recently, examinations are being conducted at the conclusion of each training session to make sure that only deserving participants receive certificates. These examinations also help the IRCBP determine those who are doing well and must be supported from those who are not doing well and might best be considered for possible replacement. The overall objective is to strengthen financial management capacity so that local governments can manage the resources that are being transferred to them and cope with the huge increase in transfers that will result once salaries also are provided as grants.

Financial management staff were part of the core group of officers whom central government assigned to local councils in 2004. Most of these officers had minimal accounting experience and few or no computing skills. These limitations posed challenges for financial management at the local council, especially for timely preparation of financial reports as required by law, implementing internal controls, and safeguarding fixed assets.

As part of the capacity building for the staff of each council, over a three–year period, these assigned treasurers were trained by the LGFD and PFMRU on a number of financial management issues, including the use of Microsoft Excel. Despite these trainings, results of periodic assessment by the LGFD were not satisfactory as internal controls remain weak with little or no separation of duties in the Finance Department. To mitigate this adverse situation, two financial management (FM) specialists from the PFMRU were assigned to monitor and supervise the treasurers of the 19 local councils. The former carried out regular visit to all the councils to ensure that proper accounting procedures were applied and the necessary working tools including computers and printers were available and in use. The FM specialists also identified training needs and ensured that the treasurers received relevant training through service providers.

The indications for the future are good, with the recent recruitment of finance officers and accountants in local councils. A series of FM and IT training courses have been delivered to these staff. Certificates are presented only to participants who attain a pre-set standard. Initially, a fully manual accounting system was in use, but gradually a homegrown Excel financial template that links cashbooks and financial statements via the general ledger has been designed and implemented. There have also been considerable improvements in councils' compliance with legal regulations, including the submission of accounts for audits. FM training will continue to be provided as decentralization deepens.

To enhance the FM regulatory framework at the local level, a draft financial administration regulation (FAR) for local councils is being prepared. It will be supported by manuals to aid the work of the council accounting staff. However, to sustain the financial capacity of the councils, development of a staff attraction and retention policy is critical and will be one focus of the future reform programs.

Achievements

Much of the success of fiscal decentralization thus far probably stems from the buy-in of the Ministry of Finance and Economic Development at the onset of the program. However, an assessment of fiscal decentralization in Sierra Leone as we approach the end of the transition reveals mixed results. There has been noticeable progress in some very important areas. However, others still face considerable challenges.

The devolution of functions to councils generally has happened in accordance with the legislative requirements. Within the limits of the tied grants that they receive to fund non-salary expenses, councils have some degree of fiscal autonomy and authority to make expenditure decisions. They also are able to formulate budgets based on broad national policy issues and the development priorities of the local community. However, councils have not yet taken (or been given) responsibility for the salaries and payroll associated with the devolved functions, and this delay is creating some issues of staff accountability. Nevertheless, the service providers know that they are answerable to the councils rather than to the MDAs for service quality and level, and generally seem happy with the decentralized arrangements.

The implementation of the revenue assignment is only partially successful. Some local governments have been able to generate additional revenues from some of the revenue sources assigned to them. However, effective implementation of this assignment has been constrained by ambiguities in the law that empowers chiefdom councils and some central government agencies to collect the same revenue. Until all central government legislation that has a relationship to decentralized governance is harmonized, effective implementation of the revenue assignment will remain constrained. The current strategy is to help councils establish reliable databases on all revenue sources available to them, particularly property tax and business licenses, and build their capacity to manage revenue collection from these databases.

The intergovernmental transfer system has worked well. A set of fair and equitable grants distribution formulae has been established and used to transfer grants to local governments. There has been little or no objection from stakeholders (local councils, MDAs, CSOs) on the formulae, and all seem happy that there is no political influence on the distributions. *The high level of transparency in the workings of the LGFD and LGFC are major contributors to the level of confidence that stakeholders have in the grant outcomes.* However, adequacy and timeliness of transfers challenge the process. In addition, the vertical allocation needs to be reviewed, as the current ad hoc shares do not seem to be equitable. Such shortfalls could undermine effective service delivery at the local level. If the intergovernmental fiscal transfer system is to function more effectively, the issues of inadequate transfers and unfunded mandates given to councils need to be addressed.

Limited progress has been made on the issue of controlling local government borrowing beyond the specification of LGA 2004. It is urgent to develop a borrowing policy and guidelines for local governments. Some local governments are borrowing in one form or another with no policy or guideline from the central government. This lack of official regulation is fiscally dangerous and must be resolved.

Monitoring missions are being undertaken by LGFD to check and advise on improvements to councils' financial management capacity, However, these missions should be undertaken more frequently (quarterly) to ensure that local governments adhere to regulations and implement the activities in their development and strategic plans. Specifically, the adherence to good financial management principles should be enforced and defaulters penalized appropriately. To do so will strengthen what has already been achieved in terms of fiscal decentralization in Sierra Leone from 2004 to 2008.

Notes

[1] Local tax collection by the Makeni City Council has increased more than 10-fold from Le 3.3 million in 2005 to Le 37.0 million in the first 6 months of 2008. Based on past experience, shop registration revenue in Freetown City Council was budgeted to be Le 17 million in 2008. However, collection methods were changed, and by June 2008 revenue from this source already had exceeded an astounding Le 500 million.

[2] Market dues are neither taxes nor licenses. They can be considered as fees paid by "small traders" and differ from local tax or licenses paid by shop-owners.

[3] Funding in 2004 was a challenge grant intended to give councils the opportunity to take advantage of the first 100-day challenge.

[4] A number of FY 2007 projects are being implemented, or their commencement has been delayed by the late transfer of funds in that year. FY 2008 is being used largely as a "catch-up" year because of the 2007 deferrals.

[5] Additional funding also is expected to be distributed in the second half of 2008.

CHAPTER 3

Administrative Decentralization: Building the Non-Financial Capacity of Local Governments

Alhassan Kanu

Managing and sustaining decentralized governance for effective delivery of services require adequate capacity in institutions, networks, organizational structures, facilities and equipment, human resources, data and information, networks and alliances, as well as a supportive and conducive legal and policy environment. Thus, the effective functioning of the new local councils could be guaranteed only if they were given the requisite capacity and environment to perform their functions and responsibilities.

With a conviction that capacity is a key requirement for effective local governance, the capacity enhancement of the local councils has received prominence since the commencement of the decentralization program in 2004. The establishment of a Capacity Building Unit within the Decentralization Secretariat in 2004 was a positive step in facilitating capacity development of the local councils. The unit has done much to strengthen the capacities of the local councils. In doing so, it also has confronted critical challenges and learned important lessons. This chapter provides a detailed account of the capacity of local governments before the passage of the Local Government Act 2004 (LGA 2004); the unit's planning for capacity building; and the capacity building strategy, achievements, challenges, and lessons learned. The chapter concludes with recommendations to strengthen the future capacity building effort.

Situation of Local Councils before Passage of Local Government Act 2004

Local government has been an integral part of governance in Sierra Leone since the colonial era. At that time, with its indirect rule, the British introduced the district council system of local governance in the protectorate (established in 1896), whereas, earlier, the colony alone (established in 1808) had had a different system of administration. The colony had been administered directly from Britain through a governor. The protectorate was administered through a system of indirect rule in which district commissioners were responsible for the administration of the districts in close collaboration with the chiefs. This administrative arrangement was strengthened during the immediate post-independence era, when district councils were given additional tasks, including developing their localities.

During that period, the local councils were categorized in three types: (a) City Council (Freetown, the capital), (b) Town Councils (Bo, Kenema, Makeni, Koidu New Sembehun, and Bonthe), and (c) District Councils (Bombali, Koinadugu, Port Loko, Kambia, Tonkolili, Kono, Kenema, Bo, Pujehun, Bonthe, Moyamba, Kailahun, and Western Area Rural).

The three categories of local councils had varying capacities in terms of staff, infrastructure, and revenue, as well as varying success rates in service delivery to their localities. Generally, all the local councils were credited for effective service delivery, evidenced by such things as the construction and management of municipal and district council schools, construction of feeder roads, and provision of pipe-borne water. Most of the local councils were well established with effective administrative systems and infrastructure.

District Councils. In 1972, just 11 years after independence, the district councils were abolished by President Siaka Stevens because they were said to be highly corrupt, politicized, and maladministered.[1] Their dissolution resulted in the transfer of their infrastructure and staff to the central government's provincial administration under the supervision of the provincial secretary and district officers. In areas with co-located councils, the town councils took over some of the infrastructure of the district councils. These arrangements continued until 2004. However, even before 2004, local district government gradually declined until only a remnant of government remained at that level. The few remaining staff provided very little service to the public.

City Council. From 1972 until 2004, the Freetown City Council functioned under a Committee of Management. Since the district councils were created, there has been an infrastructure and an administrative and staffing system in place to perform council functions. In terms of service delivery, the council witnessed oscillating degrees of effectiveness and efficiency, hingeing on the capacity of the management at any given time. For example, while the late Alfred Akibo-Betts was chair, the council witnessed its brightest period for revenue generation and service delivery. However, in later years, performance declined, and the council was often accused of being inefficient and corrupt.

Town councils. In 1972, the town councils were converted to committees of management to improve their business processes and performance. Disappointingly, the performance of the town councils worsened, and they became largely corrupt and inefficient. The major preoccupation of these committees was the collection of market dues, which then were poorly managed and accounted for. Because these committees of management were greatly influenced and, to a large extent, controlled by the central political authorities, they became a "dumping ground" for political supporters who could not be absorbed into more lucrative central government jobs. Consequently, these committees became bloated with excess staff who had little or no capacity to function effectively. The committee members were simply conduits for the political expression of the government of the day, and the committees were centers for galvanizing central government political patronage. The fact that all revenues went up to central government instead of out to provide basic services to the people greatly compromised the expenditure framework of the committees and their abilities to provide basic services for their localities. By 2004, these committees were providing very few services to the people they were supposed to be serving.

Expanded role of traditional authorities. With the decline of district and town government by the early 1970s, the traditional authorities were looked on by the people as the only remaining level of "government" that had responsibility and capacity (whether they did or not) to which the people could turn for assistance. Over time, the chiefs became more active in a range of public sector activities that the councils had previously managed but were especially active in revenue collection. However, the chiefs' activities did not carry over into maintaining service standards so public sector services gradually declined.

The centralization of power at the national level and the deterioration of local services were major determinants of the long and brutal civil war that began in 1991 and from which Sierra Leone did not emerge until 2003.

Emergence of the New Local Councils

With the worsening economic situation, pervasiveness of corruption among the committees of management, and marginalization of most citizens (especially the rural people) in decisionmaking, in 2004 the government undertook a major governance reform. It replaced the entrenched centralized system of governance by decentralization. The aims were to open up political space, to bring decisionmaking closer to the people, and to improve the transparency and accountability of public officials. It was hoped that this reform also would bring about improved and sustained service delivery.[2] The passage of the Local Government Act (LGA) in March 2004 ushered in 19 new local councils nation-wide with the mandate to coordinate the development of the localities.

The new councils came into existence at a time that the country was just recovering from the devastating conflict that had destroyed most of the infrastructure of the previous local governance institutions. Most of the district offices had been vandalized; the town councils had been ransacked; and the Freetown City Council's (FCC) enviable City Hall had been burned down. Consequently, most of the new local councils had to resort to make-shift arrangements to house their office activities.

The new district councils started with no staff with capacity since the prior councils had been nonfunctional. As a stop-gap, the district councils initially had to rely on the staff (chief administrator, deputy, and treasurer) assigned to them in 2004 by the Office of the Establishment Secretary. They were provided with some staff from the abolished district offices, but these were lower level support staff, not administrative staff. The town councils inherited a large number of staff from the previous structure, but these employees were aging and had limited management capacity. The town councils also had to rely on the assigned staff. Freetown City Council (FCC) was comparatively better off since there was a well-established administrative and management system in place and an array of technical staff responsible for key technical issues. Nevertheless, FCC, too, needed substantial capacity building.

To supplement their staffing resources, councils used other support facilities such as the National Commission for Social Action (NACSA) Volunteers and United Nations Development Programme (UNDP) Transition Support Team. The IRCBP assisted by employing "coaches" to provide day-to-day assistance to councils. They were employed full-time at the offices of all councils that had entered the scheme. The coaches assisted councils in performing their administrative functions and liaising with the Freetown-based IRCBP on capacity building and other requirements.

Upon the restoration of local councils in 2004, it was imperative to embark on an aggressive capacity building drive to address the enormous challenge of the capacity limitations. Councils had to be able to perform their roles effectively and efficiently as soon as possible to illustrate to the people that local government could improve their lives.

Planning for Capacity Building Prior to the Passage of Local Government Act 2004

A well-executed capacity building program requires proper planning based on a comprehensive needs assessment and the preparation of a responsive capacity building strategy and plan. Ordinarily, an existing decentralization policy should inform the capacity building direction and strategy. Even though the LGA was passed in 2004 and the councils already are operational, Sierra Leone's decentralization policy has yet to be comprehensively prepared. This deficiency has been a critical gap in the smooth and fully effective implementation of decentralization. As a result, very little planning for capacity building was carried out before the LGA was passed and local councils established.

Planning for Capacity Building after Passage of Local Government Act 2004

As noted in earlier chapters, passage of the Local Government Act in 2004 was accompanied by the World Bank's funding of the Institutional Reform and Capacity Building Project (IRCBP) and the establishment of the Decentralization Secretariat[3] responsible for the technical implementation of decentralization. Recognizing that the capacities of the key stakeholders needed to be developed as quickly as possible, GoSL created the Capacity Building Unit within the Decentralization Secretariat.

As a basis for the preparation of a responsive capacity building strategy, the unit identified the key challenges that needed to be addressed if any meaningful capacity building support were to be provided. They were:

- Absence of a coherent national capacity building or human resource development policy and program, implying that proper coordination of capacity building effort would be highly problematic.
- Need to coordinate capacity building activities to support the decentralization program, since different agencies (donors, national institutions, NGOs/CSOs) prefer to develop separate programs to build the capacities of the local councils.
- Aligning the capacity building program with ongoing national capacity building programs to ensure harmony and a coordinated approach.
- Establishing a system that could quickly address the diverse and significant capacity building needs of key stakeholders in a cost-conscious manner, taking

into consideration the multiple, diverse needs of all actors within the local government system.

■ Mobilizing trained personnel to support the implementation and management of the program, since there were few available professionals in the relevant disciplines in Sierra Leone, and most of these were unwilling to work in the rural areas.

■ Financing an ambitious and comprehensive capacity building program and ensuring its timely and successful implementation.

■ Developing capacities of actors at the grassroots (council wards), taking into consideration the human and financial resources required to ensure the effective functioning of those groups.

■ Deciding whether capacity building would be supply or demand-driven. If capacity building would be supply-driven, how could sustainability, appropriateness of support, and institutionalization of capacity building be addressed? If capacity building would be demand-driven, how could demand be stimulated and how could the councils be capacitated to plan and organize their capacity building activities?

■ A multidimensional capacity building program requires the participation of a variety of service providers. The challenge was to motivate the service providers to show interest in participating in the capacity building effort.

■ Strengthening the capacities of the MDAs to support decentralization and perform their changing roles within the context of decentralized governance.

■ Facilitating the awareness and understanding of citizens to fully support the decentralization program.

■ Creating an appropriate and conducive environment for local council staff to perform their roles and responsibilities, and demonstrate the knowledge and skills gained through training.

Rapid capacity building needs assessment. An appropriate capacity building strategy and program should be based on a comprehensive needs assessment of the respective institutions and actors within the decentralization context. The capacity building support for decentralization in Sierra Leone has not been based on an in-depth needs assessment, primarily because most of the key actors at the local council level had not been in place when it was commenced. In the first 18 months of the local councils' existence, they depended for technical support on staff assigned from the center (MDAs) and on facilitators from other institutions. That these staff were with the local councils on a temporary basis was the reason for GoSL's not heavily investing in a comprehensive assessment of staff needs, especially staff development needs. To get started in this environment, a rapid needs assessment was carried out to determine the generic needs of councils for training, logistics, and infrastructure. An assumption that most local councils were at zero capacity guided the interim capacity building plan implemented in the initial stages of decentralization. However, after the councils have most of their technical staff at post, a comprehensive needs assessment will be carried out.

Preparation of a capacity building strategy and plan. Capacity building within Sierra Leone's decentralization program is understood to mean a conscious effort to facilitate key stakeholders in decentralization, with specific reference to the local councils, to enhance their abilities to identify and sustainably meet development challenges. The ongoing capacity building program has not limited itself to the traditional understanding of capacity building—training or transfer of knowledge and skills—but to the wider issue of providing the necessary environment for stakeholders to effectively execute their responsibilities. Thus, the capacity building support was envisaged to cover information, education and communication, training, organizational/institutional development and strengthening, financing and financial management, physical infrastructure and tooling (logistics and equipment).

To guide the implementation of this ambitious initiative, a capacity building strategy[4] was prepared at the onset of the decentralization program. It detailed the key issues and challenges to capacity building in Sierra Leone; the goals, objectives, and indicators; key programs and priority activities; key outputs and outcomes; budget; implementation arrangements; and monitoring and evaluation (M&E) issues.

The strategy was designed with the understanding that capacity building requires a clear shared vision; unity of purpose, goals, and stakeholder aspirations; and proper planning to attain the stated goals. Training people is not productive when the organizational vision is unclear, the organizational culture is unhelpful, and structure is confusing or obtuse. It is not effective to secure resources (whether from government, donor partners, or NGOs) when an organization is not equipped to carry out its tasks. It does not help to develop management information systems (MIS) when the basic organizational attitude rejects learning through M&E in favor of frantic activity. Indeed, *capacity building is about removing obstacles and dealing with negative attitudes and behaviors.* In Sierra Leone, all of these often have been fostered or enhanced by outdated laws and regulation.

Goals and objectives of the capacity building strategy. The current capacity building strategy has two goals. The first is to provide the means to enable stakeholders to effectively execute their roles and responsibilities within decentralized government. The second is to establish the capacities to deliver services, promote development, and improve the welfare of the people, thereby contributing to poverty eradication in line with the national poverty reduction strategy (PRS).

The objectives of the capacity building strategy are to:

- Design and implement a comprehensive training program for key stakeholders in decentralization, particularly local councils and MDAs.
- Build the capacities of service providers and the media to enhance their effective participation in the decentralization program.
- Develop instructional and media materials for the implementation of training and education activities.
- Orient, sensitize, and educate relevant stakeholders on the new local government system, roles and responsibilities, functional relationships, and accountabilities. These stakeholders include MDAs, local councils, training institutions, civil society, media, NGOs, and the private sector.
- Strengthen the administrative and management capacities of the MDAs and local councils.

- Provide physical infrastructure to house local councils to create an environment in which staff can effectively perform their functions.
- Facilitate the provision of staff quarters for key personnel of the local councils.
- Provide basic tools to enhance the immediate functioning and service delivery capacity of councils.
- Provide initial working capital in the form of seed money to local councils to initiate and implement development activities (see chapter 3 for a discussion of the Local Government Development Grant Program, through which this was done).
- Support local councils to prepare responsive and participatory development plans and effectively implement and manage development projects.
- Build the capacities of councils to generate local revenue and undertake effective budgeting and financial management practices.
- Build the capacities of councils to procure goods, works, and services in line with best practices and within the framework of the national procurement guidelines.

Focus of capacity building support. The focus of the capacity building support to local councils is to ensure that they have the capacity to respond to the development needs of their locality. The long-term aim is to give them the capacity to generate substantial, sustainable, and autonomous own-source revenues and to manage these effectively in combination with fiscal transfers from central government. Capacity building also seeks to ensure that central government MDAs have the capacity to respond to the institutional transformation and develop their new policy, monitoring, and coaching roles. The support also focuses on empowering communities (including CSOs, and NGOs) to engage local councils and demand inclusive, transparent, and accountable local governance.

Key strategies for capacity building. The strategy adopted to implement the numerous capacity building programs had many parts:

- Training support included induction, orientation, training of trainers (ToT), tailor-made training programs, on-the-job coaching, workshops/seminars/conferences, participation in study tours, and follow-up support.
- The principle of learning by doing was a core strategy in training stakeholders, particularly local councils and their staff, and implied the provision of coaching and mentoring support.
- Rapid training needs assessment was carried out to assess training gaps for the provision of training support.
- Curricula were developed, and before mass-production and nation-wide application, training manuals were field-tested for all training programs. Use of service providers ensured institutionalization and sustainability of capacity building support.
- A pool of trainers was created and sustained to provide the necessary training and support.

■ Informational materials (booklets, brochures or pamphlets, posters, and newsletters) were used to effectively disseminate information.

■ Public announcements and radio discussions were used to reach the people.

■ Interface programs and sensitization and orientation workshops were organized to improve local democracy, accountability, efficiency, equity, effectiveness, and sustainability in the provision of services.

■ An effective information and communication network was implemented to promote effective coordination and collaboration among the councils. The network encompassed holding regional monthly and quarterly meetings to facilitate the exchange of experiences and ideas; organizing national local council interactive sessions, council staff exchanges, and educational visits; forming national associations geared toward advancing and defending the interests of stakeholders; and council-private sector-civil society interactions and councils forging partnerships and twinning relationships with other municipal governments outside Sierra Leone to share experiences and resources.

■ Initial support in the area of office infrastructure development focused on providing office buildings for local councils that had no permanent office structures. The second phase of infrastructure support focused on local councils that did have office structures.

■ Local councils were provided with start-up tooling support with the expectation that they would take responsibility to provide subsequent logistics and equipment. They also were encouraged to develop an efficient operations and maintenance (O&M) system to ensure the sustainable and effective use of the limited logistics and equipment at their disposal.

Providing and Developing Human Capacity

The development of human capacity was the key task in the capacity building effort for the effective implementation of the decentralization program in Sierra Leone. Obviously, local governments' abilities to achieve their performance goals depended on the quality of their human resources. In this light, targets for human capacity development were identified and supported as explained below.[5]

Councilors and Ward Committee Members

Councilors are the key actors in Sierra Leone's democratized local government. They represent the citizens and are supposed to provide political leadership and have an appreciable level of civic knowledge with an ability to manage public affairs. In Sierra Leone, many elected councilors came to office without prior management skills or knowledge of local government systems. They needed training in how to engage residents on local government issues, how to improve the resource base for the Councils, how to prepare strategic plans, how to attract investors, and how to establish enabling policy and institutional environments. To facilitate councils in acquiring the requisite skills and knowledge, GoSL provided the following supports:

■ A two-day orientation workshop on the new local government system, roles and responsibilities, and functional relationships was organized for each of the 19 local councils in the first 3 months of their operations

■ A two-week induction workshop for the political leadership of the local councils (the chair/mayor and deputy) to provide them with a broad understanding of some of the technical issues of administration, management, financing, development planning, and procurement and complementary skills;

■ Training and facilitation to prepare by-laws and standing orders to guide council business

■ A 10-day study tour to Ghana for chairs of local councils on the Inter-Ministerial Committee (IMC) on decentralization and the chief administrators of urban/town councils; another study tour to South Africa for selected local council officials

■ Executive financial management training for council mayors/chairs, and chairs of budget and finance committees

■ Training the ward committees of 13 local councils, completed in 2006.

Professional/Technical Staff of Local Councils

Local councils are required to spearhead the development aspects of their localities. This involves the performance of technical functions that require specialized expertise. The current challenge is the lack of professionals in specialized local government disciplines to support local councils in executing these technical functions. This dearth was evident from the difficulty that the Office of the Establishment Secretary confronted in assigning competent staff to the local councils in 2004 as an interim measure until the councils could recruit their permanent staff. Thus, capacity building support for technical and professional staff of local councils has targeted four categories of staff as detailed below.

CAPACITY BUILDING OF ASSIGNED STAFF

For the first two years of the life of the councils, the Office of the Establishment Secretary assigned the chief administrator, deputy chief administrator and a treasurer to each council as a stop-gap measure. The majority of the assigned chief administrators and deputies had the requisite qualifications and experience in administration and the civil service. However, they did not have in-depth knowledge in the area of local governance and the technical issues that the local councils are expected to handle. The case for the treasurers was slightly different because none of them had professional qualifications in financial management, even though some had worked in that field. To strengthen the capacities of the assigned staff, they were provided with training programs as detailed below.

■ Chief Administrators and Deputy Chief Administrators of Local Councils:
  • A two-week induction workshop on administration, management, financing, development planning, procurement, and complementary skills
  • Revenue mobilization workshop
  • Resource mobilization and budgeting training

- Computer training and application of MS Word and MS Excel for chief administrators
- Training in development planning and management for local council development planning task forces, including chief administrators
- Training on advanced procurement management
- Hands-on training for budget preparation and MTEF

■ Local Council Treasurers:
- Revenue mobilization workshop (treasurers made the initial projection of their councils' own-source revenues for 2005 during the workshop)
- Bookkeeping and accounting training for treasurers
- Resource mobilization and budgeting training
- Computer training and Application of MS Word and MS Excel
- Training on MTEF and local council budgeting
- Advanced financial management training
- Hands-on training for budget preparation and MTEF
- Since the local councils did not have auditors, the staff of the Public Financial Management Reform Unit of the IRCBP provided roaming supports to the local councils to assist the treasurers in keeping their books and checking financial management compliance.

CAPACITY BUILDING OF LOCAL COUNCILS' NEW STAFF

In 2007 the Local Government Service Commission (LGSC) supported the local councils to recruit their own technical/professional staff including the chief administrator, deputy chief administrator, finance officer, accountant, procurement officer, and statistician. The recruitment process followed the LGSC prescriptions as enshrined in the Human Resource Guidelines. From the profiles of the recruited staff, it was clear that their skills were far below those of the assigned staff. The reasons that the local councils had been unable to attract qualified and professional candidates were the poor remuneration structure and uncertainties about career advancement and opportunities for professional development. The specific assessments of the hirees follow.

Chief Administrator. All of the recruited chief administrators had the requisite qualifications listed in the advertisement. However, none of them was a trained administrator or manager. Most of them had been teachers, implying the need for training in administration and management if they were to effectively execute their functions.

Deputy Chief Administrator. All of the recruited deputy chief administrators had the requisite qualifications listed in the advertisement. However, except for Kailahun District, none had had experience in local government. As with the chief administrators, there was a need to strengthen the deputies' administrative and management capacities through training and mentoring.

Local Council Finance Officer. Some of the assigned treasurers of local councils (Port Loko, Bombali, Tonkolili, Kailahun District Councils) had applied and been recruited into the newly created office as stipulated by the HR Guidelines. All of the recruited finance officers were qualified, and those who had been assigned had received training from the IRCBP capacity building support. Nevertheless, there was a need for professional top-up training for all finance officers.

Accountant. All of the recruited accountants had the required qualifications, but none had had any experience in working for local governments. Thus, the need to orient them on local governance and decentralization was obvious. These staff had to be provided with tailor-made professional training to ensure their easy adaptation to their new roles and environment.

Procurement Officer. No applicants had the required professional qualifications. This was not surprising since courses in procurement management had been introduced only recently in one of the country's tertiary institutions, the Institute of Public Administration and Management (IPAM). Three of the recruited staff had had previous experience in procurement. They already had been working for the councils as interim procurement officers and had received some training in procurement management through IRCBP activities. There was a need for initial training of many of these staff and for periodic refresher training.

Monitoring and Evaluation Officer. None of the recruited M&E officers had ever received professional training in M&E or served as M&E officers before their recruitment. Professional training in M&E and coaching support had to be provided for these staff to ensure that they became effective as quickly as possible.

Staff inherited from district offices or previous council structures. The urban and city councils inherited staff who were already had been working in the councils. The district councils inherited staff from the previous district offices. Most of these staff were ineffective and added nothing to public sector service provision. The best way to handle these staff was unclear. One although was to assess the capacities of each staff member and lay off those deemed not suitable to the requirements of the new local councils. Another view was to retire all inherited staff who had reached the retirement age and ask for voluntary retirement from others, with the payment of benefits to both groups. The difficulty was in determining which body carried the liability for redundancy costs—the new councils or the central government? These uncertainties, which have lingered a long time, have delayed a decision with respect to what training, if any, should be given to the inherited staff. The exception was the radio operator from each Council, each of whom has received training in communication and radio operation.

Devolved staff. The hallmark of the decentralization program in Sierra Leone is the devolution of functions from the MDAs to the local councils through a properly designed framework. The process requires the transfer of all staff who had been performing the devolved functions to the local councils, that is, these staff all had to relocate from the capital to the locale to which they were assigned. These staff were expected to be fully integrated in the local council administrative system. To achieve this, orientation and induction workshops were organized for them, and interface programs were facilitated between the devolved staff and the council administrators.

Local Government Associations

Nation-wide local government associations bring together those who work in local government to share information and experiences, build support networks, initiate policy dialogue, and present a common voice for local government on policy and management issues. Strong national associations can play an important role by identifying the needs of their members, and the associations are a source of information on good local government practices. For national associations to play their advocacy role effectively, they need to know how to collect information and present facts; how to prepare policy positions and projects; and how to mobilize their members to influence change in policy, programs, and services.

DecSec facilitated local councils to form two national associations. The first is the Local Council Association of Sierra Leone (LoCASL), whose membership embraces all members of the 19 local councils (both technical and political wings). The second is the Local Council Staff Association (LoCoSA), whose members include all professional staff of the 19 local councils. Even though little support in the way of direct capacity building has yet to be realized by these two associations, there are plans to support the establishment of regional and national secretariats for them.

Ministries, Departments, and Agencies (MDAs)

The MDAs are critical for the successful implementation of Sierra Leone's decentralizations. Obviously, the decentralization reform calls for them to hand over many functions to local government and for the emergence of new roles and responsibilities at the MDA level. The responsibilities for policy formulation and review, oversight, standard-setting and monitoring local councils' performance have become more fundamental for the MDAs. MDAs' capacities to effectively perform these new functions are generally weak. The need to strengthen their capacities to effectively carry out these functions cannot be overemphasized. MDAs need to be exposed to ideas and exchange views on current central/local government policy issues. Such interchanges will aid them to appreciate the role of local government in development and the promotion of good governance, and to provide the necessary support for the smooth and timely transfer and performance of devolved functions.

Apart from the workshops held to expedite devolution and to create a forum to get agreement on how the process would be managed, very little has been done to strengthen the capacities of the MDAs for their new roles. The emphasis has been on the local councils. This imbalance in capacity building support has led to a situation in which the local councils now have more capacity than the MDAs in efficient and effective management and performance.

Parliamentarians

The lawmakers of the country are key stakeholders in the nation's decentralization program and need to be fully abreast of the progress being made. Well-informed parliamentarians can be very supportive in educating constituents to appreciate, support, and participate effectively in decentralization. There is a crucial need for the implementing agencies (MIALGRD and MOF) to interface periodically with the parliamentarians and sensitize them on the evolving roles and responsibilities of local councils and MDAs as they relate to the ongoing decentralization. However, the past interface between the implementers of the decentralization program and the parliamentarians has been weak since *no direct intervention has been undertaken to strengthen the knowledge of parliamentarians the progress of decentralization* since its commencement in 2004. Obviously, their role in sensitizing their people and supporting the ongoing decentralization program can be enhanced if their capacities to execute these important responsibilities are strengthened.

Citizens

Citizens' participation in local government affairs is essential if local governments are to be accountable for their actions and transparent in transacting business. By participating in decisionmaking and planning, demanding quality services, and holding local officials accountable for their stewardship, citizens can ensure that their local government truly represents their interests. Citizens need to be made aware of their rights and responsibilities to demand accountability from their councilors, and participate in and monitor delivery of services to their communities. They also must be aware of their role in ensuring the integrity of their representatives. For their part, councils must make citizens aware of the costs of infrastructure and services, and of the need to mobilize revenue—by paying taxes.

Over the last four years, DecSec has made efforts to sensitize and educate the citizens on the relevance of decentralization and the important role that they can play in the successful implementation of the decentralization program. A nation-wide sensitization on local government and the decentralization program was initiated in 2004, and a weekly radio program captioned "New Salone" was launched in 2005. Since then, as a result of pressure from the people, two mayors and a council chair have been forced out of office for alleged corruption and improper handling of public office.

Traditional Authorities

Traditional authorities carry tremendous influence in society since they are the "natural rulers" and hold community land in trust for the people. The chiefdom system had not undergone any major change in its role in development for a long time. As a result, much needed to be done to strengthen the chiefs' skills to foster citizens' participation. There was a need to develop the chiefs' knowledge of power relationships (who controls, where the funds come from, roles and responsibilities of citizens) and financial mechanisms for service delivery. They also needed to learn how to collect information and present facts; how to prepare proposals and projects; how to mobilize the community to demand services and participate in their implementation; and how to influence change in policy, programs, and services. Despite all of these needs, DecSec has done little to strengthen the capacity of traditional authorities, apart from sponsoring some paramount chiefs to attend workshops during the 2004 nation-wide orientation on decentralization for key stakeholders. The paramount chief from the Bombali Sebora Chiefdom of the Bombali District of the Northern Province also was sponsored by VSO Sierra Leone through DecSec to participate in a study tour to South Africa and then share his experiences with the paramount chiefs in the Bo and Bombali Districts.

Training Institutions/Service Providers

A key issue relating to human resource development for local governments is to establish an effective human resources pool and to institutionalize training courses for local governments. Training institutions and trainers lack adequate orientation to participate effectively in strengthening the capacity of local governments. Capacity-building institutions such as universities, management, and research institutions are not yet in tune with local government reforms. Professional training to work in local government in the nation's few institutions of higher learning remains compartmentalized and in many ways disconnected from the present realities of governance. Thus, *the development of capacity to provide capacity-building services needs more attention.* Tertiary institution and private sector participation in the delivery of training for local governments must be developed

To facilitate the effective involvement of service providers in the capacity building of local governments, a strategy was prepared.[6] Its central focus was to support identified service providers to develop and manage tailor-made curricula in support of local government. The objectives were to:

- Provide continued mentoring support to training providers during implementation of training courses.
- Identify and support capable institutions to design training modules on subjects relevant to the technical performance of local councils.
- Identify universities/tertiary institutions in which courses related to local government were being offered.
- Study identified training providers to obtain information and insight into their current curricula, areas of future expansion, willingness to offer courses that are relevant for local government and the necessary institutional support to design and implement training courses. Then map out an effective strategy to support them to realize their ambitions.
- Mentor institutions in strengthening their existing local government courses or expanding their curricula.
- Support training institutions in marketing their courses.

The first interaction between the IRCBP and the service providers was not held until 2007. A two-day orientation/training workshop on the local government system, decentralization program, general human resource demands of councils, and preparation of training modules was organized for selected institutions thought to have some capacity. In addition to individual trainers and facilitators, participants were drawn from tertiary institutions, technical-vocational institutions, and consulting firms.

In regard to training, an important element of the IRCBP is the Challenge Fund, which was established to fund institutions to develop course modules and to participate in local government capacity building. To date, these opportunities have not been taken up by any of the tertiary institutions in Sierra Leone.

Media

It is important to ensure that local and national media personnel are educated about decentralization issues because it is their role to inform their communities and the country, respectively, on the progress of decentralization. The capacity of the nation's media to perform this task is limited, and there is a danger that it will disseminate inaccurate or misleading information. To date, little has been done by the Information, Education and Communication Unit of DecSec to establish an effective interface between the decentralization implementation agencies and the media. Thus, it is not surprising that media coverage of decentralization activities and media efforts to sensitize people about decentralization have been very poor. The IRCBP has had a media liaison group on staff, but this group has not made effective input to promotion efforts.

Civil Society Groups

An effective strategy to strengthen the capacity of local government is not limited to local authorities. NGOs and CBOs can assume center stage in many facets of local government service delivery, job creation, and economic development. To ensure sustainable development, capacity building should be extended to such non-state actors, even down to the village level. Much effort has been made to ensure the active participation of civil society groups in decentralization. Active civil society coalitions such as the Coalition of Civil Society and Human Rights Activists were identified early in the process, and DecSec made efforts to expand their capacities through training on such issues as procurement monitoring. Improvements in their field activities also were targeted. For example, this coalition was facilitated to constitute district-based civil society monitoring teams whose capacities were developed to monitor local councils' procurement activities. Three NGOs also were engaged by the IRCBP to carry out district-based, nation-wide sensitization on decentralization.

Role of Coaches in Capacity Building

Prior to the local government elections in 2004, GoSL hired the services of the University of Birmingham (UK) to train a group of young professionals as coaches in the decentralization program. After the creation of the councils, seven of these trained coaches accepted full-time positions, initially to assist councils in the application of the Rapid Results Approach (RRA).[7] The 7 coaches were assigned to the 19 councils on a regional basis and assisted councils to design projects that were implemented within 100 days using RRA.

With the satisfactory performance of local councils in the project implementation, an additional 12 coaches were recruited and trained. One coach then was assigned to each of the 19 councils. Because of the dearth of technical capacity in the new councils and the expansive technical activities that councils are expected to undertake, the relevance of the coaches as a critical support base to the local councils gained prominence. As a result, the roles of the coaches were expanded to cover provision of technical support to the local councils in development planning, budgeting, and procurement management. The coaches also served as the link between the councils and the IRCBP implementation units and ensured that councils operated within the framework and prescriptions of the Local Government Act 2004. In some councils, coaches have been found so useful that they also have been used as support in administration, especially when the chief administrator and/or deputy were absent from council.

The contribution of the coaches to the development of the councils has been very important. They have ensured that the councils are delivering services to their localities. It is probable that local councils will need the services of the coaches until the capacities of the former have been sufficiently built and they can function independently with minimal external support.

Achievements in Infrastructure Capacity Development

After the dissolution of the district councils in 1972, local government infrastructure was used without adequate maintenance. In general, it was neglected, abandoned, misused, or converted to personal property. Much of what was left at the commencement of the war was later destroyed during that conflict. With the resuscitation of the local councils 32 years later (2004), the need for adequate infrastructure was obvious. To address these administrative infrastructure needs, an assessment of the local councils was undertaken in 2005. Based on their need for office space and other infrastructure, the councils were divided into two categories:

■ *Category A: Local councils without office infrastructure.* Western Area Rural District Council, Koidu/New Sembehun Town Council, Makeni Town Council, Bonthe District Council, and Bonthe Town Council. These councils had made temporary arrangements to occupy buildings in varying states of disrepair and were prioritized for the provision of office space.

■ *Category B: Local councils with office infrastructure.* Bombali, Kambia, Koinadugu, Kono, Tonkolili, Port Loko, Bo, Kenema, Pujehun, Moyamb, and Kailahun District Councils; Freetown City Council; and Bo and Kenema Town Councils. These councils had inherited office buildings from the former district office (DO) administrations or urban committees of management. Some of these prior councils had shared their offices with personnel from the chiefdom administration and/or the central government. For these councils, it was decided that the existing offices should be rehabilitated and new office buildings constructed to augment existing facilities.

The amount of office space available for the councils was clearly inadequate for the level of activities to be undertaken, and there was pressure from the central government for them the councils to make more space available for MDA functions. The construction and rehabilitation of offices for 8 local councils are well advanced. The Freetown City Council was supported to get its current office building rehabilitated and furnished.

In logistical support, the local councils have received a range of equipment including computers and accessories, radio sets, printers, photocopiers, generators, vehicles (boats for the riverine councils), motorbikes, refrigerators, bicycles, steel cabinets, swivel chairs, safes, megaphones, and office furniture.

Development of Local Council Administrative and Governance Capacity

Quickly following on the re-establishment of local councils, they made significant progress in administration, procurement, fiscal and budget management, and implementation of development projects. The devolution of functions (transfer of assets and personnel, and supervision of service delivery at the local level) by the MDAs to local councils gradually gained momentum within the first two years of the implementation of the devolution process (2005 and 2006).

After two years of local council existence, it became expedient to assess them to determine their institutional and management efficiencies, compliance with LGA 2004 and related regulations, and effectiveness in implementing development plans and performing other functions devolved to them. The expectation was that local councils adjudged to be weak in certain areas could benefit from the exemplary performance of the stronger ones. It was thought that learning from the good practices of the latter and identifying gaps in professional capacities that should be addressed would provide the bases for strengthening the councils as they progressed with their work.

How Local Councils' Capacity Levels Were Measured in 2006

The first comprehensive assessment of local councils using the Comprehensive Local Government Performance Assessment System (CLoGPAS) had the main objective of verifying local councils' compliance with specified minimum conditions and performance measures. The results of the assessment were expected to assist the local councils to identify their functional capacity gaps and needs as a major input in the development of an appropriate capacity building plan. The assessment also provided the basis for (a) determining which local councils had the capacity to manage discretionary development funds and therefore were eligible to access the LGDG and (b) providing incentives for local councils' enhanced performance through rewarding good performance.

Using parameters with global acceptability, the assessment also provided an opportunity for the LCs to be viewed from a global perspective as well as for reflection on the nature and level of support received and continued support required. The assessment was carried out focused on two measures: minimum conditions and performance measures.

Minimum conditions. The minimum conditions were designed with two specific goals: to look at the functional capacity of local councils to take on devolved functions and to assess whether councils are in compliance with existing regulations.

The conditions are divided into seven thematic areas:

- Financial Management
- Functional Capacity in Development Planning
- Functional Capacity in Budgeting and Accounting
- Functional Capacity in Procurement
- Transparency and Accountability
- Project Implementation
- Functional Capacity of the Local Council.

Performance measures. The performance measures captured the progress made by Councils in implementing and managing projects and programs, and reflected their abilities to meet deadlines and to appropriately document their activities. The performance measures also evaluated councils' transparency, openness, and accountability to local communities. They also are divided into seven thematic areas:

- Management, Organization and Institutional Structures
- Transparency, Openness, Participation, and Accountability
- Planning Systems and Project Implementation, M&E
- Human Resources Management
- Financial Management, Budgeting, and Accounting
- Fiscal Capacity and Local Revenue Generation
- Procurement and Contract Management.

CLoGPAS process. The coordination of CLoGPAS—including design of the assessment, training of assessors, quality assurance, data processing, and production of findings—was carried out by the CLoGPAS task team of the Institutional Reform and Capacity Building Project (IRCBP). The proposed framework and specific indicators were presented to the local councils in an analytical review seminar, held in Bo City in October 2006. The purpose of the seminar was to enable them to see the standards by which they would be assessed and to give feedback, which was incorporated in the final assessment package. In November 2006, trained assessors were deployed to all 19 local councils and to 10 MDAs.

Results of CLoGPAS 1: Levels of Capacities of Local Councils in 2006

CLoGPAS results revealed serious capacity gaps in the councils. Most of them were not able to maximize points by meeting most *Minimum Conditions* (MCs). Results achieved were:

- MC 1- Functional Capacity in Financial Management - No council met this condition.
- MC 2- Functional Capacity in Development Planning - 13 councils met this condition.
- MC 3 -Functional Capacity in Budgeting and Accounting - 1 council met this condition.
- MC 4- Functional Capacity in Procurement - 10 councils met this condition.
- MC 5- Functional Capacity in Transparency - 15 councils met this condition.
- MC 6- Functional Capacity in Project Implementation - 7 councils met this condition.
- MC 7- Local Councils' Functional Capacity - 17 councils met this condition.

For *Performance Measures*, results achieved were:

- PM 1- Management Organization and Institutional Structure - 11 councils scored above average.
- PM 2- Transparency, Openness, and Accountability - 12 councils scored above average.
- PM 3- Planning Systems and Project Implementation) - 11 councils scored above average.
- PM 4- Human Resource Management) 10 councils scored above average.
- PM 5- Financial Management, Budgeting and Accounting) 13 councils scored above average.
- PM 6- Fiscal Capacity and local revenue generation) 15 councils scored above average.
- PM 7- Procurement and Contract Management - 18 councils scored above average.

Table 3.1. Compliance with Minimum Conditions and Scores on Performance Measures

Local council	MCs met *(of 7)*	Score on PMs *(of 88)*
Bo City	4	67
Bo District	5	73
Bombali District	2	45
Bonthe City	2	62
Bonthe District	3	74
Freetown City Council	1	53
Kailahun District	5	69
Kambia District	5	48
Kenema City	4	70
Kenema District	4	73
Koidu City	3	65
Koinadugu District	3	53
Kono District	4	75
Makeni City	4	69
Moyamba District	4	64
Port Loko District	3	55
Pujehun District	4	59
Tonkolili District	3	67
Western Area Rural	0	37

The analysis above demonstrates that, despite local councils' efforts over the last three years to effectively perform their functions, the challenges had been daunting. Such challenges were, primarily, the lack of enough trained personnel to run the councils. During that period, DecSec had undertaken capacity building programs for councils' administrative and technical staff, but these programs had been only stop-gap measures. The first step toward closing the staffing gaps was the recruitment in 2007 of key council personnel facilitated by the Local Government Service Commission (LGSC). Recruitment, however, should not be an end in itself as the newly recruited staff needed training in the administrative and technical issues pertaining to the effective running of councils.

How CLoGPAS 1 Results Were Used

Minimum conditions. The minimum conditions will provide a benchmark for local councils' qualification for accessing the Local Government Development Grant (LGDG). However, 2006 CLoGPAS minimum conditions results were not used to determine the eligibility of the councils for the FY2007 grant. The first assessment was considered a wake-up call for the local councils and a grace period to learn from others and strengthen their performances. In the future, local councils must meet *all* the minimum conditions to receive the LGDG.

Performance measures. The performance measures are part of an incentive system that rewards exemplary councils with a LGDG Performance Incentive (PI) Grant to implement development projects. The results of the 2006 CLoGPAS were used to determine the allocation of a performance grant of 1 billion leones (Le 1 billion) for FY2007.

Table 3.2. LGDG Performance Incentive Grant Distribution Scale

PM score (% of 88)	Weighting factor	Eligible LCs
0–69	0	7
70–79	1	7
80–89	2	5
90–100	3	0

Five LCs that scored between 80 percent–89 percent received a PI Grant of Le 117,647,059. Seven LCs that scored between 70 percent–79 percent received Le 58,823,529. Seven LCs scored less than 70 percent so could not benefit from the LGDG Performance Incentive Grant.

The following 5 local councils—Kono, Bonthe, Kenema, Bo, and Kenema City— each received the highest allocation of Le 117,647,059. The Pujehun, WARDC, Koinadugu, FCC, Kambia, Bombali, and Port Loko District Councils received nothing.

To motivate local councils to improve their performances, the Minister of Local Government and Community Development on behalf of the Government of Sierra Leone awarded certificates to performing local councils in a well-attended public function held at the Bintumani Hotel in Freetown. The minister distributed the certificates to the local councils. This initiative had an immediate impact because, after the award ceremony, citizens started demanding explanations from their local council authorities for the inability of their councils to win an award.

Implications of CLoGPAS 1 Results for Capacity Building Gaps, Including Training Needs

The findings of CLoGPAS 1 revealed very useful information related to the effective and efficient running of the local councils. Consequently, it was imperative that capacity building programs be organized for local councils. Training needs for councils lie largely in the areas in which they had performed poorly in CLoGPAS 1. These are included financial management, budgeting and accounting, development planning, human resource management, procurement management, records management, and project planning and management.

How the Levels of Local Councils Were Measured in Local Council Stock-taking, 2008

Introduction. The institution of an annual Comprehensive Local Government Performance Assessment Systems (CLoGPAS) in 2006 laid the foundation for routine monitoring of local council performance and the provision of evidence-based information on councils' functional capacities, as would be reflected in the minimum conditions drawn from the CLoGPAS framework. The final output from the data collection further informed DecSec's capacity building interventions as the secretariat moved toward a demand-driven approach in its capacity building effort. In addition, this routine local council assessment (on minimum conditions) and monitoring will provide information to be used, first, to populate the Sierra Leone Local Council Encyclopedia,[8] and then to serve as an information-gathering mechanism to update the encyclopedia.

Table 3.3. LGDG Performance Incentive Grant by Local Council

Local council	PM score (% of 88)	PI Grant for FY2007 (Leones)
Kono	85	117,647,059
Bonthe	84	117,647,059
Kenema	83	117,647,059
Bo	83	117,647,059
Kenema City	80	117,647,059
Kailahun	78	58,823,529
Makeni City	78	58,823,529
Tonkolili	76	58,823,529
Bo City	76	58,823,529
Koidu City	74	58,823,529
Moyamba	73	58,823,529
Bonthe City	70	58,823,529
Pujehun	67	—
Port Loko	63	—
Koinadugu	60	—
FCC	60	—
Kambia	55	—
Bombali	51	—
WARDC	42	—
Total		1,000,000,000

Based on the comprehensive assessment framework used by CLoGPAS in 2006, a comprehensive stock-taking of local councils' fulfillment of the minimum conditions was conducted in the first quarter of 2008. CLoGPAS 2 had not been conducted for 2007 primarily due to the prolonged electioneering process, which had interfered seriously with the activities of the local councils and the overall implementation of decentralization. The stock-taking/assessment followed up some of the functional capacity and proficiency issues assessed during CLoGPAS 1: financial management, fiscal capacity, development planning project management, and the effectiveness of ward committees, among others.

The key objective of the 2008 assessment was to follow up some of the key capacity gaps identified in CLoGPAS 1 and, gather a wide range of information to be used to prepare the contents of the local council encyclopedia.

The specific objectives of the 2008 exercise were to:

- Assess the progress made by local councils to fulfill a range of minimum conditions in their functional and proficiency capacities to promote local good governance and service delivery.
- Initiate the process of setting up a performance-tracking system for local councils.
- Introduce the local council encyclopedia to all local councils and collect information that would constitute the contents of the encyclopedia.

- Reproduce and distribute to local councils and MDAs the proposed institutional framework reports on local council monitoring and evaluation.
- Inform the planning and implementation of CLoGPAS 2008 as well as capacity building support interventions.

Process. The stock-taking exercise was conducted between March and May 2008. Three regional teams were constituted: North/West, East, and South. Each regional team visited all of the local councils in that region and held briefing sessions with key senior staff of the local councils and members of ward committees. Eighteen of the 19 local councils were assessed because, at that time, Bo City lacked core staff (CA, and LCFO). The detailed process of engagement is described as follows:

- A team of representatives from the IRCBP held a briefing session with key senior staff (chair/mayor, deputy chair/mayor, chief administrator/deputy chief administrator, local council finance officer/accountant, statistician/M&E officer, coach, and procurement officer) of the local council. The team leader of the exercise apprised LC staff of the specifics including the purpose and importance of the exercise, documents required, and procedure (conference interviews). Different team members took leadership in certain aspects of the exercise. For instance, the LGFD representatives took the lead in discussing issues relating to LC budgeting and fiscal capacity, while the public financial management reform (PFMR) representative led the discussion on financial management.
- The exercise was conducted in a conference setting for ease of referencing. However, arrangements were made with specific LC staff when probing and further verification were required.
- Regarding the assessment of ward committees (WCs), the team worked with the Regional Capacity Building Support Coordinators (RCBSCs) to randomly select some WC executives for interviews. In view of concerns about travelling, the teams were advised to purposively select wards to which day trips could be made.
- At the end of the assessment, the team had a debriefing session with the LC officials to highlight observations made during the exercise. The highlights were prepared on an LC-specific basis for every council assessed because these inputs would inform the preparation of the final LC reports once the data analysis was completed.
- In addition to the chapter forms/completed assessment/stock-taking checklist, each team prepared and submitted a field report, which detailed the outcomes of the discussions held between the IRCBP Team and the Council representatives, to the Monitoring Unit of DecSec,
- The results of the assessment were presented at debriefing session to local council staff and other stakeholders to apprise them of the key findings and implications for capacity building and development planning.

Summarized Results of the Stock-Taking Exercise

THEME 1: FUNCTIONAL CAPACITY

- Meetings of Council
  - 17 of 19 LCs had ordinary meetings for 2007.
    - LC meetings interrupted by electoral process (August-December 2007)
  - 16 of 19 LCs that had meetings had proper documentation of minutes of meetings held.
  - Minutes of Makeni City and Kambia were not properly documented (signed by required signatories).
- Follow-up mechanisms
  - 14 of 19 LCs have some follow-up mechanism to council decisions/resolutions (action points, task teams with deadlines for reporting back to council).
  - Bombali, FCC, Moyamba, and Port Loko do not have follow-up mechanisms.
- Citizens' interest in councils' affairs
  - Nine of the 19 LCs assessed showed improvement
  - FCC, Bombali, Kailahun, Kambia, Koinadugu, Kono, Makeni City, Port Loko, Tonkolili, and WARDC showed no improvement when assessed.
  - 14 of 19 LCs have established filing systems but need improvements.
  - Kailahun, FCC, Makeni, and Port Loko have yet to establish proper filing systems.

THEME 2: DEVELOPMENT PLANNING

- Review of District Development Plans completed in 13 of 19 LCs
- Bonthe Municipal, Bonthe District, FCC, and Koinadugu DDPs not yet reviewed or review in progress.
- Only 10 LCs showed evidence of stakeholder involvement in review process; no evidence in Kenema City and Kono District Councils.
- 6 LCs made public access to revised DDP readily available: Bo District, Kenema City, Koinadugu, Makeni City, Pujehun, and Tonkolili.

THEME 3: 2007 PROJECT IMPLEMENTATION

- FY 2007 projects not completed on time due to delays in transfers to councils.
- 2007 projects rolled over to 2008.
- 13 LCs intend to use RRI as the main planning and implementation methodology.
- Preparation of local council AWP-08 is ongoing in most councils.
- Bo District, Koidu New Sembehun, Kono, Pujehun, and Tonkolili have completed AWPs for 2008.
- Only Tonkolili/Koinadugu Districts have M&E Plans.

Table 3.4. Status of Accounts and Audit, 2005 and 2006

Audit completed (1)	Audit in progress (1)	Accounts prepared (14)	Accounts preparation in progress (2)
Freetown City Council	Bombali District	Bo, Bonthe Municipal, Bonthe District, Moyamba, Pujehun, Kenema City, KNSCC, Kono, Kambia, Tonkolili, Koinadugu, Port Loko, Makeni City, and Kenema District	Kailahun District, WARDC

THEME 4: FINANCIAL MANAGEMENT, BUDGETING, AND AUDIT
- ▦ Joint 2005 and 2006 Audit
- ▦ Twelve of 19 prepared balanced budgets
  - • Budgets of Bombali, Bonthe District, Kailahun, Kambia, Kenema, and WARDC were not balanced.
- ▦ End-of month revenues banked intact in 14 of 19 councils.
  - • Four LCs do not bank intact revenues at end of month: Bombali, Bonthe Municipal, KNSCC and Tonkolili.
- ▦ Fifteen of 19 LCs make regular monthly bank reconciliations.
  - • Three do not make regular bank reconciliations: Tonkolili, Kenema District, and Bombali.
  - • Ten of 19 LCs regularly post financial documents on LC Notice Boards.
  - • Eight do not post regularly: Bombali, FCC, Kailahun, Kenema District, KNSCC, Moyamba, Port Loko, and Pujehun.

THEME 5: HUMAN RESOURCES MANAGEMENT
- ▦ Recruitment process was completed by 17 LCs.[9]
- ▦ Process was ongoing in Bo City.
- ▦ Job offers declined in 10 of 17 LCs
- ▦ Four LCs had resignations: Bo District, Kenema City, Tonkolili, and WARDC (mostly LFCO and M&E).
  - • Reasons:
    - - Low/poor remuneration
    - - Delayed/very late payment of salaries

THEME 6: FISCAL CAPACITY
- ▦ As at the time of the assessment, only 4 local councils had collected over 50 percent of their total estimated collectibles: Koinadugu District Council (75.6 percent), Bonthe District Council (71.4 percent), Koidu/New Sembehun Council (57.0 percent), and Moyamba District Council (50.3 percent).
- ▦ Four of the local councils had collected below 10 percent of their total estimated collectibles: Bonthe Municipal Council, Kambia District Council, Port Loko District Council, and Pujehun District Council.
- ▦ At the time of data collection, there was no information on the local revenues generated by two of the local councils: Kailahun District Council and Kenema District Council.

Table 3.5 and figure 3.1 indicate the total estimated collectible local revenue and the total revenue already collected by the 19 local councils.

Table 3.5. Local Council Revenue Estimate and Collection, 2007

Local council	Total estimated collectible	Total collected
Bo District	420,760,752	68,917,876
Bombali District Council	190,028,323	54077000
Bonthe District Council	161,161,267	115,081,805
Bonthe Municipal Council	58,870,000	2,508,619
Freetown City Council	2,500,000,000	1,100,000,000
Kailahun District Council	235,255,000	Not Available
Kambia District Council	225,235,000	15,294,000
Kenema City Council	1,293,853,000	541,230,242
Kenema District Council	628,947,500	Not Available
Koidu/New Sembehun Council	649,040,000	370,861,733.25
Koinadugu District Council	145,028,750	109,674,580
Kono District Council	2,699,272,436	1,193,412,007
Makeni City Council	1,976,449,527	211,291,550
Moyamba District Council	489,298,500	246,305,163
Port Loko District Council	224,587,200	16,119,210
Pujehun District Council	236,037,000	14,600,200
Tonkolili District Council	4,163,466,811	1,480,144,846

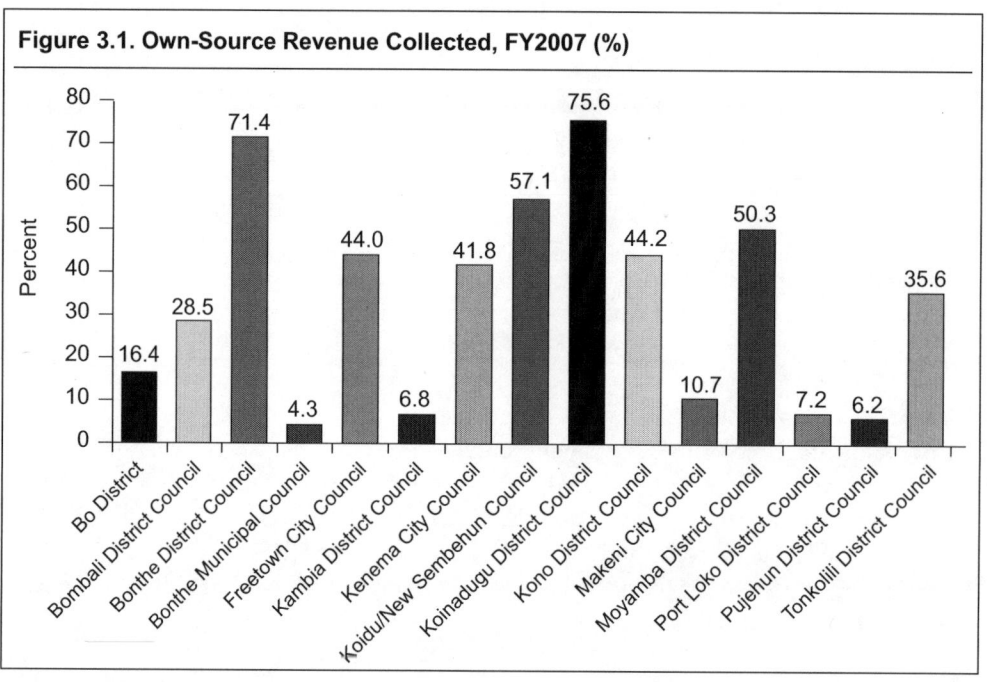

Figure 3.1. Own-Source Revenue Collected, FY2007 (%)

Source: GoSL (DecSec) 2008.

Note: Kailahun District Council and Kenema District Council could not provide their revenue data at the time of the study.

Comparison between Levels of Capacities of Local Councils in 2006 and 2008

The essence of CLoGPAS 1 in 2006 was to assess performances of local councils and to identify weaknesses that need to be strengthened through the capacity building support of the IRCBP. These measures were intended to improve the performances of councils. The expectation was that the results of the 2008 stock-taking exercise would reveal the progress made in addressing gaps in local council performance since capacity building support had been provided following the recommendations of CLoGPAS 1. From a general viewpoint, the councils have improved their performances in the respective thematic areas.

Appreciable progress in terms of local councils performing their statutory and technical functions has been noted based on the results of the stock-taking exercise, Nevertheless, much more progress would have been recorded if two severely constraining factors had not occurred:

- The extended electioneering period in 2007 affected the flow of resources from central government to local councils. Consequently, local councils were not able to implement the earmarked projects for 2007.
- In 2007 virtually all the chief administrators, their duties, and the treasurers who had been assigned to the local councils were replaced by new staff. Most of the latter are inexperienced in local government and do not have the requisite qualifications for the respective positions. Obviously, this change of staff brought turbulence to the smooth implementation of technical functions in the councils.

These two factors had a telling negative effect on the overall performance of local councils.

Critical Challenges to Capacity Building for Local Governance

Even though a great number of achievements have been made, critical roadblocks in capacity building have been identified. They are detailed below.

- A key constraint of the current capacity building support for local governance is *the absence of a policy to guide the process*. This has resulted in difficulties in the institutionalization of capacity building support.
- Capacity building has focused on the supply rather than the demand side. Shifting to a *demand-driven approach* to enhance ownership and sustainability of benefits is a key challenge.
- The Decentralization Secretariat was given the mandate by GoSL to coordinate all capacity building activities associated with decentralization. Nevertheless, the coordination of capacity building support has been extremely difficult because the different agencies involved (donor, national institutions, NGOs/CSOs) have been reluctant to harmonize their activities with the national capacity building program.
- Training activities have been carried out largely by IRCBP staff, which was not the original intention. This extra duty has placed a great pressure on project

staff since they have other technical and coordination activities to perform. This outcome also has been detrimental to the sustainability of training service provision because the outside institutions and tertiary sector have not been "forced' to provide the services.

■ Similarly, the identified Training Service Providers (TSPs) do not yet have the capacity to assist in strengthening local government performance. Some of the institutions have little or no experience in planning, implementing, and managing training. Others have no experts in the relevant technical fields. Sierra Leone's tertiary institutions are not yet ready to review their modules and curricula to include courses relating to local governance. Motivating these institutions to demonstrate interest in the capacity building effort remains a challenge.

■ Attraction and retention of technical staff by local councils has constituted a huge challenge in the capacity building drive. Local councils are unable to attract quality staff due to the unattractive conditions of service and the uncertainties surrounding staff development. Some of those who have been recruited are already leaving the councils because of dissatisfaction with the conditions of service. The challenge of attracting and retaining staff must be seriously looked at.

■ The decentralization program includes mandates to empower the people to address their poverty issues and bring about sustainable, participatory development in their localities. Available funding has limited the support that can be directed to strengthen the ward committees and facilitate them to undertake their functions. Lack of funding constitutes a major bottleneck to capacity building support.

■ A major challenge in the ongoing capacity building support to local councils is ensuring that materials and equipment supplied to them are used for the purposes for which they were intended and are managed effectively. DecSec has received a number of complaints related to either misuse of Council property or inaccessibility of staff to logistics supplied to Councils for the purpose of Council activities.

■ Local councils are required by LGA 2004 to establish four mandatory departments, but not all 19 local councils have met this target. Only two departments (Administration and Finance and Budget) have been partially established. Support to ensure the effective establishment of the other two departments (Development Planning and Management and Internal Audit) is ongoing.

■ Networking among local councils and their staff to facilitate cross-fertilization of ideas, joint planning and implementation of projects, shared learning, and experience-sharing has yet to be effectively institutionalized. The framework to facilitate networking among local councils, that is, the Associations, has yet to become fully operational.

■ A civil society district-based monitoring team has been formed in each of the 14 administrative districts, and these teams have been given some training in procurement monitoring. Nevertheless, the capacity of these groups to effectively perform their roles is still very weak, due primarily to the lack of logistics to support their operations.

■ Creating citizens' awareness about the local government system and the decentralization program, and strengthening the media to effectively promote general public education, has been a major challenge during the last four years and needs much greater effort going forward.

Lessons Learned in Capacity Development

In building the capacity of the councils and other institutions associated with decentralization of governance in Sierra Leone, a number of lessons have been acquired. The details are provided below.

■ *Integrated approach to capacity building.* Developing skills and providing the environment to demonstrate the skills and knowledge acquired through training was a strategy that provided results by enhancing the effectiveness of council staff. For example, the provision of basic infrastructure and equipment for councils enhanced their capacity to translate knowledge gained and skills acquired in training to concrete outcomes.

■ *Learning by doing.* When Councils were given the challenge to plan, implement, and manage on their activities with structures external support, they were able to do things for themselves, learn, and build on their experiences. For example, when the local councils were created, they were provided with limited support to implement development projects using RRA. That experience went a long way to unleash their latent capacities and build their confidence to plan, implement, and manage development projects.

■ *Effective sensitization of citizens to ensure that they hold their Councils accountable.* The emphasis on sensitizing the citizens to the essence of the ongoing decentralization process, and their roles and responsibilities in it, paid great dividends. Through their civil society groups, citizens were able to hold their local councils accountable for their actions. A case in point was the Makeni City Council procurement issue that brought about the resignation of the mayor and the transfer of key council staff.

■ *Shift of supply-driven to demand-driven approach.* When local councils were new, most started from scratch. The DecSec Capacity Building Unit adopted the supply-driven approach to capacity building to ensure that each council got the support necessary to ensure its early and effective operation. After a number of years of operation, the gradual shift from supply-driven to demand-driven capacity development makes great sense. Once each local council has the capacity to demand the capacity building support that it needs most and organize its own capacity building program, greater institutionalization of capacity building in the councils will take root.

■ *Timely preparation of capacity building and human resource policy.* A key constraint on the current capacity building support has been the absence of a capacity building and HR policy to guide provision of the support. As a consequence, the coordination of capacity building is highly problematic. Before the commencement of capacity building associated with the next phase of decentralization is begun, it is critical that the necessary policy and regulatory provisions are made.

■ *Preparation of a comprehensive capacity building strategy.* The preparation of a comprehensive capacity building strategy to guide the implementation of past activities was very helpful. A clear direction was mapped out at the outset of the decentralization program.

■ *Use and maintenance of equipment.* Due to the absence of clear guidelines for recipients, the use and maintenance of equipment given to councils was not done properly. As a consequence, many assets were stored by individuals who were not using them, while the technical staff were starved of the basic working tools.

Future Possible Changes to Capacity Development

Changing the Focus of Capacity Building

Now that local councils have been established and are operational, there is a need to widen the emphasis on capacity building. While continuing the support necessary to strengthen the capacities of local councils, other key actors such as the MDAs should be focused on to build capacity, as there is now an imbalance in capacity between the local councils and the MDAs. The MDAs need to perform critical functions to ensure that the devolution succeeds. They need capacity development to assist them with policy formulation, standard-setting, quality assurance, and monitoring and evaluation.

The new capacity building framework should prioritize strengthening the capacities of grassroots institutions such as the ward committees and the village development committees (VDCs). These structures are crucial to ensure participatory planning, implementation, and management of local development. Strengthening their capacity should include training and support to apply new skills.

Preparing a Policy on Capacity Building for Local Government

A capacity building policy is required to guide activities. The policy should ensure that interventions are effectively harmonized and coordinated to avoid unnecessary duplication and multiple approaches in building the capacities of those involved in local governance. The policy should provide a framework in which elected and appointed officials in local governments will receive training and acquire necessary skills. The Local Government Policy that is being developed will seek to identify the gaps in skills necessary to address problems; to attract, absorb, and manage financial, human, and information resources; and to operate programs effectively. The policy also should detail the evaluation of program outcomes to guide future activities. Councils and other stakeholders wishing to undertake capacity building activities in local governments will be expected to follow the policy.

Needs Assessment as Basis to Design a More Focused Training Plan for Council Staff

To ensure that capacity building is more focused and appropriate, a comprehensive needs assessment will need to be carried out to ensure identification of specific council needs. The needs assessment will enable the development of a specific capacity building program for each council and mapping its demands for training against a benchmark assessment.

Moving to a Demand-Driven Approach to Capacity Building

To ensure that capacity building is sustainable, there should be a gradual move from supply-driven to demand-driven interventions. The latter will ensure ownership of capacity building support by the councils and that capacity building activities for a given council will be more appropriate and effective. The focus will be to move the councils to appreciate the need for them to invest in capacity building. Such a development will result in councils' identifying their capacity building needs and preparing annual plans and budgets for capacity building.

Strengthening the Participation of Training Providers: Tertiary Institutions

As noted earlier, tertiary institutions offer very few professional courses related to local government. If these institutions are to become key sources for training professional staff who will work in the local councils, the universities and colleges will need to be encouraged and facilitated to expand their curricula and tailor courses to train local government professionals. Interface between the tertiary institutions and the decentralization implementing agencies should be strengthened so that the institutions appreciate their potential role in the capacity building of local government.

An important mechanism for encouraging innovation within tertiary education systems is the availability of *challenge fund grants*. This fund could introduce or accelerate adaptive change within teaching, learning, and research programs. As flexible additions to normal operating budgets, challenge fund grants offer rare opportunities for experimentation and innovation within the tertiary sector. The challenge grant scheme should be pursued, as envisaged under the IRCBP Trust Fund, to motivate tertiary institutions to institutionalize training courses related to local governance.

Streamline Use and Management of Capacity Building Support

The purpose of providing infrastructure and equipment to councils will be realized only if these assets are put to effective use by the local councils. Guidelines for the use of council assets should be prepared and included in the capacity building policy. The capacities of local councils to effectively manage their assets and equipment should be strengthened.

Intensify Sensitizing Citizens to Decentralization

The information, dissemination, sensitization, and education of the population on decentralization should be intensified. The participation of civil society groups and the media in these processes should be encouraged and strengthened. There is need to prepare an IEC Strategy that is implementable within the context of the Sierra Leone decentralization framework.

Strengthen Records Management Capacities of Local Councils

Managing records at both the MDA and local council levels is a major area of concern. Few government institutions in the nation have cultivated an attitude of effective records management or have the required infrastructure to support such a system.

Strengthening councils' records management should constitute a key focus area in the new capacity building framework.

Strengthen the Monitoring of Capacity Building Support to Local Councils

Monitoring capacity building support to local councils should be strengthened to ensure that planned capacity building activities are implemented adequately and achieve their aims. The monitoring should also check the compliance of councils with the eligibility criteria under which they receive capacity building support. Periodic evaluations of capacity building outcomes should determine the impact of interventions and inform the regular review of capacity building efforts and strategies.

Building the Capacities of MIALGRD and MoF to Perform Their Functions

The monitoring role of the Ministry of Internal Affairs, Local Government, and Rural Development (MIALGRD) has not been effectively executed over the last four years, due primarily to the fact that the ministry has very few capable technical staff. The ministry's human resource capacity must be re-examined, and the requisite complementary support in the form of logistics, equipment, and training must be provided to strengthen it. The role of the MoF has been provided for more effectively, but the imminent cessation of the Public Financial Management Reform Unit (PFMRU) component of the IRCBP may mean a loss of some capacity to assist councils in performing their accounting and financial management responsibilities. This gap must be filled.

Conclusion

Over the last four years, the capacity building effort to support decentralization has contributed significantly to the establishment and functionality of the 19 local councils. The foundation for improved performance of local government in the next few years largely has been laid. However, the capacity building process has confronted two key challenges that must be addressed if the performance of local councils and other governance actors is to be improved and sustained.

- The poor coordination of capacity building support is a key concern that must be addressed through policy and legislation.
- Funding for capacity building support should be critically looked at as the requirement for future activities is substantial and will require a very large financial investment.

It is clear that there is need for shift in the focus of capacity building. The MDAs, critical stakeholders for the success of the decentralization program, will need to be sufficiently strengthened to enhance their abilities to effectively perform their changing roles in accordance with the devolution process. The need to gradually shift from a supply-driven capacity building to a demand-driven system is essential for the ownership of capacity building support by the beneficiaries and the provision of appropriate capacity building support that will bring about more meaningful outcomes.

The implementation of the capacity building support over the last four years also has generated many useful lessons that will inform the current review of the capacity building strategy and serve as useful inputs for the continuation of such support.

Notes

[1] Tangri 1978, 165–73.

[2] World Bank 2003, 43–44.

[3] The Decentralization Secretariat is both a Directorate of the Ministry of Internal Affairs, Local Government and Rural Development, and a unit of the IRCBP.

[4] For details, refer to IRCBP 2005a.

[5] For details on the achievements of the capacity building support to decentralization, refer to the IRCBP quarterly, annual, and mid-term evaluation reports from 2004–08.

[6] For details of the strategy, refer to GoSL 2007. It addresses the involvement of service providers in capacity building under decentralization.

[7] Introduced by a consulting firm, the Rapid Results Approach (RRA) methodology was adapted by the IRCBP for the Sierra Leone decentralization.

[8] The Local Council Encyclopedia provides comprehensive information on Sierra Leone's national decentralization reform process and how local councils are responding to development challenges in their respective localities. The project seeks to design 19 web pages for the local councils. The initial version can be accessed at http://www.insomniacdesign.com/wbslio/html/index.asp.

[9] Recruitment took place in only 17 councils. Two councils did not carry out recruitment due to their disagreement with the role that LGSC was playing in the recruitment process.

CHAPTER 4

Decentralization in Practice

Katherine Whiteside Casey

Generating hypotheses about the likely impacts of decentralization requires a realistic assessment of how much influence the local councils could have exerted over public service delivery.[1] Councils' influence, in turn, depends on the extent to which they actually control functions and finances. For the three critical sectors—health, agriculture, and education—this chapter documents when functions devolved, how much public funding the local councils manage directly, and what activities the councils have undertaken. In so doing, the analysis focuses the broad hypotheses concerning how decentralization might improve governance on specific areas in which local councils have had sufficient time, resources, and authority to enact real changes on the ground. Chapter 5 examines these more specific hypotheses in depth.

Overview: Motivating Hypotheses and the Size of the Pie

The overarching objective of decentralization is to bring the government closer to the people, thereby improving service delivery, increasing accountability of government agents, and enhancing public voice in governance issues. More specifically, by reducing the management distance from Freetown to district headquarters, decentralization intends to: (a) improve the efficiency of work plan approval, financing, and implementation; (b) enhance oversight and thus the reach of public goods distribution; and (c) increase oversight of employees, thereby motivating better staff performance. Taken together, these translate to higher quality service delivery, improved public access to services, and thus greater citizen satisfaction with public services. In addition, by bringing the government closer to the people, decentralization seeks to: (a) enhance citizens' access to politicians and thus increase the former's influence over decisions and (b) increase citizens' access to information about the government, thereby enabling them to better assess and monitor government activities. Through this combination of voice and information, decentralization aims to increase citizens' ability to demand better services and hold their representatives accountable for public sector performance. For each of the three key sectors, it is important to track the extent to which decentralization actually delivers these hypothesized benefits.

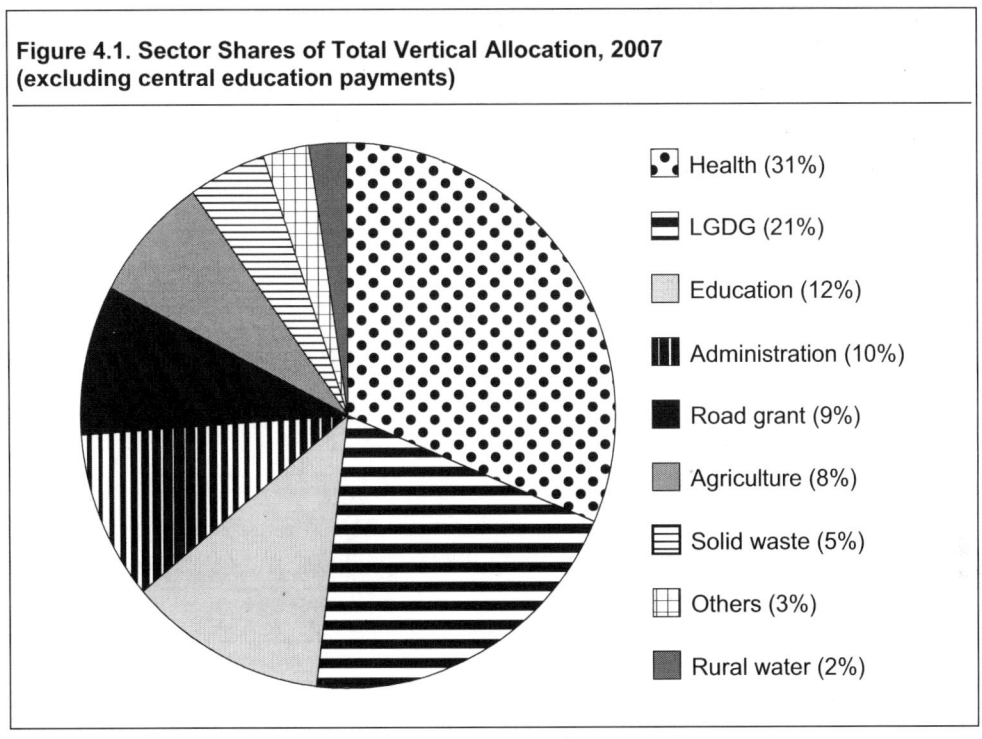

Figure 4.1. Sector Shares of Total Vertical Allocation, 2007 (excluding central education payments)

Health (31%)

LGDG (21%)

Education (12%)

Administration (10%)

Road grant (9%)

Agriculture (8%)

Solid waste (5%)

Others (3%)

Rural water (2%)

Local councils' ability to deliver such improvements depends crucially on how much public funding falls under their control. In the 2007 government budget, the total vertical allocation from central to local government was 59,228,800,000 Leones (Le), roughly equivalent to US$20 million.[2] To service a population of nearly 5 million, this amounts to only approximately $4 per capita. Figure 4.1 shows the division of these devolved funds by sector. Note that health accounts for the largest share of the vertical transfer (31 percent), followed by education (12 percent), roads (9 percent), and agriculture (8 percent).[3] Other large areas of the government budget, such as salaries and development expenditures, remain under central control during the transition.

Untied Local Government Development Grants (LGDGs), which local councils are free to use for any activity in their development plans, account for approximately one-fifth of the vertical transfers. Over the last few years, the councils have allocated these funds across a variety of sectors. For 2004–06 grants, road rehabilitation and transport projects account for the largest share (28 percent), followed by agricultural projects and markets (13 percent each).[4] Other areas of spending include solid waste (8 percent), education (5 percent), and water (5 percent). Perhaps because the tied grants for health are relatively large, councils have not prioritized health activities for their discretionary funds (only 2 percent).

Table 4.1. Statutory Timetable for Transfer of Health Sector Functions and the Date of First Fiscal Transfer

Function (Activities) to devolve	Year LCs to assume function	Date of first financial transfer to LC accounts
Registration of births and deaths	2005	Sep-05
Public health information, education and communication	2005	Sep-05
Environmental healthcare (water and sanitation)	2005	Sep-05
Maintenance of non-technical equipment	2005	—
Primary healthcare (district peripheral health units)	2005	Sep-05
Facilities management	2005	Sep-05
Procurement of equipment and drugs	2007	
Secondary healthcare	2008	—

Noting the overall size and division of funds, the next three sections delve into the details of devolution by sector. Specifically, they document (a) when the first tied grants for specific functions were transferred to local council accounts, particularly in comparison to the assumption date specified in the Statutory Instrument of 2004 (SI); (b) how much of the sector financing local councils currently control, compared to how much is controlled by the relevant central ministry and donors; and (c) main local council activities in each sector funded by both the tied grants and untied discretionary LGDGs. The last two sections then explore possible reasons for the large variation in progress apparent across sectors and identify areas in which decentralization is most likely to have impacted service delivery.

Devolution of Healthcare

The Ministry of Health and Sanitation (MoHS) stands out as the only ministry to devolve its scheduled functions on time. Moreover, it has transferred a greater proportion of its resources to councils than has any other ministry. MoHS transferred the first tied grants for 5 of the 6 functions slated for 2005 to local council accounts in September 2005. Given the late date, councils implemented few related activities in 2005 and began substantive primary healthcare work early in 2006. Management of the district peripheral health units (PHUs) accounted for the largest share of the tied health grants (85 percent in 2006) and council efforts in the sector.[5] The remaining 4 functions each accounted for 3 to 5 percent of the 2006 devolved health budget.

Three areas of nonsalary health sector financing were included in GoSL's 2007 budget: resources allocated to ministries, departments, and agencies (MDAs) to implement their work plans, transfers to local councils tied to the individual functions listed above, and development expenditures for specific donor-funded projects.[6] Considering the first two sources only, local councils currently control 23 percent of the nondevelopment health expenditures allocated to central and local government.[7] Focusing on primary healthcare, councils control 62 percent of the resources for this significant function.

Figure 4.2. National Health Budget, 2007

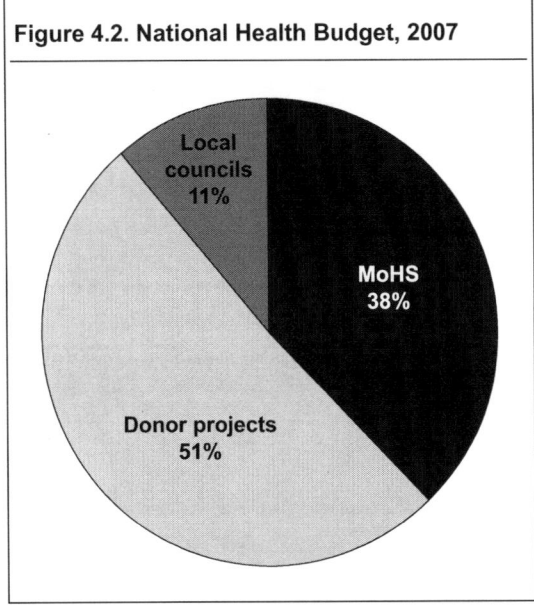

However, the picture looks a bit different when development expenditures also are considered. Figure 4.2 shows that councils control only 11 percent of the national pool across these three funding streams (which do not include NGO spending in the sector). The MoHS Director of Financial Services views these development expenditures as falling under the control of the central government in collaboration with contributing donor partners. Funds for specific activities under these projects are disbursed from the center to the district-level MoHS offices. However, soon this arrangement likely will adjust to incorporate local government. In the meantime, LGDGs provide discretionary funding to councils to support development projects that councils identify in their areas. During the transition, the grants partially compensate for the lack of devolution of the sectoral development budgets. As noted above, the tied health grants account for the largest share (31 percent) of the total vertical allocation from central to local government.

An important consideration in evaluating local governments' abilities to maintain the same quality and coverage of health services is the relative size of functional budgets pre- and post-devolution. In particular, LGA 04 stipulates that, through 2008:

> Parliament shall appropriate to local councils as a tied grant for each
> devolved service, at least that amount necessary to continue the
> operation and maintenance of that service at the standard to which
> it was provided in the year prior to its devolution (Section 47.1).

Thus, the relevant comparison for health is the actual 2004 MoHS expenditures for the five functions that devolved and the subsequent 2005 budget allocation and actual disbursements to councils for the same set. The 2004 actual expenditures by the MoHS for civil registration (births and deaths), environmental healthcare, primary healthcare, facilities management, and public health IEC (waste disposal) totaled Le 2,269,585,570. The total budgetary allocation to local councils for 2005 devolved health functions was Le 8,100,620,000, of which Le 3,868,884,000 was disbursed. The figures show that the level of actual funding was maintained, and, in fact, increased by more than half (170 percent of base).[8] Furthermore, this hike exceeded the overall increase in total actual health expenditures for the ministry alone in 2004, compared to that for the central and local government combined in 2005 (137 percent of base).

Since late 2005, local councils have been using these funds in partnership with the District Health Management Teams (DHMTs) to implement activities under all five functions for which they received tied grants. The most important area of work relates to management of the PHUs, for which councils collaborate in implementing vaccination campaigns, distributing bed nets, and constructing and equipping primary health clinics. For environmental healthcare, councils have funded water wells and public taps, constructed public toilets, and organized solid waste management schemes. Councils also are active in public health education, hosting information sessions on disease prevention (for malaria, HIV/AIDS, and cholera) and public hygiene. Finally, councils organized birth registration campaigns, most notably in Kono, in which the district council worked with UNICEF to register 45,000 children. Two functions—procurement of drugs and secondary healthcare—have not yet devolved to councils.

Devolution of Agricultural Services

While the Ministry of Agriculture and Food Security (MAFS) lags behind the MoHS, it has surpassed the Ministry of Education, Science and Technology (MEST)[9] in devolving functions and financing to the local councils. MAFS devolved functions under three divisions: Crops, Livestock, and Land and Water. The first sets of tied grants were lodged in local council accounts in May 2006 and March 2007. However, for each of the three divisions, the central ministry retains control over some activities and financing in the 2007 budget. Since the MAFS budget, both pre- and post-devolution, is not itemized by function, table 4.2 provides dates of financial transfers by division only. Furthermore, no clear policy directive specifies which functions and underlying activities are retained at central level, which are shared between the two levels of government, and which are fully devolved to local councils. As a result, discrepancies exist between the views of central MAFS officials regarding what has and has not been devolved and the activities of local councils. This lack of clarity, combined with differences in terrain and livestock populations, causes additional variation across councils in the kinds of agricultural projects implemented.

In addition to the divisions listed above, the SI also covers Forestry, which has since been removed from the MAFS and established as the standalone National Commission on Environment and Forestry. No funds have yet devolved to councils for forestry activities.

Excluding donor-funded development expenditures, the local councils control 16 percent of the 2007 total nonsalary agricultural budget allocated to central and local government.[10] Focusing on the functions specified for devolution, councils controlled 67 percent of Crops Division funds, 55 percent of Livestock Division funds, and 21 percent of Land and Water Division funds for 2007 (figure 4.3). However, including the development expenditures reveals that the vast majority of finances in the sector are tied to specific donor-funded projects.

Table 4.2. Statutory Timetable for Transfer of Agriculture Sector Functions and the First Year of Fiscal Transfer

Function (Activities) to devolve	Year LCs to assume function	Date of first financial transfer to LC accounts
Crops Division		May 2006
Extension services	2005–2007	
Tree and cash crop nurseries	2006	
Plantation development and maintenance	2007	
Input delivery services	2005–2006	
Vegetable production	2007–2008	
Food science and nutrition	2007–2008	
Post-harvest and agro-processing	2005	
Marketing	2006	
Farmers training	2005–2006	
Staff training	2006	
Seed production and multiplication	2008	
Produce inspection, grading and licenses	2008	
Off-farm income generation	2008	
Land and Water Division		March 2007
Small scale swamp development	2007–2008	
Small scale IVS/upland rehabilitation	2008	
Livestock Division		May 2006
Animal health	2005–2007	
Animal production	2007–2008	
Cattle settlement schemes	2005	
Settlement of crop/livestock disputes	2005	
Administration of livestock markets	2005	

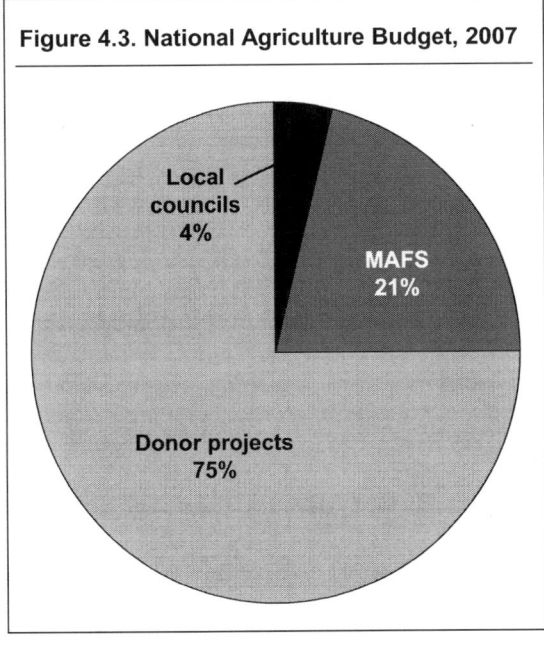

Figure 4.3. National Agriculture Budget, 2007

Local councils 4%

MAFS 21%

Donor projects 75%

Without an itemized budget, it is impossible to track whether the actual level of pre-devolution funding by function was maintained, as legislated by the LGA. However, MAFS and Local Government Finance Department (LGFD) staff worked together to determine an equitable sharing arrangement between central and local government for the first set of transfers (2006). They did this under the assumption that all functions scheduled for 2005 would fall completely under local council responsibility, while the others would remain fully under central ministry control—a division that is not clear in practice. They then gave relative priority weights to each function and used these to divide the overall budget envelope across central and local accounts. In this way, the LGA provision was implemented in spirit, even though it was not possible in letter. As seen above, agriculture accounts for 8 percent of the total vertical transfer from central to local government. In addition, several councils undertook agricultural activities—mainly rice production and markets—with untied LGDG funds, which accounted for 11 percent of the total number of these projects in 2004, 42 percent in 2005, and 20 percent in 2006. Thus, while tied agriculture grants are a modest contributor to the overall vertical transfer envelope, the sector remains a high priority for discretionary funds.

Although MAFS began transferring tied grants in mid–06, local councils had begun implementing agricultural activities using un-tied LGDG as early as 2004. The main council-supported initiatives under the Crops Division included extension services, delivery of farming inputs, cash group and vegetable production, and provision of processing equipment. More specifically, several councils purchased motorbikes and bicycles to extend the reach of field extension workers, and supported farmer trainings in post-harvest loss reduction and modern farming techniques. The largest activity under input delivery was the local procurement, distribution, and recovery of seed rice loans in 2006. This local initiative represented a significant shift in procedure from earlier centralized MAFS distribution campaigns. In terms of production, most councils fund ward-level rice or cassava farms and vegetable plots for women's groups. Last, regarding post-harvest processing, several councils purchased equipment such as rice mills and cassava graters and built grain stores and drying floors.

For the Livestock Division, typical activities included (a) animal healthcare, mainly vaccination and treatment of cattle, goats, sheep, dogs, and chickens; (b) animal production, including cattle ranches, poultry units, and goat distribution; and (c) cattle settlement schemes, which aim to prevent disputes between crop farmers and cattle herders, an area traditionally under the chiefdoms. Finally, since the Land and Water functions began to devolve only in 2007 and the tied transfers are very small, there is little council activity under this division. Nonetheless, several councils are involved in swamp development and inland valley swamp (IVS) rice cultivation.

Devolution of Education

Devolution of education is very recent and much delayed. The first direct transfers to local council accounts were not sent until 2007. In a speech given on June 1, 2007, the Minister of Education formally transferred responsibility for primary and junior secondary schools to the local councils through the Ministry of Local Government and Community Development (MLGCD). In the following weeks, MEST issued devolution guidelines, revised district-level organizational charts with accompanying lists of devolved and retained personnel, and school, pupil and teacher rosters. The Permanent Secretary of MLGCD officially presented these documents to councils in the last week of July. Furthermore, as measured by direct control of financial resources by councils, devolution of education has progressed very little since 2004 (table 4.3). As a result, during a survey of councilors in mid–2007, expressions of frustration with the slow process of devolution and eagerness to take control of more primary education responsibilities arose repeatedly.[11]

Table 4.3. Statutory Timetable for Transfer of Education Sector Functions and Date of First Fiscal Transfer

Function (Activities) to devolve	Year LCs to assume function	Date of first financial transfer to LC accounts
Primary Education		
Payment of examination fees	2005	---
Payment of school fees subsidies	2005	---
Payment of staff salaries	2006 (2005 for DEC)	---
Provision of furniture	2006 (2005 for DEC)	---
Provision of teaching and learning materials	2005	---
Provision of textbooks	2006	---
Recruitment of teachers	2005	---
Rehabilitation/reconstruction of schools	2005	---
Staff development (study leave)	2005	---
School supervision		
Inspection of teachers and curriculum	2007	Mar-07
Inspection of pupils	2007	Mar-07
Government libraries		
Establishment of Boards	2007	Mar-07
Supervisory monitoring	2007	Mar-07
Staff training	2007	---

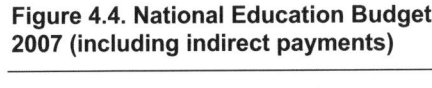

Figure 4.4. National Education Budget, 2007 (including indirect payments)

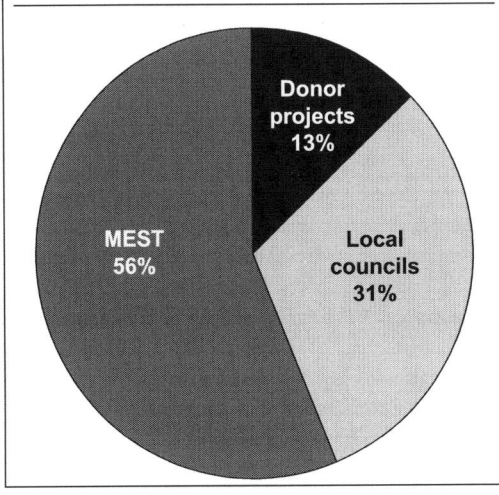

Funds in the national budget for school fees subsidies, examination fees, teaching and learning materials (TLM), and textbooks all appear under the local councils for 2006 and 2007. Nevertheless, these payments actually were made centrally on their behalf. Thus, although MEST no longer controls these resources, local councils also have little direct influence. In fact, the picture of how much financial control councils have in the education sector changes markedly when the above 4 items are included or excluded. When they are excluded, local control drops from 31 percent to 5 percent. Figures 4.4 and 4.5 show the shares of nonsalary recurrent and development expenditures controlled directly and indirectly by councils and by MEST, and of those tied to donor-funded projects.

The only monies local councils controlled directly come from a Le 4 billion overestimate of the 2007 schools fees subsidies budget.[12] LGFD reallocated these savings to school supervision and government libraries (which were unfunded) and two discretionary line items of education administration and development. Regarding education's share of local government budgets, these education grants (excluding indirect payments) account for 12 percent of the total vertical allocation to councils. Finally, local councils do not prioritize education projects for their discretionary spending: to date, they have allocated only 5 percent of LGDGs toward education.

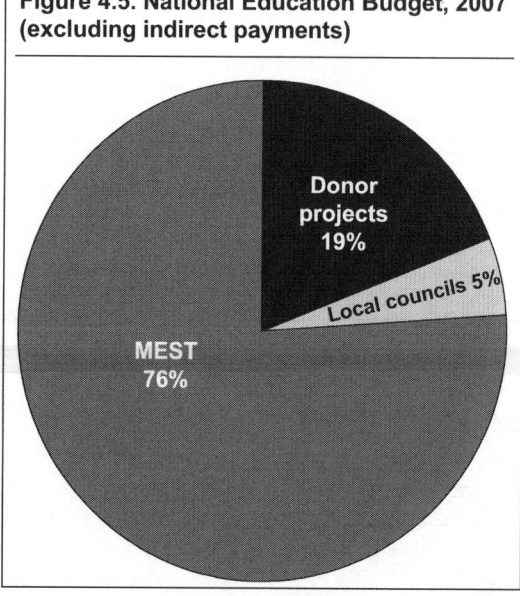

Figure 4.5. National Education Budget, 2007 (excluding indirect payments)

Donor projects 19%

Local councils 5%

MEST 76%

Although local council activity in education is much more limited than in the other two sectors, the two main areas of council involvement are the distribution of teaching and learning materials (TLM) and verification of teacher and student rosters. Regarding the former, decentralization has brought three main changes: it incorporated local council representatives in the procurement committee for textbooks and TLM; shifted the contractor delivery point from Freetown to the local council offices; and allowed councils to manage the distribution. In moving the supplies from district headquarters to schools, councils chose different allocation formulae and distribution mechanisms. For the latter, councilors and district education staff visited schools to clean up the list of teachers (to eventually rid the payroll of "ghost" teachers), and provide a more accurate assessment of enrollment rates. A few councils have further used discretionary funds to purchase classroom furniture and construct vocational centers and primary schools. With new funds transferred for the 2007–08 academic year to cover school supervision, development, and administration, council activity in the sector is expected to increase.

Reasons for Differential Progress across Sectors

The most immediate explanation for the health sector's lead in decentralization is its decade-long head start. The MoHS began deconcentrating—that is, giving greater responsibility and autonomy to district-level ministry staff—in the early 1990s. In preparatory research for its Health and Population Project (HPP), which started in 1986, the World Bank identified over-centralization of the MoHS as a key constraint to improving health provision.[13] Around the same time, Sierra Leone joined in the Bamako Initiative, which emphasized community involvement in determining affordable, sustainable rates of cost-recovery for drugs and in improving maternal and child health. These shifts toward a more local approach were reflected in the National

Health Policy issued in June 1993 (revised 2002), which aimed to "decentralize the administrative structure of the health care delivery system," an effort that culminated in "the creation of District Health Boards which will only function within the framework of less stringent central control." This movement extended to higher tiers of health care with the enactment of the Hospital Boards Act (2003), which introduced district-level boards for secondary health care. Thus, by the time that LGA 04 was passed, district medical officers (DMOs) had experienced several years of increasing responsibility for and control over the district health programs, notably more so than their district-level counterparts in the other two sectors. After 2004, confidence accumulated through learning by doing, enhanced by the security of high levels of education, likely gave the DMOs a stronger negotiating position to push their central MoHS superiors to decentralize even further.

The LCs are near unanimous in the view that the health sector has made the most progress in decentralizing. Their most common explanation for the difference in progress relates to MoHS staff qualifications and compliance. The LCs cite the "will power of the politicians," their "belie[f] in consultation with council," the "willingness of MoHS to devolve," and their "openness to Council's personnel at all times." Other explanations involve the ministry's widespread presence in the field and greater volume of funds to disburse.[14]

Regarding agriculture, when pressed to explain why MAFS devolved more slowly than MoHS and why the progress of the former has been less extensive, both central and district officials tend to cite the relatively small amount of funding for agriculture. They further report that the quarterly allocations for the various agricultural divisions are too small and arrive late. Nationwide, some 500 staff service roughly 730,000 farming households, yielding a ratio of 1 extension worker to approximately 1,400 farming households.[15] This acute resource constraint impedes service provision and appears to be further slowing decentralization.

Finally, for education, central and district officials in the ministry blame (a) the sheer size of the primary school system with its attendant administrative challenges, and (b) the significant role of private providers for their slow progress in decentralizing. Others cite political resistance within MEST as an important cause of the delay.

- MEST is responsible for overseeing around 5,000 primary schools nationwide, which is roughly 5 times the number of government primary health clinics. This vast number is accompanied by an unwieldy and ineffective administrative system that puts the exact roster of schools, teachers, and pupils continuously under investigation. Ministry officials argued for a central administrative clean-up before devolving primary education to councils. Decentralization advocates countered with the local knowledge and efficiency advantages in devolving sooner and letting the councils manage the roster verification process. Either way, the administrative confusion with the accompanying debates may be one reason for the delayed hand-over.
- MEST officials cite the vast majority of private providers in education as a second limiting factor to the extent of decentralization. One district deputy director draws an analogy to MoHS being in charge of all private pharmacies

in the country, and emphasizes that MEST's role is more limited to oversight as opposed to service implementation. While this is less convincing as an argument concerning the progress of decentralization, it touches on an important issue of how to motivate local government interest and activity where there is little money for direct project implementation. Councils have less interest in monitoring the performance of sector programs in which their own funds are not invested. With major inputs—salaries, subsidies, and examination fees—handled centrally and less control over the budgetary and operational decisions of frontline (private) providers, it seems probable that local government involvement in primary education will remain limited in comparison to the other two sectors. It will be interesting to see whether this passivity changes with the new funds for education development, supervision, and administration transferred to councils in 2007.

■   Local councilors and others outside the ministry tend to cite political resistance within MEST as the most important reason for slow progress. Compared to the other two ministries, which also must grapple with issues of loss of control and power, MEST may face greater challenges in mobilizing the necessary political will at all levels to push decentralization forward.

Likely Areas of Decentralization Impacts

To frame the analysis in chapter 5, the preceding discussion identifies several areas in which decentralization likely affected the quality and reach of public services. First, given the early and sustained transfers of tied funding for health, it seems reasonable to expect some positive change in healthcare provision if the original hypotheses about decentralization are correct. The health sector was already heavily devolved with significant autonomy at the district level. Therefore, we expect decentralization not so much to change what is being done in primary health, but to improve the efficiency with which work plans are executed and the reach of services and resources. More specifically, district-level health employees repeatedly emphasize the elimination of bureaucratic delays in accessing resources from Freetown as the most significant contribution of decentralization. Moving budgetary and activity approval to the district level closes the gap between planning and implementation, enabling district teams to spend more time and energy doing their jobs. Furthermore, delivering and storing drugs and supplies at district-level facilities may have reduced supply chain leakages and thus increased the availability of resources. Finally, district and clinic staff suggest that the provision of outreach incentives has expanded the catchment area of clinics and the number of clients who benefit from their services.

Summing up these operational improvements, the Director of Primary Healthcare reports that, in three recent supervisory visits, he was impressed to see that clinics are implementing nearly 80 percent of their planned activities, a notable increase over previous years.[16] Similarly, the District Medical Officer from Kenema remarked that "Decentralization makes you more effective and less expensive."[17] Thus, for health, chapter 5 investigates whether (a) closing the management gap from Freetown to local councils improves the efficiency of DHMT work plan approval, implementation, and oversight; (b) local councils' role in overseeing resource distribution improves the reach of health supplies to clinics; (c) local council and DHMT clinic rehabilitation/construction and outreach activities improve public access to and use of government clinics; (d) local council support extends the reach of birth and death registration; and (e) the combination of these and other service delivery improvements enhances public satisfaction with the healthcare they receive at government facilities.

In comparison to health, the amount of money transferred to councils for agriculture was smaller and arrived later, so expectations of change should be more muted. Specifically, as ministry functions and finances began to devolve only in May 2006, councils have had less of an opportunity to make operational or management changes to impact the delivery of the scheduled functions. However, from as early as 2005, councils prioritized agricultural projects and markets in their discretionary funding, so if they spent effectively, they should have created some impacts in these areas. In terms of management, district-level agricultural staff members frequently cite two major improvements from decentralization: easier, although still imperfect, access to resources; and greater mobility and logistical support to extend the reach of extension workers and project monitoring. While they note that bureaucratic delays, especially untimely disbursement of funds, continue to impede efficient implementation of their work plans, they do suggest that decentralization has eased this burden. In addition, replacing the monthly meetings of District Directors of Agriculture in Freetown with district-level meetings among members of the District Agriculture Office staff and local council Agriculture subcommittees gives some evidence of increasing local autonomy. Central MAFS employees admit that this decrease in direct reporting has not been met with a commensurate increase in their oversight and monitoring activities, an area they flag for improvement. Chapter 5 investigates whether these changes in management practice and local council investments have expanded the reach of frontline extension staff and improved farmers' access to drying floors, markets, and grain stores.

Finally, given the limited progress in devolving education, it would be unreasonable to expect decentralization to have had an impact on service delivery. Furthermore, any discovered changes in education outcomes are likely attributable to other actors or initiatives beyond the local councils. The only area that may be experiencing impacts attributable to decentralization is the distribution of textbooks and teaching and learning materials. Since local councils chose both different allocation formulae and distribution mechanisms, it will be interesting to explore changes over time in cross-council variation in the equity and reach of supply allocations. While data on this hypothesis is not yet available, the IRCBP Evaluations Unit plans to collect and analyze these indicators during the 2008–09 academic year.

Notes

[1] This chapter draws from Whiteside 2007.

[2] Vertical allocation refers to central-local government transfers so does not include local council own revenue. The total envelope reported excludes indirect (central) payments for education examination fees, school fees subsidies, and procurement of textbooks and teaching and learning materials.

[3] GoSL 2006.

[4] RRI Implementation Reports for 2004, 2005, and 2006 LGDG funds. In these reports, financial data is available for only 80% of LGDG projects.

[5] Local Government Finance Department (LGFD).

[6] All national budget figures are from GoSL 2006.

[7] Retained central ministry line items include Administration Division, Human Resources Management, Primary Health Care Services (Maternal and Child Health/EPI, Malaria Prevention, and STI/HIV/AIDS Prevention), Secondary Healthcare, and Support Services (Drugs and Medical Supplies).

[8] 2004 MoHS actuals from principal accountant, MoHS, and acting subaccountant, MoHS; and 2005 local council actuals from the Local Government Finance Department (LGFD).

[9] Renamed the Ministry of Education, Youth and Sports (MEYS) after the 2007 national elections.

[10] Retained central ministry budget items include Office of the Permanent Secretary, Food Security Division, Planning, Evaluation, Monitoring and Statistics, and Support to Agricultural Institutions.

[11] The Decentralization Watch Survey (July 2007) interviewed roughly 5 representatives from each of the 19 local councils. All subsequent references to local council opinions draw on this survey and personal interviews by the author.

[12] Interview with Director, LGFD.

[13] Interview with Director of Planning and Information, MoHS.

[14] Whiteside 2007.

[15] GoSL 2006a, GoSL 2004b.

[16] Interview with author, June 2007.

[17] Interview with author, July 2007.

CHAPTER 5

Impact of Decentralization on Public Services: Evidence to Date

Elizabeth Foster and Rachel Glennester

Chapter 4 explored the extent to which decentralization has taken place in various sectors and identified areas in which Sierra Leone's decentralization can be expected to raise the quality of services. This chapter intensifies investigation of these areas. We develop specific hypotheses of the ways in which decentralization may have affected these areas, in terms of both overall changes in performance and the patterns of performance that might be seen if these changes had been driven by decentralization. A key point to keep in mind throughout this chapter is that, until now, there has been no decentralization of the employment, promotion, or dismissal of service providers in any sector. As staff pay is one of the largest elements in the budget for any area of service provision, this limits the extent to which the decentralization that has taken place can influence services.

How Might Decentralization Be Predicted to Impact Services?

In assessing whether and how the decentralization that has taken place has impacted public services, it is useful to think through how and what we might expect it to impact. In the literature, the main reasons for thinking that decentralization might improve public services are:

- Decentralization allows for greater diversity in the type of public services delivered and how they are delivered so that services can more closely reflect the different priorities of different regions of the country.
- By reducing the distance (both geographically and bureaucratically) between frontline service providers and managers, decentralization can reduce the cost of monitoring by superiors, and can increase the speed and efficiency with which managers respond to needs on the ground.
- Decentralization can also make services more accountable to the local population by reducing the distance that individual citizens must travel to complain about services and the number of bureaucratic layers that they have to go through to make their complaint.
- If a central government has a particular interest or strong support base in certain regions and there is a risk of favoritism, decentralization can help

ensure that money for public services is spread more evenly among regions than might otherwise be the case, for example, by introducing transparent resource allocation to districts.

When measuring the impact of decentralization, it is important to be aware of its potential pitfalls. The useful discussion of these in Bardhan (2002) can be summarized as follows[1]:

- Decentralization could undermine national cohesion by making people identify themselves more by their region than by their nation.
- It can be more efficient to have one organization than many small ones (what economists refer to as economies of scale in production). In this case, decentralization can lead to inefficiencies, extra costs, and reinventing the wheel.
- Because decentralization encourages governments to treat all districts equally, it can undermine the government's ability to redistribute between rich and poor regions. This is the flip side of iv) above.
- Implementation capacity and technical skills may be limited at the lower levels of government so that decentralization could reduce the quality of public services, particularly in areas in which technical skills are important. Not only will the average *quality* of technical skills be lower but also the *variation in skill level* among different services at the district level is likely to be higher than when all services are run by the center.
- Decentralization can allow local elites undue influence over resources. This is a particular concern when a technocratic central bureaucracy is replaced by a local system under the unchecked influence of a local elite.

Data

In this chapter, we use data from the National Public Services (NPS) survey, carried out in February/March 2005 and May/June 2007. The NPS covered a nationally representative sample of 6,350 households, with a minimum of 40 households each per local council area. It was structured so that half the questionnaires were answered by women and the other half by men. This chapter also uses data from the 2005, 2006, and 2008 Clinic Surveys.[2] Together, these data sources provide information on *access* to services in different sectors as well as *satisfaction* with these services. The Clinic Surveys provide detailed information on many different dimensions of service quality in health before and after decentralization. The survey covers a nationally representative sample of clinics and includes such indicators as personnel absence rates, drugs in stock, material condition of the clinic, and frequency of supervision visits. Once the second round of the equivalent survey for education quality is completed, it will be possible to compare how these detailed measures of quality compare in these two sectors, one of which has decentralized and one of which has not.

Testable Hypotheses

At a very broad level, some of the existing literature summarized above suggests that decentralization should correlate with improved delivery of public services (ii and iii). Other literature suggests that it should correlate with reduced quality of services (b, d, and e). To address this divergence of views, the first hypothesis that we test is:

Hypothesis 1. Service quality will improve as decentralization progresses.

Decentralization in Sierra Leone is occurring at a time that the country is recovering from a devastating civil war and donors are supporting substantial reconstruction efforts. For these reasons, an improvement in public service quality might be expected with or without decentralization. It is difficult to determine how much of any improvement might be due to decentralization. The fact that different sectors in Sierra Leone decentralized at different times suggests a more precise hypothesis, namely:

HYPOTHESIS 1A: THE SERVICES THAT HAVE EXPERIENCED MORE DECENTRALIZATION HAVE SEEN GREATER IMPROVEMENTS THAN THE SERVICES THAT HAVE EXPERIENCED LESS DECENTRALIZATION. The literature also has mixed predictions about whether decentralization will be associated with more or less inequality of provision of public services (i and d suggest increased inequality in outcomes from decentralization; iv suggests greater convergence of outcomes with decentralization). This suggests our second testable hypothesis:

Hypothesis 2: Inequality of public service provision across regions is reduced with decentralization.

Finally, some data enable us to examine potential mechanisms through which decentralization might work. Advantages of decentralization ii and iii work through reduced geographic or bureaucratic distance. Some areas of the country saw dramatic reductions in the distance to the center of power; others saw relatively little change, suggesting a potential test:

HYPOTHESIS 2A: AREAS THAT HAVE EXPERIENCED THE LARGEST REDUCTION IN THE DISTANCE TO POWER HAVE SEEN THE GREATEST IMPROVEMENTS IN PUBLIC SERVICE QUALITY. Reduced bureaucratic distance (for example, the reduced number of layers of approval that a health worker has to go through to get a roof repaired) is often mentioned in Sierra Leone as a benefit of decentralization (chapter 3). As this benefit applies equally to all parts of the country, it is hard to test for it quantitatively. We do, however, have information on whether decentralization changes the person to whom people go when they have a problem.

HYPOTHESIS 2B: DECENTRALIZATION CHANGES TO WHOM PEOPLE REPORT PROBLEMS. We also can directly test whether more supervisory visits took place in health after decentralization than before. Once data from the education sector is available, it will be possible to compare the changes in supervision frequency in sectors that have seen more and less decentralization.

HYPOTHESIS 2C: SERVICES THAT HAVE BEEN DECENTRALIZED SEE INCREASED MONITORING FROM SUPERVISORS.

Outcomes: Public Service Quality Has Improved across Most Sectors

Table 5.1 summarizes key indicators across many different sectors from the NPS and shows that the majority has improved between 2005 and 2007, with many seeing dramatic improvements. The only indicator to decline significantly is the percentage of the population who has spoken to an agricultural extension worker. At the same time, other agricultural indicators have shown large improvements. The only sector to see no overall improvement is the registration of births and deaths. This average for births and deaths hides sharp improvements in some local council areas and sharp declines in others.

Table 5.1. Access and Quality of Public Services, 2005–07 (%)

	2005	2007	Difference Significance
Education			
Access to school within 30 minutes walking	68.4	73.9	5.5 **
Access to school within 60 minutes walking	87.0	87.5	0.5
Satisfaction with primary schools	87.7	94.4	6.7 **
Health			
Access to health clinic within 30 minutes	29.9	34.2	4.4 **
Access to health clinic within 60 minutes	48.4	53.7	5.3 **
Satisfaction with health clinic (% satisfied)	81.2	90.9	9.7 **
Registration of births and deaths			
Births registered (%)	44.8	43.4	−1.4
Deaths registered (%)	23.4	23.7	0.3
Agriculture			
Spoken to an extension worker in the past year	23.1	17.6	−5.5 **
Storage, access to enough space (farming hh only)	8.2	11.6	3.4 **
Drying floor space, access to enough space (farming hh only)	12.1	19.6	7.4 **
Transport/roads			
Drivable road within 30 minutes walking	65.8	73.2	7.3 **
Nearest drivable road passable all year	56.4	68.1	11.7 **
Transport at least once a day on nearest drivable road	57.1	60.0	2.9 **
Markets			
Market area within 60 minutes	32.7	45.6	13.0 **
Water			
Water source within 15 minutes	61.0	73.4	12.4 **

Detailed data from the three health surveys show that almost all key indicators of quality improved from 2005–08. The only indicator to decline over this period was use, and this decrease was not statistically significant. The NPS surveys also show a decreased used of government clinics and which appears to be due to the increase in the number of nongovernmental hospitals and clinics available during the period. All other indicators showed a significant improvement between 2005 and 2008[3] and the percentage of clinics with working refrigerators (the focus of a large EC program), the percent of staff positions filled, and the percent of clinics with all basic supplies in stock increased steadily in throughout the period.

Have Public Services Improved More in Sectors That Have Seen More Decentralization?

Table 5.2 summarizes the extent to which services have been decentralized and whether these sectors have seen improvements. Sectors that have no negative indicators also tended to experience improvements of a larger magnitude. For example, we only have one indicator for water, but it improved by more than 12 percentage points.

Table 5.2. Does Greater Sector Decentralization Correlate with Greater Public Service Improvement?

Sector	Govt. resources through LCs (excl. salaries and donors (%)	Clear division of responsibilities	Decentralization of roles and funding	Service quality change	Allocation LCs own resources	Sector spending by donors (%)
Education	0	yes	Nothing as of June 2007	+	5	13
Health Primary health	11 62	yes	Central: salaries and drugs LCs: repair, supervision	++	2	51
Agriculture	21 to 67	no	Salaries not devolved dispute over what functions devolved	Mixed	13	75
Registration of births and deaths	100	yes	Money and functions devolved, not staff	0 Big improve-ments and falls, by LC	n/a	Big in some LCs
Roads	0	medium	No devolution, but LCs use own money for roads	+	28	NA
Markets	NA	medium	Chiefs, not national govt, traditionally responsible	++	13	Some NaCSA
Water	40	yes	Partial devolution of	++	5	yes

Sources: Decentralization Watch, NPS Report 2007.
Notes: "++" = all indicators in that sector saw significant improvement; "+" = majority of indicators in the NPS improved; "mixed" = some went up while others went down; 0 = no significant improvement found; n/a = information not available 1. From 2007 annual budget for Government of Sierra Leone as summarized in Decentralization Watch. 2. Small grants for school libraries were given to councils in 2007.

Table 5.2 also summarizes other relevant factors for judging the role that decentralization has played in these improvements, such as whether the division of responsibilities between the center and local councils is clear and how big a role donors play in the sector. For agriculture, although some funding has been decentralized, the lack of clarity of roles is a major impediment to decentralization being able to feed through into an improvement in services. In addition, donor projects in agriculture massively outweigh spending by either central or local government, suggesting that any improvement may reflect donor activity rather than council activity.

Another factor to take into account is the extent to which local councils have spent their own money on a particular sector. For example, none of the central budget for roads has been decentralized, but local councils are spending a lot of their own resources on road improvements. Thus, some of the improvements in access to drivable roads could reflect activity by councils (especially as central spending tends to focus on upgrading trunk roads, whereas council spending tends to focus on improving local roads and access to main trunk roads). Later in this chapter, we find that improvements in roads were concentrated in those parts of the country that had experienced a big reduction in the distance to political power (namely, areas that were close to district headquarters but far from Freetown), suggesting that local councils may be responsible for some of these improvements.

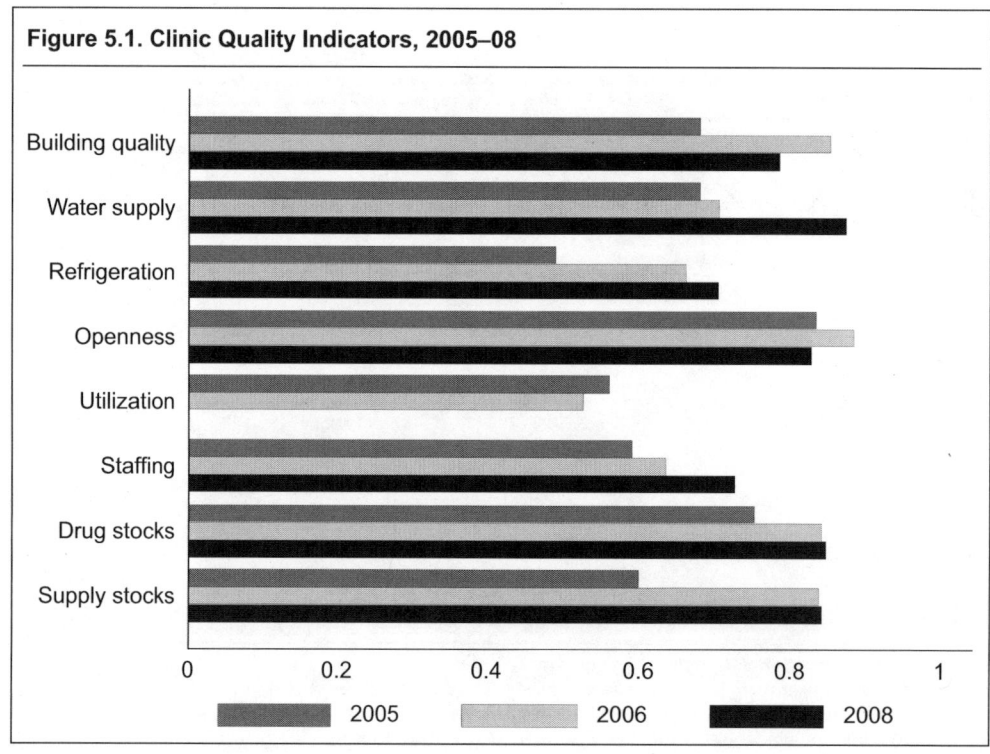

Figure 5.1. Clinic Quality Indicators, 2005–08

Turning to the extent of decentralization by sector, education has seen the least movement toward decentralization; health and agriculture have seen partial decentralization; and the registration of births and deaths has seen the most decentralization. As mentioned above, all staff in all sectors are still hired, paid, and dismissed by central government. This fact means that decentralization is still far from complete, even in health and agriculture. Roles and responsibilities are particularly unclear in agriculture. Services have improved most in health, markets, roads, and water. Several of the areas that have seen stronger improvements also have been the foci of local councils' discretionary spending (although the budget for discretionary spending is small compared to national—and, particularly, donor—budgets). Similarly, other areas that have seen strong improvements have received substantial donor support. For agriculture, the strong donor presence is not associated with large improvements in all indicators. However, given the multidimensional nature of this sector, it is possible that donors have focused on elements of agriculture that are not picked up in the NPS.

No very strong relationship between the extent to which a sector devolved and the extent of improvements comes through from this analysis. However, the absence of a clear correlation is not so surprising given the complexity of the various factors at play, including the clarity of roles, discretionary funding by councils, and the very different size and priorities of the different sectors.

On this last point, health and education arguably are the most comparable. They had similar indicators of access and, prior to decentralization, and each was the responsibility of central government rather than of chiefs or parastatals. Nevertheless, they have disparate levels of decentralization. A comparison of just these two sectors suggests that health, which decentralized, has done better, but this does not necessarily mean that this relatively positive performance has been due to decentralization (box 5.1)

Box 5.1. Why Has Health Decentralized Relatively Better Than Education?

It is suggestive that decentralization in primary health care has been accompanied by relatively larger improvements than those seen in education, which did not decentralize. Nonetheless, these relatively larger improvements cannot necessarily be taken as proof that decentralization improves public service delivery. First, levels of access and satisfaction were lower in health care to begin with, making it easier to effect improvements. Local councils have not spent money on building new clinics and thus can not take credit for increased access to clinics.

More fundamentally, although both were scheduled to devolve in 2005, it is not accidental that primary health care devolved whereas primary education did not. The health sector was better prepared for decentralization. MEST had begun to devolve internally to district health officials before the advent of political decentralization. In contrast, the education sector was much less committed to decentralization. It also is much larger, with between 4 and 5 times as many primary schools as there are clinics. The much greater size of the sector makes it much harder logistically to turn primary schools over to local councils and harder to effect real improvements in the sector. There is no guarantee that the education sector will see the same relative benefits as the health sector, even after it decentralizes.

Areas with Initially Low Levels of Service Have Experienced Catch-up in Some Sectors

If decentralization helps to spread resources more evenly across the country, then areas of the country in which services have lagged should experience some catch-up. In particular, satisfaction in health, registration of births, and access to roads saw their largest gains among those who had previously been in the bottom third of the distribution. However, this finding also is consistent with there having been measurement error in the data, rather than true catch-up or reduced inequality. Mismeasurement can mean that outliers in one year revert to more normal levels in the next ("reversion to the mean"). Unfortunately there is little that can be done to tease out whether the gains seen in the bottom third of the distribution are due mainly to allocation of resources to deprived areas or reversion to the mean due to measurement error. Aggregation of data can help. We therefore examined our indicators at the community level rather than the individual level. We also examined the level of variance in our indicators in the two years for which data are available and found overall no change in variance, suggesting no significant changes in inequality.

An alternative approach is to look at whether poorer or more remote communities saw larger improvements in decentralized service quality. This approach does not suffer from mismeasurement reversion to the mean. We found that poorer communities did not see greater improvements in decentralized services. On the contrary, in education, which is still controlled from the central government, richer communities saw much larger gains on average. For some indicators (access to clinics and access to water source), more remote communities saw greater improvements. For others (registration of deaths and access to storage and drying floor space for agricultural produce), the reverse was true.

Evidence on the Mechanisms through which Decentralization May Impact Services

First we test hypothesis 2a: the areas that have had the largest reduction in geographical distance to power see the biggest gains in service quality.

With decentralization, different parts of the country experienced very different changes in their geographic distance to power. At the extreme, residents of Freetown saw decentralized services move from the central government in Freetown to the Freetown City Council (FCC). This shift may have reduced *bureaucratic distance* (there were fewer layers of bureaucracy for people to go through), but not *geographic distance* to power. In contrast, residents of Kailahun became able to walk to lobby councilors compared to taking transport for many hours to Freetown. Similarly, councilors in Kailahun were much closer to the services for which they were responsible for than were officials in Freetown.

Therefore, we measured the change in the distance to power as the distance to Freetown minus the distance to the council office. We used two measures of distance: one in miles and one in estimated travel time.[4] The advantage of using miles is that it is available for all locations and is accurately measured. The disadvantage with this method is that the time and cost of traveling a given distance varies greatly with the quality of the road and the availability of public transport. The time-taken measure also is not perfect as it will vary considerably by season and mode of transport. We therefore show the results for both measures. There is quite a bit of difference between the results of the two measures partly because the samples are different (there are many missing values for change in the distance to power as measured by travel time).

For the sectors impacted by decentralization, there appears to be a weak correlation between improvements and reductions in the distance to power. Seven of 22 indicators are significant and positive. Registration of births improves by 9.6 percentage points for every 100 miles reduction in the distance to the center of power. This result holds true even if Koidu (which is far from Freetown and experienced a big UNICEF project to promote birth registration) is dropped from the analysis. Contact with an extension worker (which declined overall) and registration of deaths (which declined in a number of local councils) saw a significant correlation but in the opposite direction, that is, declines worsened in areas that experienced a larger reduction in the distance to power.

As a control, we tested for a correlation between the distance differences between Freetown and local council headquarters for education indicators, which had experienced no decentralization. Encouragingly, we found no correlation.

Table 5.3. Correlation between Improved Services and Changes in Distance to Power *(%)*

	Improvement from 100-mile reduction to center of power	Improvement from 3- hour reduction to center of power
No decentralization		
Access to primary school	−3.45	0.63
Satisfaction with primary schools	−1.61	0.64
Decentralization		
Access to clinic	3.35	1.06**
Satisfaction with clinic	1.28	1.06**
Registration of birth	9.61**	−0.12
Registration of death	0.08	−0.93**
Contact with extension worker	−2.21	−2.21**
Access to enough storage space	0.94	0.14
Access to enough drying floor space	3.68**	−0.38
Access to markets	−0.24	0.05
Access to roads	9.2**	1.15
Nearest road passable all year	5.92	2.78**
Access to drinking water	−1.84	2.18**

Note: ** = estimate of difference is statistically significant at the 95% confidence level.

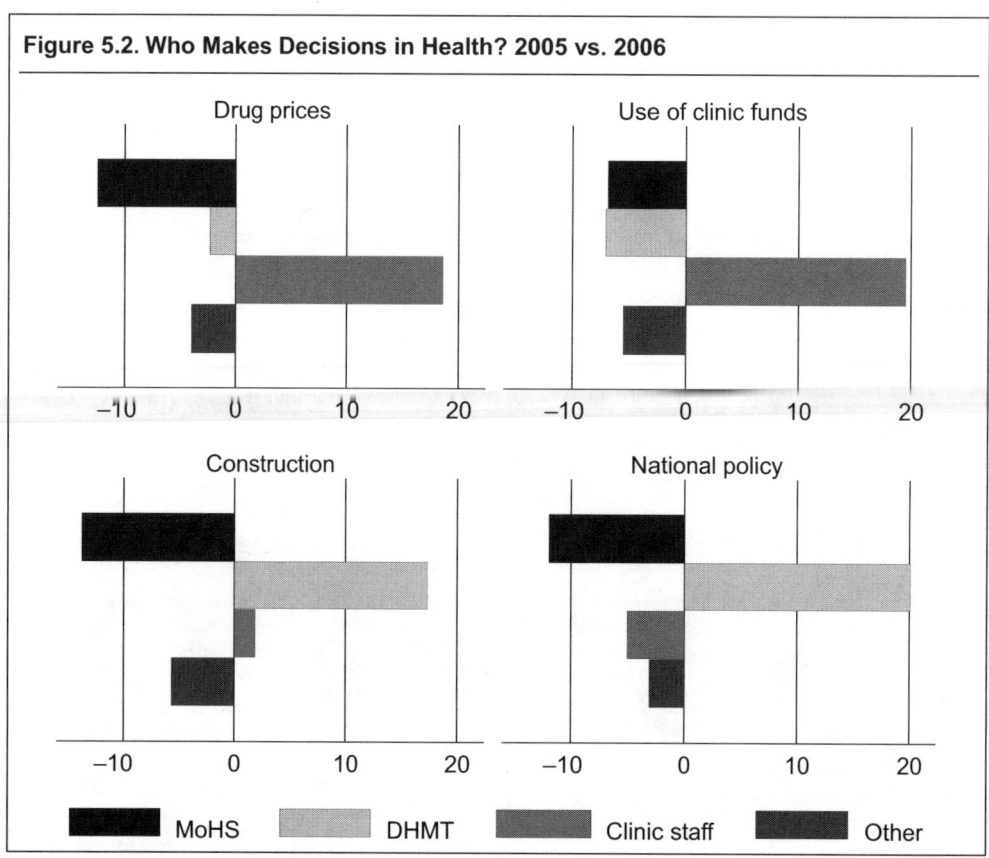

Figure 5.2. Who Makes Decisions in Health? 2005 vs. 2006

Has Decentralization Been Accompanied by Increased Supervision?

The evidence to answer this question comes from the Clinic Surveys as they have sufficient detail to look at issues such as supervision. As a first check, it appears that the changes in formal authority in health have translated into changes in perceived authority on the ground. Figure 6.2 shows that clinic staff believe that the Ministry of Health and Sanitation has less direct say in a number of decisions in the clinics, whereas the District Health Management Teams (DHMTs) and clinic staff both are perceived to have increased their influence between 2005 and 2006. However, there is considerable variety in who people think are in charge of what—suggesting some lack of clarity in roles. These data support the findings from focus groups that decentralization has meant a shift in power to DHMTs more than to local councilors.

Over time, the general trend seems to be that the percent of clinics visited by the central ministry is declining somewhat, and the percent visited by DHMTs is increasing somewhat. DHMTs have claimed that increased flexibility in funding has led them to be able to increase supervision of clinics. In the first year of their term in office, local councils visited over half of all clinics but after that, the percent of clinics visited in the last year dropped dramatically.

Table 5.4. Supervision Visits to Clinics, 2005–08 *(%)*

Year	Clinics Visited in the previous year by		
	Ministry of Health and Sanitation	District Health Management Teams	Local councils
2005	51	70	53
2006	61	81	43
2008	45	78	25

Are Providers or Households Turning to Local Councils When They Have Problems with Services?

Households are not turning to their elected local politicians when they have problems with public services in health and education. Household respondents who reported that they had been dissatisfied with the *primary schools* that their children had attended were most likely to complain only to the head teachers of the schools. Sixteen percent of parents did complain to their local councils—slightly more than complained to the chief, district education officer, or village headman. In contrast, household respondents who were dissatisfied with *primary health care* were most likely to complain to the village headman or chiefdom officials. Only 9 percent complained to their local councils. These were the outcomes, despite the fact that local councils control substantial discretionary funding for primary health care so should be more able to address problems in the health sector than in education.

Staff at clinics are not turning to the local councils for assistance. Instead, they rely on their own efforts or on their District Health Management Team. The clinic survey asked clinic staff about 6 different types of problems that they might face. In no case did more than 2 percent of staff members say that they would turn to their local councils to help resolve the situation. Even when the problem was with the district-level ministry staff (such as not enough drugs being supplied to the clinics), almost no clinic staff reported that they would approach their local councils. Between 2006 and 2008, staff at clinics became more likely to turn to the DHMTs, and less likely to turn to either the central ministry or the local councils. In other words, concerning reporting, decentralization seems to have led to more discretion and authority for district health teams than for local councils. This outcome be conscious on the part of local councils (for example local councilors may consider that the district medical teams have more technical skills than they do about health), or it may be that district health teams are simply in a better position to manage local clinics than are local councilors. As local councilors become more experienced, it will be interesting to see whether they start to play a bigger role in health decisionmaking.

Conclusion

It is impossible to know what Sierra Leone would look like in the absence of decentralization. It, therefore, also is impossible to say precisely how much of the general improvement in public services observed in Sierra Leone over the past few years has been due to decentralization. At the very least, *decentralization has been compatible with consistent improvements in public service delivery.* Any attempt to say whether improvements in services have been greater in sectors that have seen more decentralization than those that have not yet devolved is complicated by multiple factors:

■ Measures of improvement may not be comparable among sectors.
■ Many improvements have been funded by donors, not by central or local government.
■ Local councils have invested their own resources in areas that have not yet received decentralized funding
■ A critical component of service delivery in all sectors—staff hiring, promotion, and discipline—has not been decentralized in any sector. This absence makes it hard to draw distinctions among sectors.

When we look at the geographic spread of improvements, the signs are encouraging. There is weak evidence that services have improved most in areas that are close to local councils (and district medical teams) but far from Freetown. This evidence suggests that decentralization may have helped spread development out from the capital and its surroundings. Given the importance of improving the regularity with which service providers show up to work and how they provide services, it is disappointing to find that, so far, decentralization has not been associated with increased supervision visits in the health sector (the only sector for which we have data on supervision visits).

It is important to recognize that the evidence presented here is just an early snapshot of an evolving process. Decentralization is still at an early stage, evidenced by the fact that all government staff are still paid, hired, and dismissed by central government, even in the sectors that have decentralized the most. A change in government and a large turnover in local councilors may well bring additional changes to how decentralization evolves and to its impact on frontline services. Further tracking of service levels will enable the longer term implications to be followed and more detailed and comparative analyses to be done on the impacts of decentralization.

Notes

[1] Bardhan 2002.

[2] At the time of writing, the 2008 Clinic Survey had not been fully cleaned, so only some of the variables from this survey have been included in the analysis here.

[3] Building quality and openness show a small and statistically insignificant decline between 2006–08, but they do not reverse the overall statistically significant increase considering 2005–08.

[4] Missing values in the distances to Freetown and the local council office were filled by estimating distance along the roads on maps, so there are many fewer missing values for this measure than for change in time to the center of power.

CHAPTER 6

Civic Engagement
in Local Governance

Yongmei Zhou and Ye Zhang

In his farewell speech in Parliament in 2007, President Ahmad Tejan Kabbah said,

> ...fiscal decentralization and political decentralization [are] bringing
> hope again to the once alienated and criminally marginalized rural
> masses. They can now boast of owning and controlling their
> destiny, compared to days when all was decided at the central
> government level.

As is clear from the previous chapters, decentralization has certainly empowered political and bureaucratic elites in rural areas through elections and devolution of resources and responsibilities. Has decentralization brought government to the doorsteps of the rural population, or has decentralization stopped at the council headquarters? Is the rural population engaged in local governance and holding their councils accountable? This chapter examines these questions. Our primary sources of data are the two rounds of National Public Services Surveys in 2005 and 2007, data from the National Electoral Commission (NEC), as well as the Comprehensive Local Government Performance Assessment undertaken by the IRCBP.[1] After providing background on the key motivations behind political and fiscal decentralization, we present an analysis of whether decentralization has created opportunities for citizens to engage with local authorities, voice their concerns, monitor government operations, and reward or punish their elected representatives via elections.

Political Motivation of Decentralization and Electoral Outcome of 2004 Local Council Elections

Many people believe that Sierra Leone's governance problem is primarily a problem of exclusion and corruption[2] and that diamonds financed the 1991–2002 civil war rather than caused it. In the decades preceding that war, concentration and abuse of power and resources among the Freetown elites had generated widespread deprivation and disenchantment in the provinces. In addition, rural youth, especially "strangers,"[3] were subject to suppressive gerontocracies within their villages.[4] Lack of food security, education, and jobs made such rural youth easy targets for rebel recruitment.

As was the choice of proportional representation in the first post-conflict parliamentary elections, re-establishment of elected local councils after a 32-year hiatus was driven primarily by the political need to share power and resources between Freetown and the provinces, and among parties and ethnic groups. It also was driven by a pragmatic recognition that a centralized system simply could not overcome widespread poverty and deliver the peace dividends that people were expecting.

Soon after the national elections in May 2002, GoSL initiated a series of national and regional consultations and deliberations, focusing on the modality of local council elections. As was expected, restoring elected local councils was a popular policy across the country. However, an overwhelming majority of people were disenchanted with political parties so preferred non-partisan elections. Nevertheless, parties fought against the popular sentiment and enshrined partisan elections in the Local Government Act (March 2004).

Given the fragile security situation, it was decided that the first country-wide local council elections would be organized before the United Nations Peace Force withdrew at the end of 2004. To beat the start of the rainy season between June and November, the date for the first local council elections was fixed for May 22, 2004.

As a result, the elections were hurriedly organized, just two months after the president had signed the LGA. To varying degrees, parties' headquarters dictated local candidates, often blocking competent and popular people from standing. In total, 1,112 candidates registered with the National Electoral Commission (NEC). In 84 of 394 (21 percent) of constituencies, councilors were elected unopposed. Elections in urban constituencies were more competitive. Areas not dominated by the Sierra Leone People's Party (SLPP) also saw more competitive elections. Post-election investigations revealed ballot stuffing in a large number of polling stations across the country.[5] Voter turnout, reported as 55 percent by the NEC, was less enthusiastic than the 76 percent turnout at the national elections two years earlier. The quality of the first group of councilors was somewhat disappointing. Many councilors were illiterate.

Despite the limitations, the 2004 elections offered ethnic minorities an opportunity to participate in local governance. Ethnic conflicts in Sierra Leone are much less frequent than in many other African countries. Nevertheless, there is a strong perception that national politics tends to be a "winner takes all" game in which northern tribes (the most prominent being Timne) and southern tribes (the most prominent being Mende) take turns governing the country and are perceived to be exclusionary in exercising power.[6] Political decentralization allowed direct participation of ethnic minorities in local governance. Smaller ethnic groups such as Kono, Loko, and Sherbro, were elected to leadership in their local councils.

Election of women and youth to local leadership positions was limited, although slightly better than at the national level. Women occupied 12.7 percent of council seats in the 2004 elections, as opposed to 10 percent in Parliament. Urban councils generally had more female councilors than did rural areas. Based on the data collected by DecSec, the average age of councilors in each council was between 46 and 51 years (see figure 6.12 for the age profile of the councilors based on the data collected by DecSec). In Sierra Leone, whose national leaders and traditional leaders (chiefs) usually were elderly, the first group of councilors was seen as the "young" generation of leaders on the political scene.

Fiscal Decentralization as a Policy Choice to Improve Effectiveness of Public Spending

For technocrats in the Ministry of Finance, fiscal decentralization became a pragmatic solution to the persistent problems of theft and corruption in the public expenditure system. Since the late 1990s, the Ministry of Finance had taken significant actions to improve the ways that public spending was managed. Allocations to rural areas for post-war reconstruction and primary services were among the top priorities in GoSL's budget. However, subsequent Public Expenditure Tracking Studies (PETS) conducted by MoF uncovered that the significant amount of public spending on education, health, and agriculture had not reached the intended beneficiaries. PETS 2002 discovered that:

- A shocking less than 10 percent of all essential drugs purchased and distributed by the central government was confirmed by district medical officers (DMOs) as having reached the district.
- A shocking less than 5 percent of all essential drugs could be confirmed by peripheral health units (PHUs) as having reached them.
- Only 72 percent of teaching and learning materials had reached intended schools from District Education Offices and had arrived 170 days (almost 6 months) later than contracted.

PETS 2003 uncovered that only 8 percent of seed rice had arrived before planting season and 35 percent during planting season, whereas 57 percent had arrived after planting season was over.

The line ministries were seen as the main culprits for the thefts and inefficiencies. MoF embraced fiscal decentralization as a way to bypass the "leaky pipes" in the spending system. Thus, MoF established an intergovernmental fiscal transfer system (chapter 3). Grants to finance decentralized functions such as primary health and agricultural extension services were disbursed directly from the central treasury to the local council accounts, thereby avoiding potential leakage and diversion between Freetown and the councils. Despite the limited size of council budgets, fiscal decentralization finally put into the hands of elected local representatives real resources to manage and to account for. LGA 04 requires local councils and wards to post on public notice boards in their offices information on their financial accounts, assets, tax rates, meeting minutes, and development plans. A local council's compliance with the disclosure request is one of the conditions for it to receive untied grants from the central government. This legal requirement created a regulatory enabling environment for civic activism.

Has Decentralization Brought Government to the Doorsteps of the Rural Masses?

Given Sierra Leone's small size (71,740 square km) and population (5 million), the degree to which a large number of rural communities are physically, economically, and politically isolated is staggering. Among the 753 communities surveyed by the IRCBP National Public Services Survey, 27 percent are more than 30 minutes' walk from the nearest drivable road, 62 percent do not have a market, and 31 percent do not have cell phone coverage. The survey took place two months before the heated national elections in August 2007. During the entire year preceding the survey, 59 percent of the communities had not been visited by any government VIPs from Freetown, whether Cabinet member, Member of Parliament, or one of the top three presidential candidates.

Poverty in Sierra Leone is widespread and access to public services is almost universally poor. However, *remote communities,* defined as those more than 30 minutes' walk from a drivable road, *are extremely deprived.* For example:

- Only 48 percent of remote communities have primary schools, as opposed to 83 percent for non-remote communities.
- Only 7 percent of remote communities have secondary schools, as opposed to 46 percent for non-remote communities.
- Only 15 percent of remote communities have clinics or hospitals, as opposed to 55 percent of non-remote communities.
- Only 46 percent communities have latrines, as opposed to 74 percent of non-remote communities.

The map in the appendix is another illustration of the extreme deprivation outside the Western Area, especially in rural areas off the beaten track.

Remote communities also are more isolated politically. The NPS Survey took place in June 2007, two months before a heated contestation for the Presidency and parliamentary seats. Only 15 percent of remote communities reported any visit during the previous year by a presidential candidate, as opposed to 44 percent for non-remote communities. While 53 percent non-remote communities reported such visits by a Cabinet member, the number was 23 percent for remote communities.

Table 6.1. Sierra Leone's Many Isolated Communities

Isolating characteristics	Communities (%)
More than 30 minutes' walk from nearest drivable road	27
WITHOUT a market	62
WITHOUT cell phone coverage	31
NOT visited by President, Vice President, or government minister in past year	77
NOT visited by Member of Parliament in past year	76
NOT visited by any of top three Presidential candidates (Ernest Koroma, Soloman Berewa, Charles Margai) in past year	68
NOT visited by any of above categories of central government VIPs	59

Source: NPS Survey 2007.

Local councils did provide citizens with new opportunities for contact with the state. The two maps below present the footprints of Freetown VIPs (presidential candidates, MPs, and Cabinet ministers) vis-à-vis local councilors during the year preceding the June 2007 National Public Services (NPS) household survey. The shaded areas on the map (figure 6.1) are enumeration areas covered by the NPS Survey in 2007. In the map at the top, very light gray areas indicate areas not visited by any Freetown VIPs during that year; medium light gray areas were visited by one out of three types of Freetown VIPs; medium dark gray areas were visited by two out of three types of Freetown VIPs; and the black areas were visited by all three types of Freetown VIPs. In the map at the bottom, the very light gray areas indicate enumeration areas not visited by their councilors; and the dark gray areas, areas that were visited by the councilors. Clearly, councilors had more presence than Freetown VIPs and their presence and outreach made a visible difference in remote areas. In contrast, Freetown VIPs stayed near the main roads and gave their attention to resource-rich areas, such as diamond centers in Kono and Kenema.

Outreach efforts by councilors vary significantly. In Koidu City, all respondents reported visits by councilors to their communities, compared to less than 35 percent of residents of Kenema City and Freetown City. In the rural areas, only 4 percent of respondents in Western Rural Area reported councilor visits; in contrast, 78 percent respondents in Koinadugu reported such visits.

Although on average local councilors' presence is felt more widely in remote areas than the presence of Freetown VIPs and even paramount chiefs, councilors, too, tend to pay more attention to communities within easy reach. The exceptions are the remote communities that produced councilors (figure 6.15 in appendix). Interestingly, these communities are visited by Freetown VIPs and paramount chiefs more often than are non-remote communities. The disappointing fact is that nearly 30 percent of councilors' home communities had not been visited by their own representatives. Frequently, an absentee councilor had won the election as a local "big man" but then relocated to reside in a large town or Freetown.

Have local councils brought development to their communities? Kargbo's chapter 2 and Whiteside Casey's chapter 4 detail the development initiatives that local councils have undertaken. Field monitoring by the IRCBP shows that a majority of the projects have been satisfactory. Many of them were financed by the Local Government Development Grant and were implemented using the Rapid Results Approach (RRA). The 100-day Rapid Results Initiatives (RRIs) created buzz around the project areas. Their participatory planning and implementation approach as well as visible results in a short time were in sharp contrast to the usual central government projects, which had been slow or of poor quality.[7] Unfortunately, the total funding of the LGDG for 2004–06 was less than US$4 million, so only some people could benefit from these small-scale initiatives.

Figure 6.1. Visits to Remote Areas by Freetown VIPs (top map) Compared to Local Councilors (bottom map), 2006–07

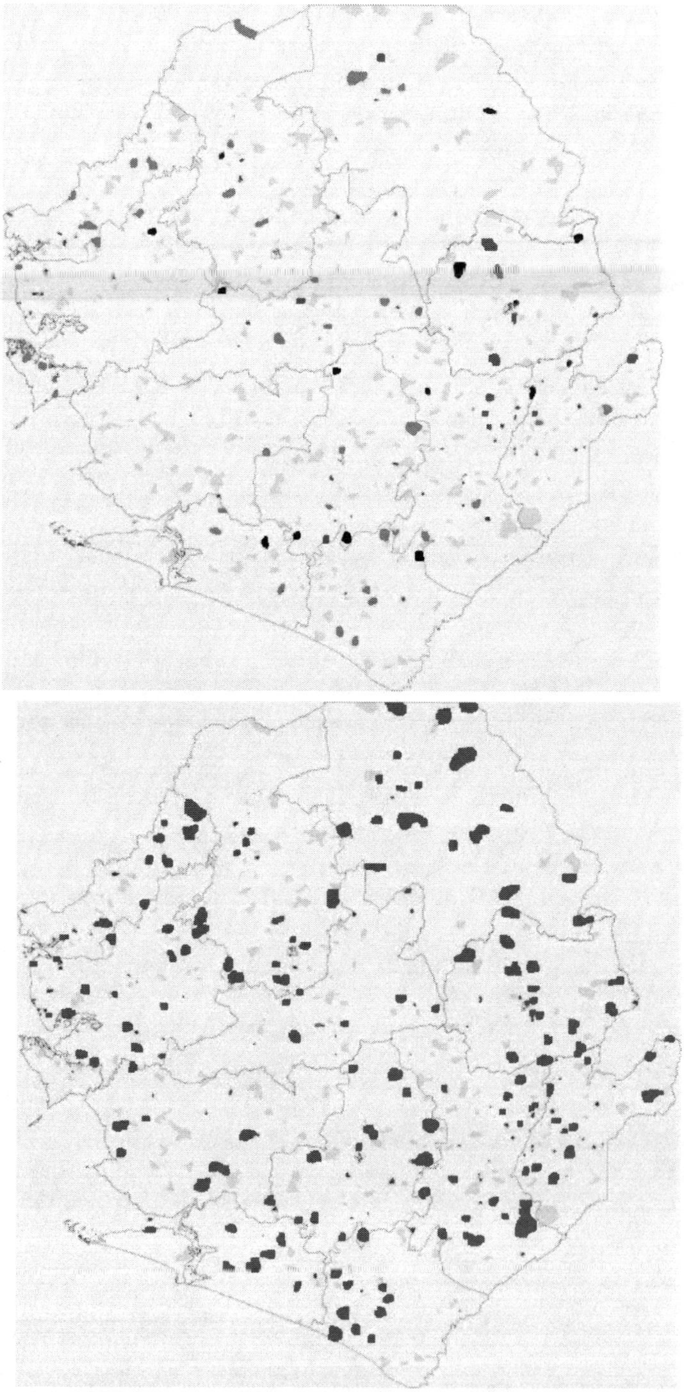

Councils did not seem to have particular bias against remote communities in deciding beneficiaries of council spending. Eighteen percent of respondents living in remote communities reported awareness of at least one such project, the same as the national share. Among people who know of council projects, 73 percent of respondents in remote communities reported being beneficiaries of such projects, again similar to the national ratio.

Have People Felt the Presence of the Local Councils?

In June 2007, three years into the tenure of the first group of councilors, the national average of respondents who knew the name of their councilor was 36 percent, ranging from only 5 percent in Freetown to 65 percent in Pujehun. In general, a rural population is more likely to be able to name its councilors then people in big towns. Among urban councils, people in Koidu (center of a diamond area), Makeni (the central point of the northern region), and Bonthe Town (an island town) are more likely to be able to name their councilors. Correlation between reported councilor visits and council name recognition is positive.

The 2007 NPS Survey examined people's perceptions of their councils. There is some evidence that constituent outreach improves name recognition and a responsive image of councilors. Correlation between reported councilor visits and perception of their responsiveness is positive.

Figure 6.2 presents scorecards given by the different types of communities. Respondents from the remote communities that had produced councilors had far better views of their councils than did the other communities. This is especially true with regard to whether the respondents felt that their local councils listened to them.

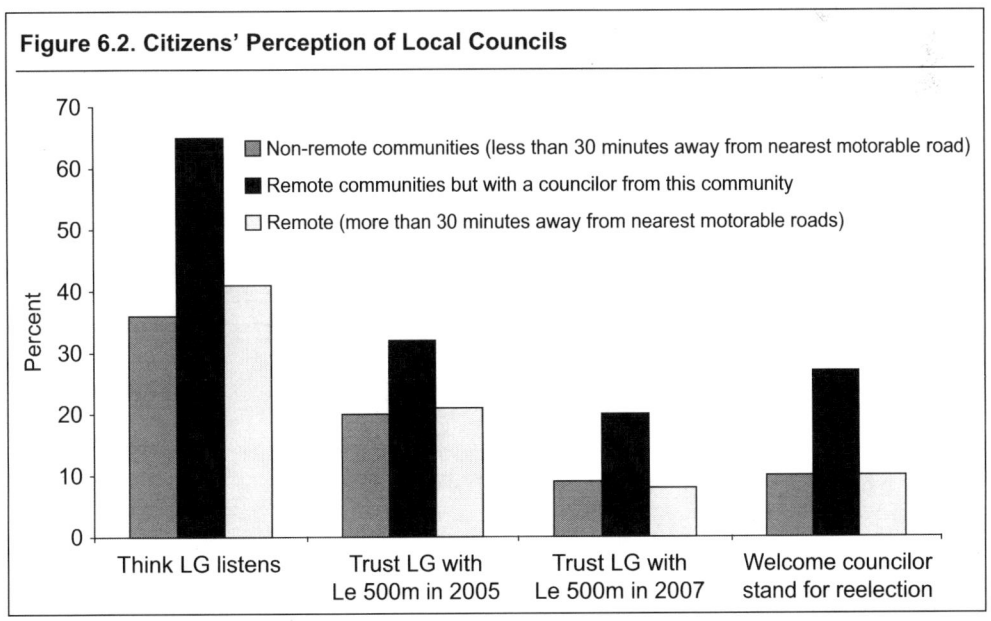

Figure 6.2. Citizens' Perception of Local Councils

Source: 2007 NPS Survey.

In general, *citizens did not trust their councils.* Respondents were asked to give their opinions of how their council would spend 500 million Leones (approximately $170,000) for a project in the area (figure 6.3). A score of 3 meant: "The council would spend all the money and do a great job." A score of 2 meant "The council would take a little money but do a good job." A score of 1 meant: "The council would take most of the money and do a bad job," and a score of 0 meant "The council would just take all the money." The national average was 1.3 out of 3. Even the relatively more trusted councils (Makeni City and Bonthe City, with a score of 2) were far from receiving people's full confidence of financial accountability.

Are more transparent and better managed councils perceived more favorably by their citizens? In November 2006, the IRCBP undertook a Comprehensive Local Government Performance Assessment to document evolving governance practice in each council. In particular, the assessment documented council compliance with central government guidelines on planning, budgeting, financial management, procurement, human resource management, community participation, and transparency of council operations (see Kanu's chapter 3). The correlations between the average level of trust in council/councilor and a council's management performance measures were not consistently positive (table 6.2).

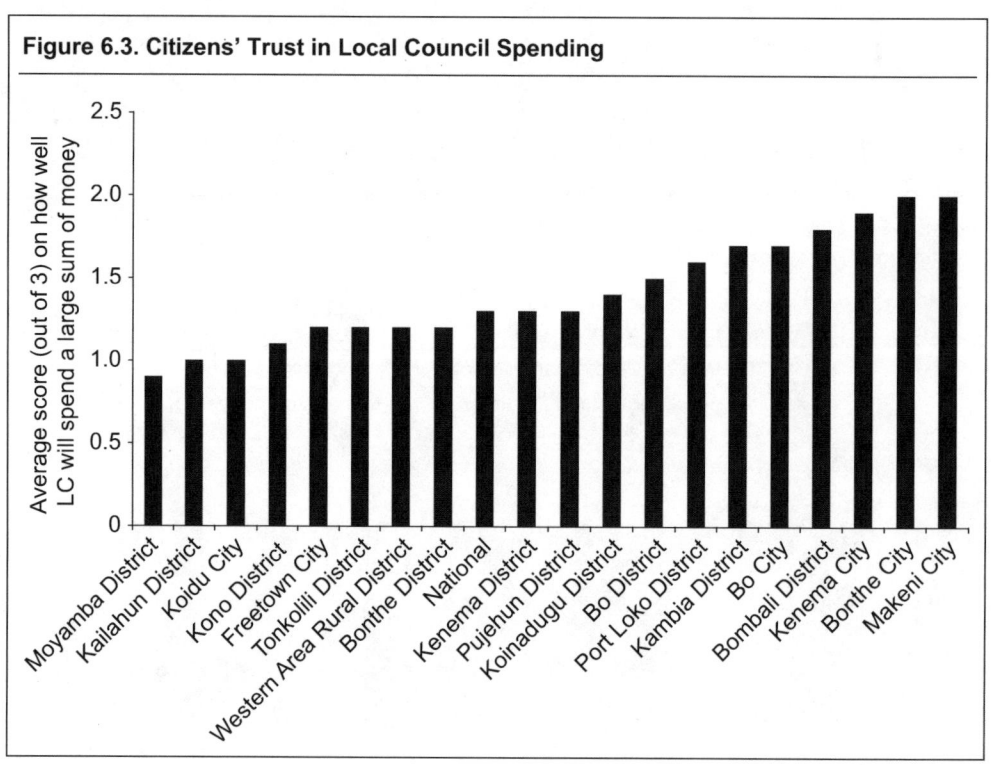

Figure 6.3. Citizens' Trust in Local Council Spending

Source: 2007 NPS Survey.

Table 6.2. Correlations between November 2006 Local Council Management Performance Measures and June 2007 Average Citizen Perception of Council and Councilor

	LC perceived as responsive	Trust councilor	Trust LC spending
Financial management	0.15	−0.23	0.04
Transparency	0.33	0.22	0.28
Project implementation	0.37	0.33	0.26
Budgeting and auditing	−0.03	0.24	−0.04
Fiscal capacity	−0.07	0.29	0.25
Procurement	0.06	0.06	0.12

Source: "Decentralization Watch" analysis of 2007 IRCBP National Public Services Survey data, and K. Whiteside Casey's chapter 4.

Transparency and project implementation performance did correlate positively with the three perception measures: responsiveness of council, trustworthiness of councilor, and trust worthiness of councils in money matters. Procurement integrity was marginally positively correlated with the perception measures. Other measures of management performance—financial management, budgeting and auditing, and fiscal capacity—were not always positively correlated with the perception measures.

There are at least three explanations for these findings:

■ The performance measures used in the Comprehensive Local Government Performance Assessment are imperfect measures of management capacity and governance practice. Citizens' perception could be affected by factors that are not captured by the assessment's list of "good governance" measures.
■ Citizens may not be fully aware of their council's governance practices.

Comparing the findings from the two national household surveys in 2005 and 2007, there seems to have been a drop in awareness and trust in local councils. While in 2005, 87 percent of respondents had heard of the local councils, by 2007, this ratio had dropped to 70 percent. Table 6.3 shows that, in early 2005, councils had a strong lead over central government in citizens' views of their own ability to influence government decisions, confidence in government spending money effectively, and trust of government officials. However, by mid–07, local government had lost this initial vote of confidence in perceived spending effectiveness and had fallen significantly behind central government in citizen influence and trust.[8]

Specifically, citizens' views of *central government* spending did not change significantly over time, whereas the initial 7.7 percent inclination toward local government in 2005 disappeared by 2007. Regarding public influence and trust, the initial margin in favor of local government actually *reversed* to favor central government.

Table 6.3. Public Perception of Central Government and Local Council: Changes from 2005–07 *(%)*

	2005			2007			Change over time	
	Local govt	Central govt	LC-CG gap	Local govt	Central govt	LC-CG gap	Local govt	Central govt
Feel govt will spend Le 500 million effectively	52.4	44.7	7.7	45.6	46.7	−1.1	−6.8	2.0
Feel they can influence govt decisions	50.2	37.3	**12.9**	40.1	46.1	**−6.0**	**−10.1**	**8.8**
Trust govt officials	62.5	53.8	**8.7**	34.6	42.6	**−8.0**	**−27.9**	**−11.2**

Source: "Decentralization Watch" analysis of 2007 IRCBP National Public Services Survey data, and K. Whiteside Casey's chapter 4.

Given the modest improvements in service delivery during the initial phase of the decentralization program (documented in Whiteside chapter 4 and Foster and Glennester chapter 5), the sharp decline in public confidence is puzzling. In the 2007 "Decentralization Watch," Whiteside Casey hypothesized that the disconnect came because the high expectations of local councils generated by the 2004 elections could not be met as a result of limited and delayed transfers of responsibilities and financing from the central government. The financial figures in tables 4.1, 4.2, and 4.3 show that local councils have substantial control over only a few specific line items, such as clinics and group services, and that, overall, they remain small players in the sectors.

Given that all councils have limited resource to address the vast development needs in their constituencies, do the citizens aware of their efforts and constraints perceive them more favorably? Table 6.4 presents the same indicators as table 6.3, but for only the subset of respondents who had knowledge of council initiatives.[9]

Table 6.4. Perception of Central Government and Local Councils among Those Who Have More Interactions with Local Councils (%)

	2005			2007			Change over time	
	Local govt	Central govt	LC-CG gap	Local govt	Central govt	LC-CG gap	Local govt	Central govt
Only the 18% of respondents who know of a local council project (75% of them are beneficiaries)								
Feel govt will spend Le 500 million effectively	56.5	48.1	8.4	67.5	58.0	9.5	11.0	9.9
Only respondents who have met a councilor or participated in a council-organized meeting								
Feel they can influence govt decisions	52.6	39.2	13.4	71.1	58.6	12.5	18.5	19.4
Trust govt officials	67.2	57.8	9.4	44.6	50.1	−5.5	−22.6	−7.7

Sources: "Decentralization Watch" analysis of 2007 IRCBP National Public Services data and K. Whiteside Casey.

In fact, people who know about specific council activities have a *positive* and *improving* view of their local government's performance. Among those who knew of a local council project, the proportion who had some confidence in local council spending increased by 11 percent between 2005 and 2007. In addition, for this subsample, the lead of local over central government increased from 8.4 percent to 9.5 percent.

Do people who have contact with councils perceive them more favorably? Looking only at the respondents who had spoken to a councilor or participated in a meeting organized by the council, table 6.4 shows that these people now feel that they have more influence over local government decisions than before and that they have more influence over local, compared to central government, decisions. While trust fell over time for this group, it fell by less than it did for all respondents taken together.

These observations give us comfort that constituent outreach and (presumably useful) development initiatives by councilors are consistent with their constituents' more responsive and trustworthy image of their elected representatives.

There is an alternative explanation for the relatively more upbeat assessment of the local councils among those who are more knowledgeable or benefited from council initiatives. The correlation could be driven by an independent phenomenon of a higher level of trust that some Salone people tend to have in a community member.[10] Communities that had produced councilors may trust their own "son of the soil" and, by extension, the council, regardless of the development performance of the councilors. Indeed, this explanation is consistent with the more upbeat assessment in communities that had produced councilors (figure 6.2).

If there is such loyalty, councilors seemed to have repaid it by bringing council projects first to their home communities. Figure 6.4 shows that among all respondents to the 2007 NPS survey, over 22 percent of those who reported their councilors as residing in their communities also reported benefiting from a council project. This ratio is 5 percentage points higher than those who reported councilors as residing in district headquarters; 9 percentage points higher than those who reported councilors as living in nearby communities or chiefdom headquarters, and 11–12 percentage points higher than those who reported councilors living in other districts or in Freetown. These results confirm the advantage of communities in which their own councilors reside. A close second best seems to be communities whose own councilors reside in the district headquarters, presumably with more opportunities to participate in district-level decisionmaking and the ability to lobby for resources for their constituent communities.

The natural tendency to give first preference to their home communities is not driven by equity considerations, because councilors in remote areas tend to come from relatively better off areas (often small towns) that have better access to basic facilities than other remote communities (figure 6.5).

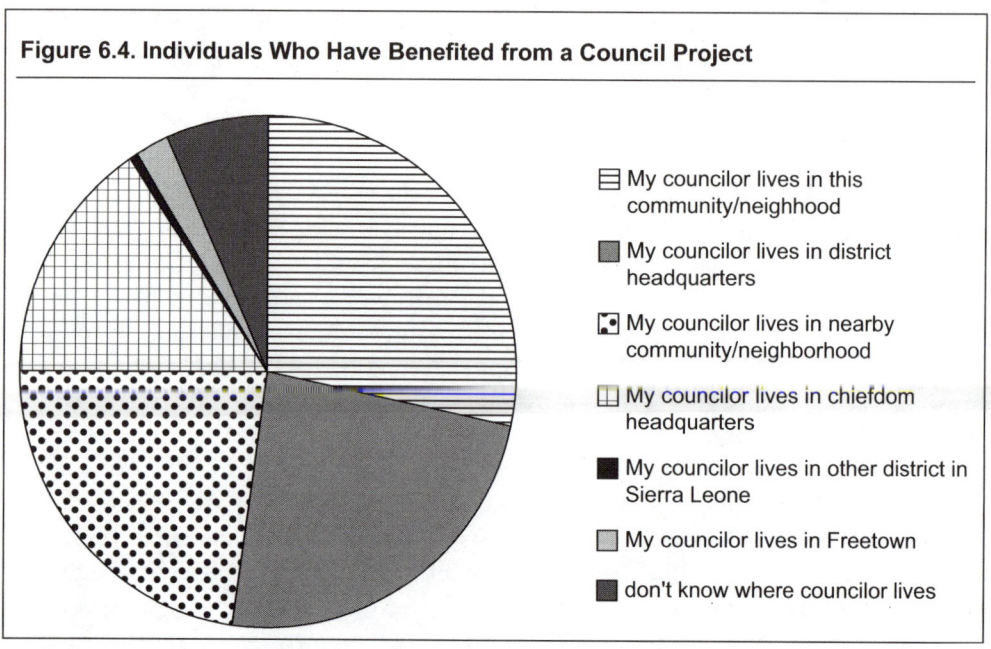

Figure 6.4. Individuals Who Have Benefited from a Council Project

⊟ My councilor lives in this community/neighhood

▨ My councilor lives in district headquarters

☒ My councilor lives in nearby community/neighborhood

⊞ My councilor lives in chiefdom headquarters

■ My councilor lives in other district in Sierra Leone

☐ My councilor lives in Freetown

▨ don't know where councilor lives

Source: 2007 NPS survey.

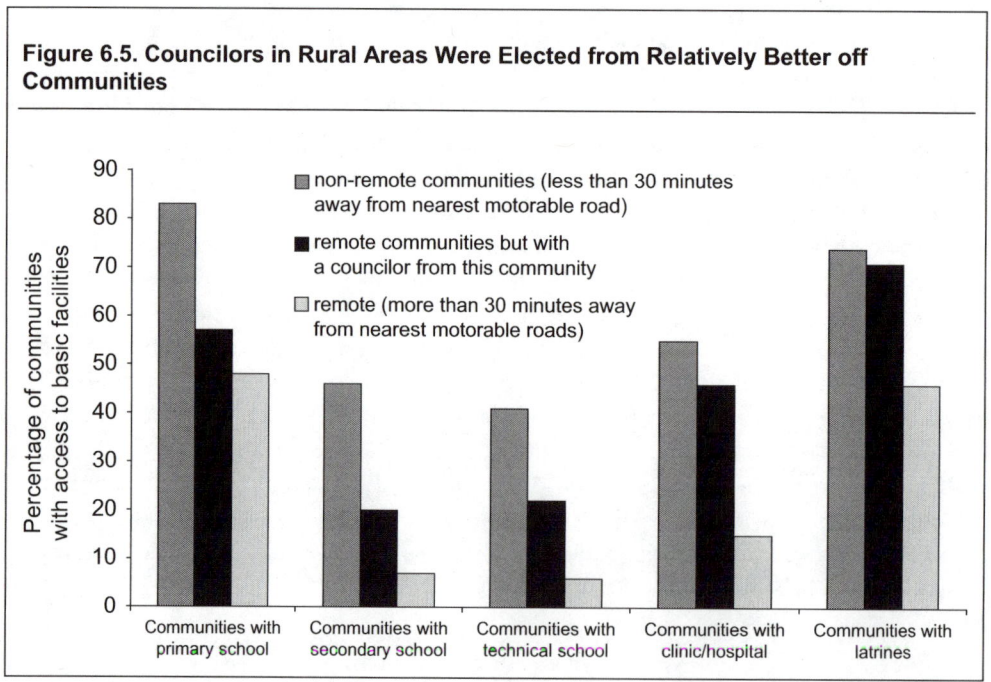

Figure 6.5. Councilors in Rural Areas Were Elected from Relatively Better off Communities

■ non-remote communities (less than 30 minutes away from nearest motorable road)

■ remote communities but with a councilor from this community

☐ remote (more than 30 minutes away from nearest motorable roads)

Source: 2007 NPS survey.

On the other hand, when the development need is overwhelming in all communities, helping his/her own hometown from which s/he feels the most pressure to deliver government resources is not surprising. Either as a result of higher level of intrinsic trust and/or reward for good performance, 27 percent of the councilors were believed to be popular for reelection, as opposed to 10 percent nation-wide. However, there is a cost to this preference, as other segments of the constituencies have a less sanguine view of their councilors and council.

Civic Activism at the Grassroots

For decentralization to improve the quality of public services, one assumption is that citizens would take advantage of the greater access to information and authority and become active in demanding service improvement and government accountability. However, civic activism cannot be taken for granted in a nascent democracy in which adult literacy is only 37 percent.

The NPS 2007 shows that people generally demand government accountability and accept civic duties. Sixty-seven percent of people agreed that "As citizens, we should be more active in questioning the leaders" and disagreed with the statement that "In our country these days, we should have more respect for authority." Ninety-one percent of people thought, "It's wrong to pay a bribe to any government official," as opposed to "In our country, it's normal to pay a bribe to a government official to encourage them [sic]."

In reality, given their lack of trust in them, are citizens active in monitoring and questioning their elected representatives? Our data showed that not many people took advantage of current participation and disclosure requirements imposed on local councils by the Local Government Act (2004). Nationally, while 52 percent of respondents reported visits by councilors to their communities, only 26 percent of respondents had either talked to a local councilor or attended a meeting organized by their councilor.

As noted earlier, the 2006 Comprehensive Local Government Performance Assessment (CLoGPAS) documented that 15 of the 19 councils were posting information on public notice boards at the council offices and in each ward as required by LGA. The information included their financial accounts, assets, tax rates, meeting minutes, and development plans. Disappointingly, among those who had heard about the local councils, only 6.6 percent had ever visited the notice boards. Mass communication has yet to become the main source of information on government in Sierra Leone, and people rely primarily on family and relatives for information on government (IRCBP 2008). This reality is likely to indicate both a lack of interest by citizens in council governance and a need for councils to search out more proactive ways of disclosure and dissemination. This reality also may explain why "good governance" practices as defined by the 2006 CLoGPAS did not necessarily correlate positively with citizens' perception.

Are Salone people apathetic? Far from it. According to respondents' self-reports in the NPS 2005 survey, approximately 60 percent across the country claim interest in national and local politics. In remote areas that had produced councilors, more than 80 percent of respondents reported interest in national and local politics. Self-reported participation in elections is uniformly high, usually near 95 percent.

Remoteness did not diminish villagers' interest in national or local politics. They also reported similar levels of participation in the 2002 national elections and the 2004 local government elections. In fact, self-reported voters in these areas are more likely to know the names of their chosen representatives. Sixty-five percent of the self-reported voters in remote communities can name their local councilor, vs. 52 percent in the non-remote areas. Similarly, self-reported voters are more likely to know the names of the candidates for presidential elections (67 percent versus 41 percent, respectively, in 2007).

Respondents in the National Public Services surveys in February/March 2005 and May/June 2007, as well as in the household surveys in Bombali and Bonthe in December 2005, consistently reported more than 90 percent participation of the respondents in the national and local council elections (figure 6.6). Actual turnout data from NEC are much lower: 76 percent turnout for the 2002 national elections, 55 percent for the 2004 local council elections, and 38.8 percent for the 2008 local council elections. The consistent discrepancies between self-reports and actual participation may indicate evolving social norms regarding electoral participation as a civic responsibility. This explanation is consistent with the results from the 2007 BBC Elections Survey, in which 90 percent of respondents (aged 23+) reported having voted in the previous national election and over 90 percent placed a high value on the importance of voting.

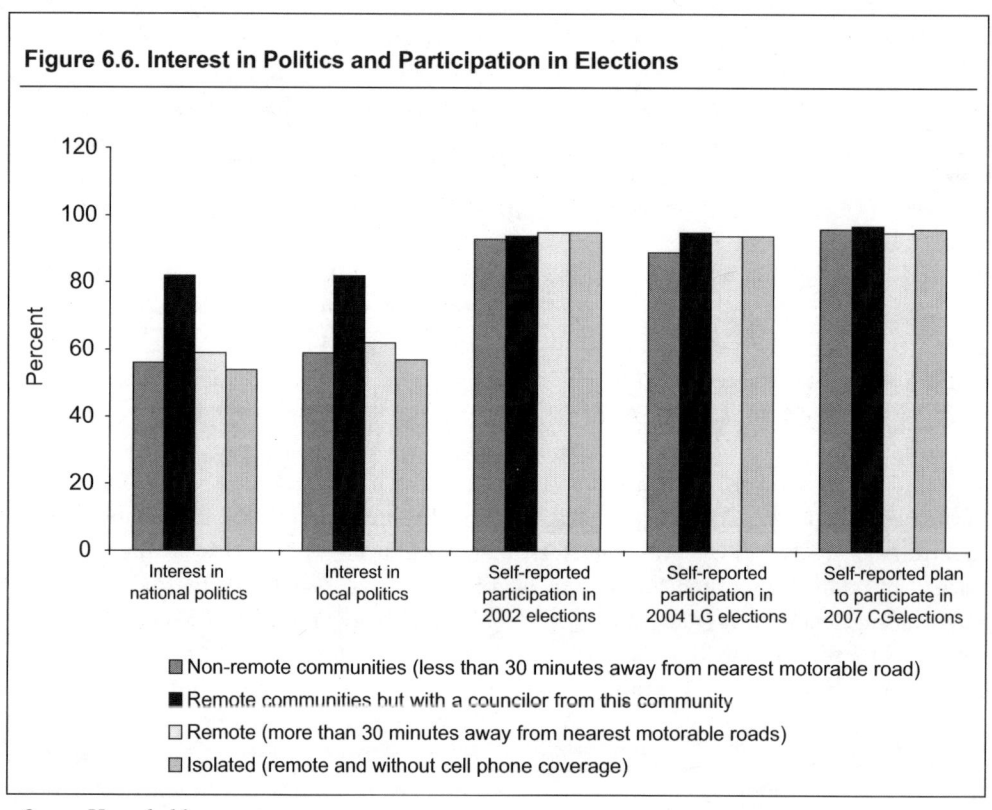

Figure 6.6. Interest in Politics and Participation in Elections

Non-remote communities (less than 30 minutes away from nearest motorable road)
Remote communities but with a councilor from this community
Remote (more than 30 minutes away from nearest motorable roads)
Isolated (remote and without cell phone coverage)

Source: Household surveys.

Activism may have been impeded by citizens' lack of confidence to engage with authorities or lack of knowledge about effective channels for complaint. Salone people usually resort to local authorities rather than to media or justice institutions to address their dissatisfactions. In the NPS 2007 Survey, just over half among those who were unsatisfied with some aspect of education had complained. Twenty-eight percent complained to the head teacher, and 12–16 percent complained to each of the village chief, chiefdom official, district education inspector, and local councilor. Of those who didn't complain, 46 percent reported that it was because they didn't know to whom to complain, and another 40 percent because they would not be heard. As some respondents in the GoBifo Survey in 2005 put it, when observing corruption, they "leave it to God."[11] As in many other poor democracies with high illiteracy, people in leadership position often are regarded as Big Men and expected to have wealth that they cannot accumulate without corruption. Qualitative research under the Justice for the Poor Program also documented cases in which the few brave people who did pursue justice were more likely than not frustrated, and sometimes put in harm's way, by their experience (Manning 2007).

Civic participation and self-perceived influence on local governance show visible gender and generational gaps. A detailed survey of 2,400 households in Bombali and Bonthe in December 2005 recorded the percentages of people who had attended a community meeting in the previous year and spoken at the last meeting (figure 6.7). Percentages ranged from 9 percent for women under 24, to 20 percent for women aged 25–35, to 21 percent for women above 36. For men, the range was from 22 percent for men under 24, to 42 percent for men aged 25–35, to 51 percent for men above 36. While 52 percent of men above age 36 believed that they had some or a little chance (rather than no chance) to change unjust local council law, this ratio was higher for younger men: 44 percent for men aged 25–35 and 35 percent for men under 24. For women, the range in women who saw themselves as politically self-empowered was 36 percent—37 percent for women above 25 and 31 percent for women under 24.

Similar gender gaps and age gaps are observed in self-perceived influence on chiefdom law. Women's participation in community meetings and their contributions to discussions are significantly lower than those of men. A gender gap of over 20 percent is observed in perceived self-empowerment to name a local councilor or council chair.

Are the People Disciplining Their Representatives via Elections?

One of the most critical questions for an electoral democracy is whether voters care about the performance of their elected representatives and whether they reward or punish the incumbents' performance in the next election. Observers of Sierra Leone's elections, especially national elections, can hardly ignore the role that ethnicity plays in electoral behavior. For example, the national elections of 2007 demonstrate a striking divide between political parties along ethnic lines.

Figure 6.7. Gender and Gaps in Political Awareness, Participation, and Self-Perceived Influence

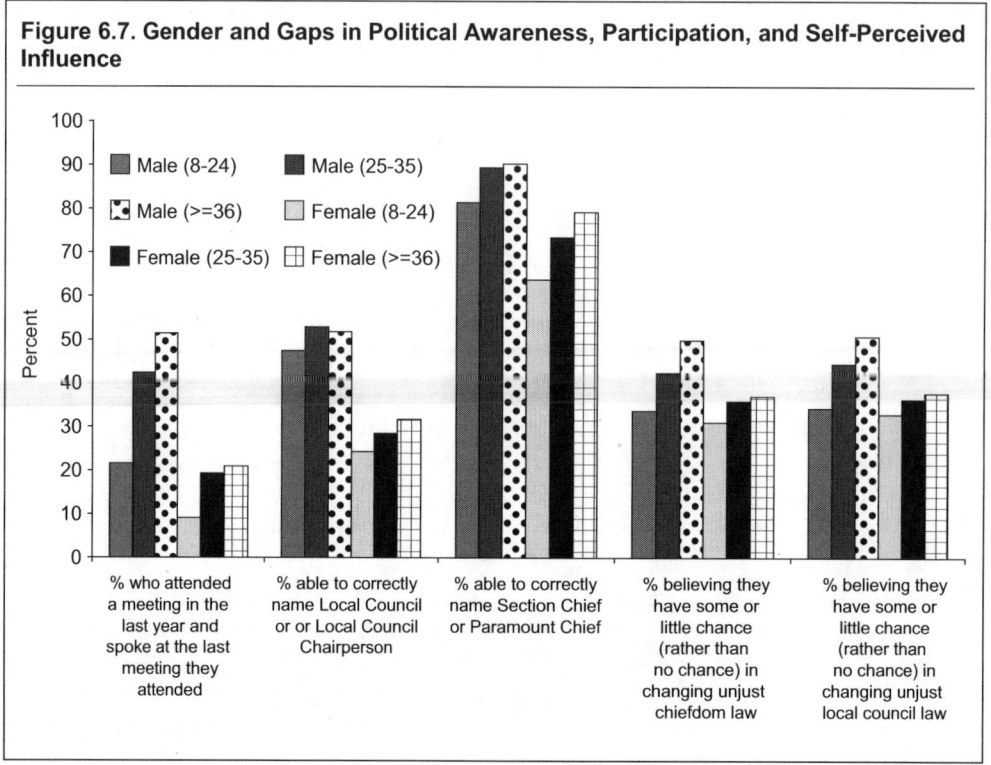

Source: Household surveys.

Figure 6.8 shows the distribution of dominant ethnicities in the enumeration area. There is a clear pattern of ethnic homogeneity in southern districts. Mende is the dominant group in almost the entire southern region, except in Bonthe and the western end of Moyamba where Sherbro dominates. Kono is largely dominated by Kono, but the mining areas have attracted other ethnic groups as well. Timne is dominant in Port Loko, Tonkolili, and parts of Kambia and Bombali. Koinadugu has a dominant presence of Limba.

Figure 6.9 shows that the northern and western blocks were handily captured by the All People's Congress (APC), while the southern and eastern blocks were captured largely by the Sierre Leone People's Party (SLPP). The exceptions were Bonthe and Pujehun and part of Moyamba and Bo, which voted for the People's Movement for Democratic Change (PMDC), an offshoot of the SLPP.

Figure 6.8. Distribution of Dominant Ethnic Groups

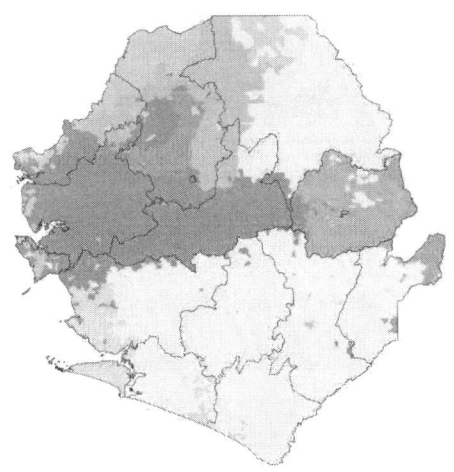

Source: 2004 Census data.

Figure 6.9. Map of Parliamentary Election Results, 2007

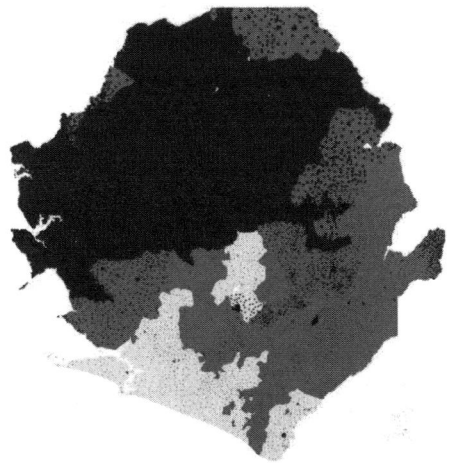

Source: National Electoral Commission data.
Notes: Black area = APC seats; dark gray area = SLPP seats; light gray areas = PMDC seats. Overlay: Density and expanse of black dots correspond to % of votes captured by the APC candidates of that constituency.

Strong ethnic correlation in voting behavior does not necessarily mean blind loyalty. In Bonthe, Pujehun, southwest of Moyamba, and parts of Bo, the "no confidence" sentiment against the SLPP was demonstrated through votes for PMDC, an offshoot of the SLPP. Incidentally, the rebellious areas in the south also happened to be the most deprived areas under the SLPP regime (figure 6.10). The massive votes for the APC in the northern region could be interpreted as either blind ethnic loyalty or a massive block vote of "no confidence" against the then-incumbent SLPP government.

How do people explain their voting behavior? The household survey by the GoBifo and IRCBP in Bonthe and Bombali Districts in December asked people about their main reasons for voting their preferred presidential candidate in 2002 and for their preferred candidate in 2004. In the national election, the candidate's political party was the most important reason for votes. A candidate's promise of development was the second most important reason. For the local council election, the most important reason was a candidate's promise of development, whereas the importance of the candidate's political party declined to the second. Ethnicity of candidates did not feature prominently in the responses.

Figure 6.10. Community Access to Basic Facilities

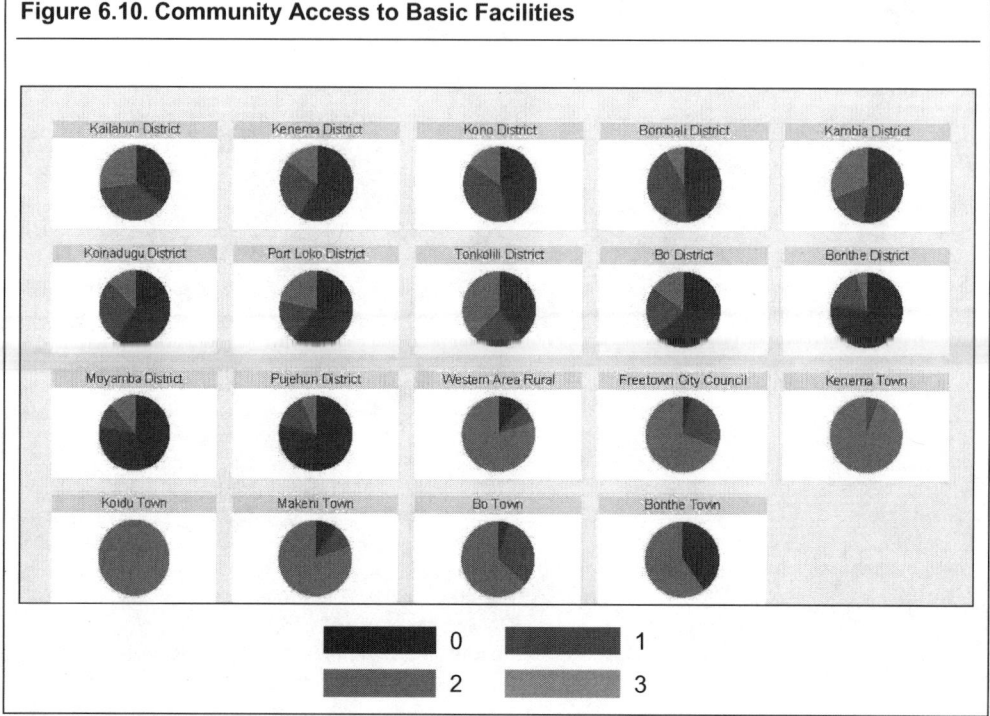

Source: IRCBP National Public Services Survey 2007, the Community Module.
Notes: Existence of three types of facilities in local councils: a) primary school, b) clinic/hospital and c) latrines.

In the National Public Services survey of June 2007, opinion leaders were asked whether their community would like the incumbent councilor or someone else to run in the 2008 council election and the reasons for their preference. Only 17 percent of them responded that they would definitely like the same councilor, whereas 35 percent said they would not want the same councilor, 23 percent said that opinion was divided in the community, and 24 percent did not know.

Among the respondents who explained why they would not like their councilors to stand for reelection, 62 percent listed "he/she did not bring any development" as the reason. Another 14 percent listed "s/he doesn't talk with/visit people around here" as the reason. Among those who would like the councilor to stand for reelection, 53 percent cited the reason "s/he has done a lot for the community." It appears that citizens did care about whether their elected representatives listened to them and played an active role in channeling development resources to their communities. These citizens were ready to reward or punish the behavior. This finding is consistent with the observation earlier that beneficiaries of council initiatives seem to have a better impression of their councils.

The local council elections in July 2008 were slightly more competitive than the elections in 2004. The number of uncontested wards dropped from 84 to 38. Political parties tried to capture grassroots positions one year after hotly contested presidential and parliamentary elections in 2007 and a peaceful transfer of power from a SLPP government to an APC government. Preliminary figures from a recent survey of councilors and candidates suggest that, among 133 local councilors who had reported intention to contest for reelection, 60 percent were returned to office.[12] The implication is that only 80 incumbents came back for a second term. The second-term veterans count as approximately 20 percent of the first group of councilors. It seems that, in aggregate, the opinion leaders were not far off in their reading of their communities' preference for a councilor to hold a second term. Future research on the reelection success or failure of the last group of councilors will give us more insight on people's voting behavior.

Table 6.5. First Most Important Reason for Choosing to Vote by Local Council

Bombali

Reason	Presidential Election	LG Election
Political Party	0.41	0.328
Reputation/Achievement in Previous Job	0.044	0.045
Promises of Development	0.349	0.342
Ethnicity	0.042	0.118
Chief Told Me to Vote	0.079	0.079
"Good" Reason"	0.42	0.412

Bothe District

Reason	Presidential Election	LG Election
Political Party	0.454	0.368
Reputation/Achievement in Previous Job	0.131	0.083
Promises of Development	0.334	0.385
Ethnicity	0.005	0.057
Chief Told Me to Vote	0.038	0.036
"Good" Reason	0.492	0.504

Bothe Town

Reason	Presidential Election	LG Election
Political Party	0.505	0.364
Reputation/Achievement in Previous Job	0.22	0.13
Promises of Development	0.242	0.481
Ethnicity	0	0
Chief Told Me to Vote	0.011	0
"Good" Reason	0.473	0.61

Note: * The variable "Good Reason: is the union of reason #2, #3, and #7. Sec GoBiFo Household Survey (P. 22) for more information.

**Table 6.6. Reasons to Reelect or Replace Local Councilors:
Views of Opinion Leaders (%)**

Opinion leaders citing the reason for wanting the same councilor to run in the 2008 council elections		Opinion leaders citing the reason for wanting someone else to run in the 2008 council elections	
No one better to replace incumbent	39	Someone else can do better	21
Incumbent has done much for community	53	Incumbent did not bring development	62
Incumbent has connections in Freetown	2	Incumbent was corrupt	1
Other	6	Incumbent ignored community	14
		Other	1

Conclusions

In a small country such as Sierra Leone, it may surprise people how many communities are almost entirely cut off from regular interactions with the rest of the country through transport, telecommunications, markets, or contact with the state. The 2004 local council elections brought government closer to people. The presence of these councils has been felt across the country, especially in rural areas off the beaten track that hitherto were neglected by central government authorities. Local councils provided rare opportunities for rural citizens to interact with authorities and have their voices heard.

In remote areas, the benefits of decentralization accrued primarily to the home villages (or, rather, towns) of elected councilors. Rural villages represented by someone living in a different town or village within the constituency still require effective representation. Not only do these villages see less of their councilors, but also they also are less likely to benefit from council projects.

Where there is more outreach or development initiative on the part of councilors, citizens are more likely to perceive their councils as responsive and trustworthy and have more confidence in their own influence over council decisions. People also are more likely to express support for their councilors' reelection.

Across the country, citizens' trust in local councils is low and followed a declining trend between 2005 and 2007. This drop seems to be associated with lack of citizen awareness about council achievement. People who know about council projects have a positive and improving view of local government's performance both in absolute terms and in comparison to central government.

Participation in local elections is widespread. Nevertheless, although much information about local council operations is public, citizens are not yet actively monitoring council operations. They also are not very confident in engaging the authorities and changing the status quo. Younger people are less confident than middle-aged people and the oldest people. Women are less confident than men. These gender and generational gaps also appear in citizens' voices in public fora.

Of course, these observations are a small slice of the long-term evolution of a society. The attitudinal survey reveals a rather liberal political attitude across the country relating to women's participation in politics and to youth leadership, as well as tolerance for corruption and a more questioning civic society (NPS Survey Report 2008).

The local council elections in 2008 resulted in more women councilors. Compared to their 12.7 percent representation during 2004–08, their winning of 18.9 percent of seats in the 2008 elections is significant progress. This trend of change is consistent with the liberal attitude toward female leadership documented in the NPS 2007 Survey. Seventy-nine percent agreed that "Women can be good politicians and should be encouraged to stand in elections," as opposed to "Women should stay home and take care of their families."

Similarly gerontocracy is giving way to youthful leadership. In 2007 the newly elected President Ernest Koroma formed a much younger political and technocratic leadership group around him. In 2008 people voted in a younger group of councilors. This change also is consistent with a more tolerant attitude toward young leaders: 76 percent of voters agreed that "Responsible young people can be good leaders," as opposed to "Only older people are mature enough to be leaders."

Whatever the citizens know about their councilors' performance, they seem to give the most consideration to whether they have brought development to their communities. The huge turnover in the 2008 elections is quite consistent with what the local opinion leaders predicted a year ahead of the elections. Such widespread acceptance of democratic values gives us hope that Sierra Leone is heading toward a more inclusive and accountable polity.

Annex 6.1. Figures from Chapter 6

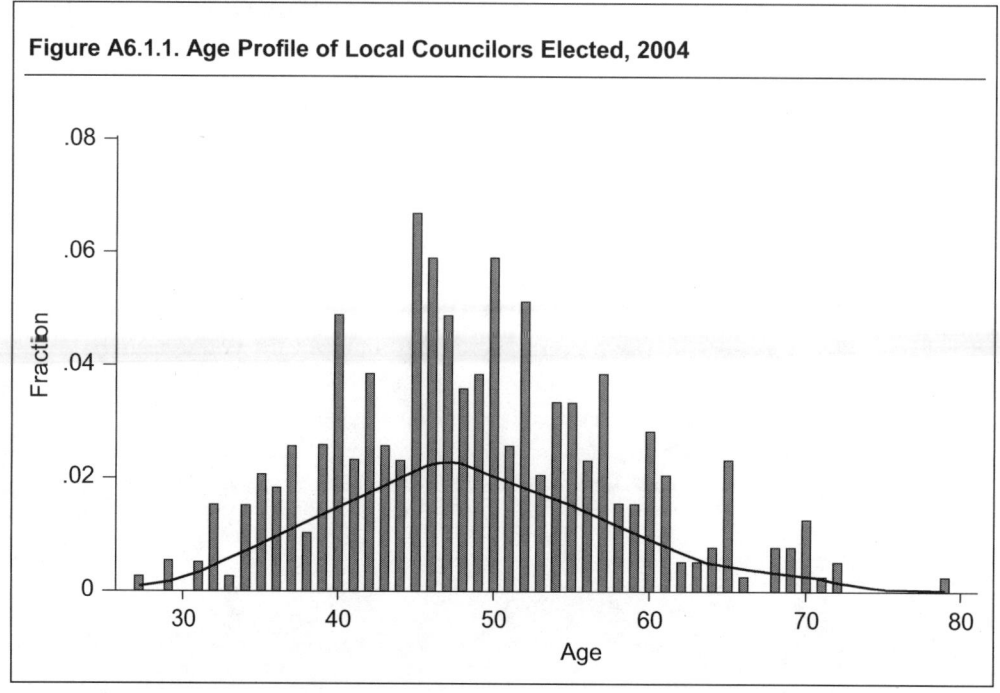

Figure A6.1.1. Age Profile of Local Councilors Elected, 2004

Source: Profiles of local councilors, Decentralization Secretariat.

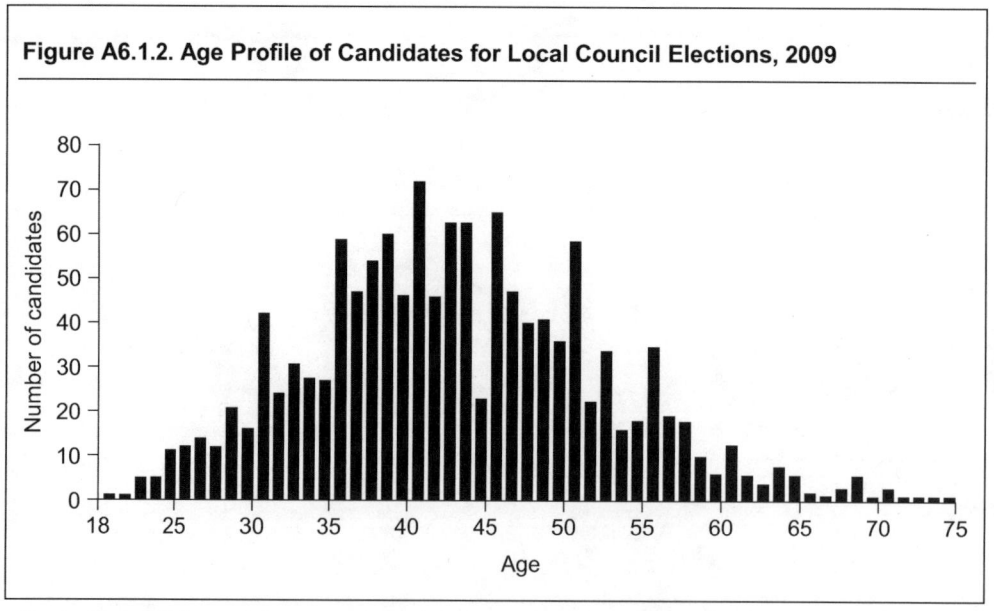

Figure A6.1.2. Age Profile of Candidates for Local Council Elections, 2009

Source: National Electoral Commission, candidate nomination statistics.
Note: The oldest candidate is Alex P. Amara, an 80-year-old PMDC Councillor candidate running in Bonthe. The youngest candidate is Theophilus Belmoh, an 18-year-old SLPP Councillor candidate running in Western Urban.

Figure A1.3 is a map of Sierra Leone overlaid by its major road network. Outside Freetown and Western Rural Area, most of the communities with no fewer than two of the three public facilities are along major roads. Communities off the roads are deprived.

Figure A6.1.3. Sierra Leone: Land of Deprivation

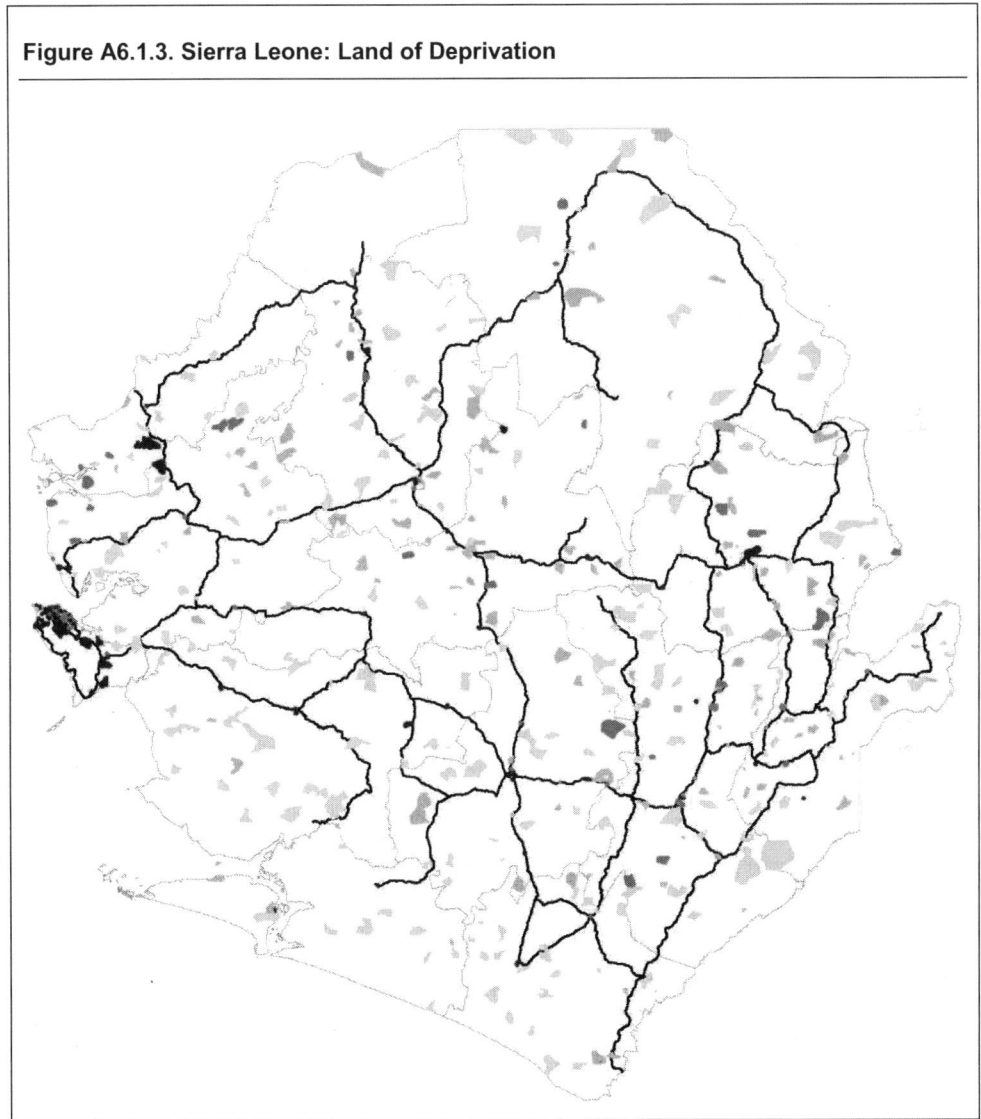

Source: The GIS data are from Sierra Leone statistics.

Notes: The colored areas are the enumeration areas covered by the National Public Service Survey of 2007. The 4 colors (gray, light gray, dark gray, black) indicate the number of 3 basic public facilities that are available in the communities: elementary school, latrine, clinic/hospital. Gray = 0; light gray= 1; dark gray = 2; and black = 3.

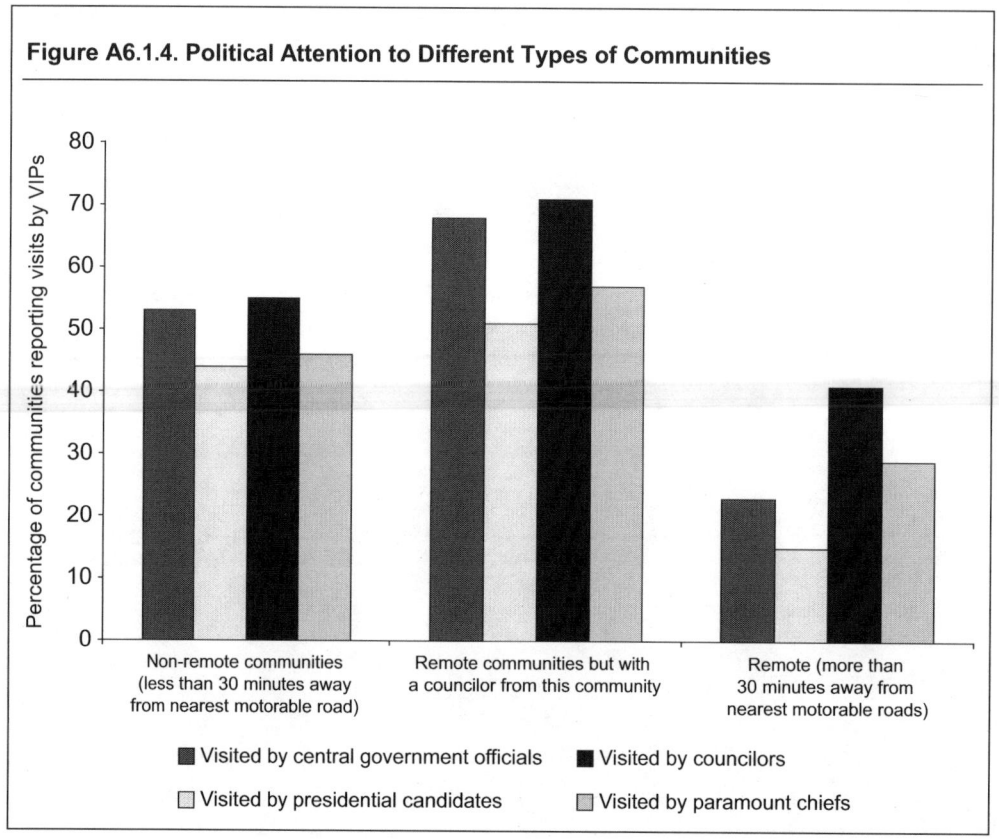

Figure A6.1.4. Political Attention to Different Types of Communities

Notes

[1] See Annex 1 for a description of these datasets.

[2] This was the official view expressed by Vice President Solomon E. Berewa at the Paris Consultative Group Meeting in 2006. It also is the view of some researchers (Keen 2005) and popular media.

[3] In rural Sierra Leone, a "stranger" refers to someone who is not an indigene.

[4] Richards 1996.

[5] Investigation of patterns of ballot stuffing shows that it benefited all parties. It appears that it most likely happened with the collusion of polling agents and some party people, especially where the (very weak) opposition parties in the locality had failed to appoint a monitor for the polling station. See the Statement from the Chief Electoral Commissioner/Chair for the Press Conference on May 20, 2005. See detailed analysis in IFES 2004.

[6] For example, during Albert Margai's rule during 1964–67, Mende dominated the Cabinet. Mende's officers in the army increased from 26 percent to 52 percent. Under the subsequent Siaka Stevens' rule, he aggressively installed northerners (Time and Limba) in power. He shut down the profitable railroad to the south-east, cutting off trade between Mende regions and Freetown.

[7] World Bank 2006a.

[8] The trust questions were not identical in the two surveys. In the 2005 NPS, respondents were asked "Suppose the ____ (local government in this area, or the central government) was given a

large amount of money, say 500 million Leones. Do you believe they will spend the money in an effective way that will benefit the needs of your council area?" A trust score was computed as 1 if the answer was "They would spend the money effectively," 0.5 if the answer was "Maybe, but they would only spend some of the money or spend it somewhat effectively," or 0 if the answer was "No, they wouldn't spend any of it at all effectively."

In the 2007 NPS, the respondents were asked "If the ___ (local council, or paramount chief, or the government in Freetown) was given 500 million Leones to complete a project in this area, do you believe they would spend all the money doing a good job on the project or would they cut some of the money?" A trust score was computed as 1 if the answer was "They would do a great job and spend all the money," 0.667 if the answer was "They would do a good job but cut a little money," 0.333 if the answer was "They would do a bad job and cut most of the money," or 0 if the answer was "They would just take all the money".

[9] In table 6.4, 18 percent of respondents knew of at least 1 project of the local council. Among them, 72 percent had benefited directly from the projects. The most commonly mentioned projects were roads and transportation projects, followed by schools and markets. These are consistent with the most popular types of projects that local councils chose to implement using their main source of discretionary funding, the LGDG. For 2004–06 grants, road rehabilitation and transport projects accounted for the largest share (28 percent). They were followed by agricultural projects, which, when combined with markets, accounted for 26 percent of the discretionary funding.[9] Other areas of spending included solid waste (8 percent), education (5 percent), and water (5 percent).

[10] IRCBP 2007(a). With a trust score of 1 (lowest trust) to 5 (highest trust), the national average trust score for "people from your own community/neighborhood" was 4.4, whereas the score for "people from outside your community/neighborhood" was 3.2.

[11] "GoBifo" is a Krio word meaning "to move forward." Started in 2005, the GoBifo Project is sponsored by the Japan Social Development Fund (JSDF) and administered by the World Bank to strengthen social capital, post conflict, in the pilot districts of Bombali and Bonthe. www.ircbp.sl/drwebsite/publish/article_459.shtml. The GoBifo project is managed by DecSec.

[12] Communication with K. Whiteside.

CHAPTER 7

Landscape of Local Authority in Sierra Leone: How "Traditional" and "Modern" Justice and Governance Systems Interact

Ryann Elizabeth Manning

The topic of this chapter, [1] in the words of one reviewer, is "one of the most discussed sociological and societal issues in African studies: ...the relationship between traditional institutions and new institutions."[2] In the annals of academia and the villages and cities of African countries, this discussion often takes the form of a normative debate about what this relationship *should* be: to what extent tradition should cede to modernity, or modernity should yield to the dictates of traditional norms; and what should be the mix of the two.

This debate is certainly alive and well in Sierra Leone. Much has been said and written about the abuses of the chieftaincy system and customary law, including the history of chieftaincy as a tool of colonial rule; exploitation of youth labor; exclusion of "strangers" and young men from weak lineages from access to land or marriage; imposition of harsh and arbitrary fines; and discriminatory practices against women.[3] Many have argued that abusive and autocratic practices by traditional authorities helped to fuel the civil war that ravaged Sierra Leone in the 1990s by driving aggrieved young men from their villages and into the various armed factions, in rebellion against a social system that trapped them in a rural underclass.[4] On the other hand, many people see the traditional justice and governance systems as important mechanisms for maintaining peace and social order, particularly in rural areas.[5] (This viewpoint is not necessarily incompatible with an acknowledgment of the kinds of abuses outlined above; many people argue that the chieftaincy is an important system despite such abuses.) Some on this side see the war as resulting from a breakdown in this social order,[6] and argue for strengthening chieftaincy systems to consolidate peace and promote development today.[7]

The primary intention of this chapter is not to argue for any particular side in the "tradition versus modernity" debate—not least because, as described below, the two are actually integrated, interdependent, and even fused. Instead, the intention is to paint a description of the landscape of local authority in Sierra Leone, especially for those not familiar with this landscape, and to provide new data about how local justice and governance operate on the ground today, with a focus on the interaction between traditional authorities and the new local councils.[8]

What this landscape shows is that the reality of local authority in Sierra Leone is not an antagonistic and mutually incompatible duality between the modern and the traditional, but a complex and dynamic hybrid of the two. Local governance and justice in Sierra Leone involve a complex array of institutions and individuals, who draw their structure and legitimacy from a range of systems and heritages—customary, colonial, and modern—and interact with one another in a rich and sometimes unpredictable manner. New "modern" systems, most prominently the local councils reinstated in 2004 after a hiatus of 30 years, adapt to operate with and alongside more "traditional" systems, which themselves transform over time. This process of mutual accommodation results in a hybrid system different from what was intended by either in isolation.

The traditional justice and governance system, although highly imperfect, is relatively familiar to and accessible by the average community members whom it is meant to serve. Most of these are poor, illiterate, and largely disconnected from both the capital, Freetown, and the decentralized state institutions located in provincial and district headquarters. These community members are quite willing to tolerate the complexity and apparent contradictions of having modern institutions operating alongside traditional institutions.[9] Indeed, the people show a willingness to "forum shop" for the system that best meets the needs of a particular situation.

If this chapter takes a normative position, it is that there is some need for reform of both the traditional and the modern governance and justice systems operating in local Sierra Leone, as both fall far short of effectively meeting the needs of communities and individuals. This is hardly a controversial position. In fact, there seems to be some consensus around the need for reform among even the strongest supporters of both traditional and modern authority structures, and even their most strident critics typically do not advocate complete abolishment. The author also takes the view that this reform should increase the voice and agency of members of society who are excluded or poorly served by local governance and justice mechanisms.

The question of how such reform should take place, how quickly, with what scope, and to what degree, will be left for others—particularly Sierra Leoneans—to debate. It is hoped only that this chapter offers data to help inform the debate and questions to provoke a more constructive conversation; and also that this data is helpful to those trying to deliver services or otherwise engage with rural and peri-urban Sierra Leone.

Research Methodology

This chapter is based primarily on research conducted in 2006 and 2007 as part of the World Bank's Justice for the Poor and Understanding Processes of Change in Local Governance (J4P/LG) project.[10] This project was implemented in partnership with the Campaign for Good Governance and Timap for Justice,[11] two civil society groups in Sierra Leone. Research was conducted throughout the country in a range of rural and peri-urban areas to reflect Sierra Leone's geographic, ethnic, and socioeconomic diversity. (Very little research was conducted in the larger urban areas.) The bulk of research was carried out by a team of local researchers who had received intensive training in qualitative research methods at the outset of the project and who worked under close supervision and support from international Justice for the Poor members.

Research was primarily qualitative and used anthropological and ethnographic techniques, particularly in-depth, semi-structured interviews and participant observation. The team did not conduct formally constituted focus group discussions. However, the nature of communal village life meant that individual interviews sometimes turned into group discussions. The four main research sites were in the Bombali (Northern Province), Moyamba and Bo (Southern Province), and Western Area Rural Districts. During either the preliminary scoping research or core qualitative research, or in the administration of a study of local customary law courts, team members also spent time in another 5 of Sierra Leone's 13 districts, for a total of 9 districts included in the research. In total, original qualitative research contributing to this chapter totaled approximately 83 distinct person-weeks of time. Core research covered approximately 31 villages in 4 chiefdoms and involved at least 460 interviews with 360 individuals. Other related research, particularly the preliminary scoping research, involved dozens of additional interviews in a wide range of locations.[12]

Mapping Local Authority Structures in Sierra Leone

This section will provide an overview of local authority structures in Sierra Leone. Some of these authorities have formally and legally constituted positions; others have informal (but often no less powerful) mandates. As a visual map of this network, figure 7.1 outlines the most important institutions and individuals involved in local governance and justice.[13] Although necessarily a simplification, figure 7.1 highlights the fact that the institutions considered "local" or "decentralized" from the perspective of Freetown—local councils, local courts, Paramount Chiefs—are relatively high in the hierarchy of authorities from the perspective of the people.

Figure 7.1 roughly places these institutions along a spectrum from formal to informal, although it is important to acknowledge that there is a great deal of gray in these distinctions. All structures listed on the right side, down to local councils and local courts, are formally constituted bodies with legally defined mandates. On the left side is a network of mostly "traditional" authorities with a range of formality.

Local Courts

Focusing on the bottom (more local) part of figure 7.1 and starting on the right side, we find local councils and local courts. Local councils will be discussed in a later section. Local courts, also known as native administration (NA) courts, are the lowest level of the formally recognized justice system. Although numbers vary, a chiefdom typically has one or two local courts.[14] The administration of local courts is governed by the Local Courts Act of 1963, which also outlines jurisdictional limits and an appeal process leading in principle through the court system up to the Supreme Court, although such appeals are extremely rare. Substantively, the courts hear cases on the basis of customary law, which is unwritten and varies from chiefdom to chiefdom.

Figure 7.1. Most Important Institutions and Actors in Local Governance from a Villager's Perspective

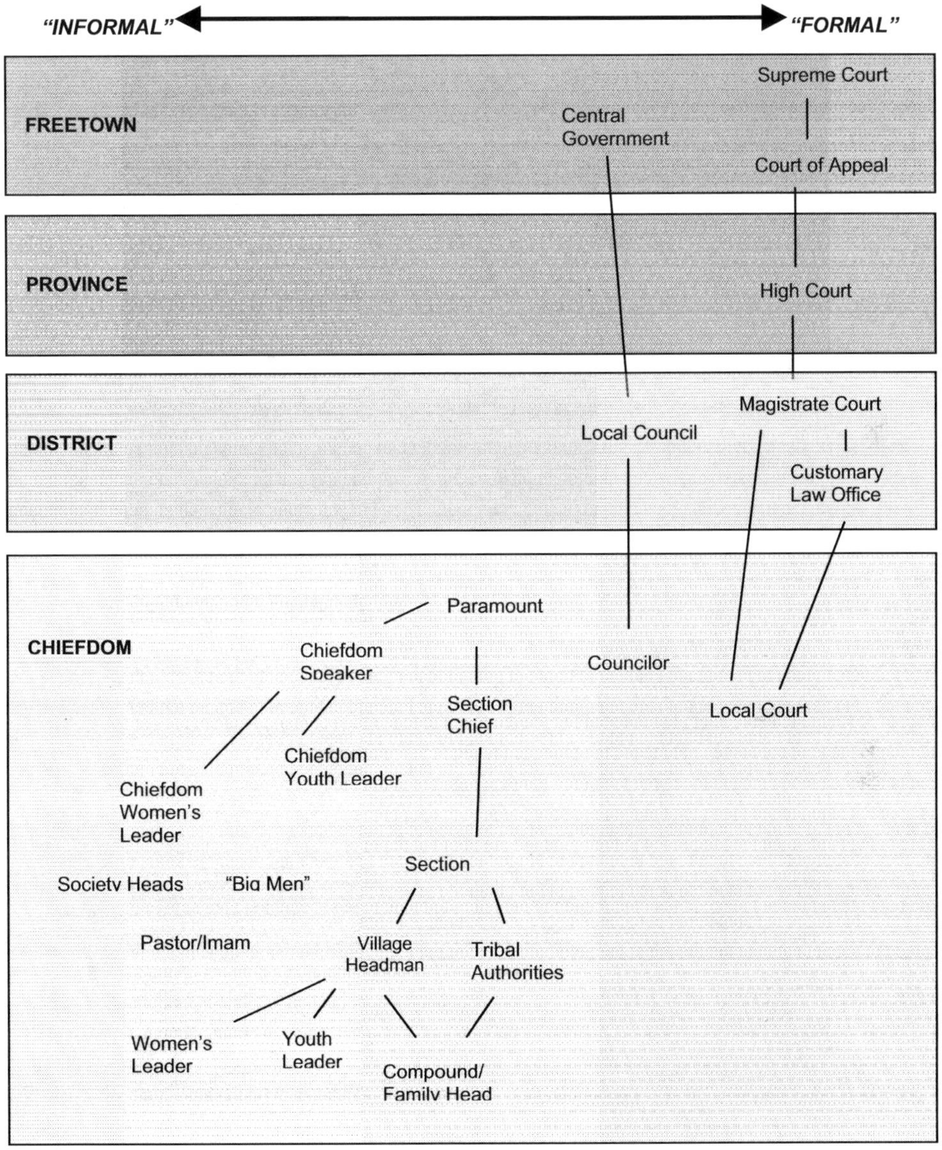

On paper, the administration of local courts may appear very formal and well organized, but in practice the courts often overstep the bounds of their official mandate—for example, by hearing cases they should not, or levying fines that far exceed the allowable amount[15]—or otherwise act outside the law. Court chairmen and members often are illiterate and have little to no training on the laws and regulations that govern local courts,[16] even though the GoSL and civil society recently provided ad hoc training. Supervision of the courts is minimal, so problems usually come to light only when the parties involved appeal to the district appeals court or contest to the customary law office.[17] Local courts also lack sufficient judicial independence. Their ties to local governance systems, particularly chiefdom authorities, often render them prone to influence and bias. Chiefs wield a great deal of power over the local courts in many, although not all, chiefdoms,[18] and rely on these courts to help them exert authority over chiefdom residents.[19] Chiefs also are known to interfere directly in court proceedings.[20]

Paramount Chiefs

On the left side of figure 7.1 at the district level is a network of mostly "traditional" authorities with a range of formality. The most formal is the Paramount Chief. Outside of the Western Area,[21] Sierra Leone is divided into 149 chiefdoms, each ruled by a single Paramount Chief, considered the top authority in his or her chiefdom. Per statutory requirement, Paramount Chiefs are elected by Tribal Authorities (TAs), also known as chiefdom councilors. The qualifications and election processes for Paramount Chieftaincy are laid down in law and regulation and supervised by the central government,[22] although qualification is still sometimes hotly contested.[23]

The position of Paramount Chieftaincy and its associated responsibilities are established by law in a series of acts, many of them predating independence,[24] and are enshrined in the 1991 national Constitution.[25] According to recent government documents, the roles of Paramount Chiefs can be delineated as follows (the last three in consultation with chiefdom committees and chairpersons of local courts):

- Uphold and maintain traditions, customs, and practices of the chiefdom
- Serve as custodians of land for the people of the chiefdom
- Settle disputes
- Maintain law and order
- Deal with land and customary and traditional matters in the chiefdom.[26]

In practice, the chief is the primary representative of his or her chiefdom to outsiders having any dealings with the chiefdom, including NGOs and other development agents, government representatives, politicians, and mining companies and other commercial interests. Essentially, and with few exceptions, it is impossible to do anything in a chiefdom without the knowledge and approval of the chief. Most chiefdom resources also fall under the authority of the Paramount Chief, although it is the chiefdom treasury clerk[27] who actually keeps all chiefdom accounts. Many chiefs also fulfill traditional and ceremonial tasks, particularly in relation to the secret societies. The latter are particularly important in the North, where Paramount Chieftaincy is considered sacred.[28]

Paramount Chiefs also play a major role in resolving disputes. As noted above, chiefs no longer have the legal right to operate a court,[29] but they are allowed to mediate or arbitrate, and often still adjudicate, despite the legal prohibition. According to a 2007 National Household Survey (NHS), 6 percent of all cases and 13 percent of land disputes reported outside of the family are reported first to the Paramount Chief.[30] Of cases that are reported elsewhere first but then to a second authority, 19 percent are reported second to the Paramount Chief. Given that most communities have a strong preference for resolving disputes at the lowest possible level, Paramount Chiefs usually hear only relatively major or intractable cases,[31] as well as grievances in which someone from outside the chiefdom has wronged members of the chiefdom.[32] It also is usually more expensive to bring a case to the Paramount Chief than to a lower chief.[33]

Section and Town Chiefs

Paramount Chiefs rule through a network of subchiefs and chiefdom functionaries at chiefdom, section (each chiefdom is divided into between 5–15 sections[34]), and town or village level. These functionaries are somewhat less formally mandated than the Paramount Chief, although many are recognized by legislation,[35] and all are considered quite "official" by local community members. Some (specifically chiefdom treasury clerks and court clerks) are actually employed as civil servants by the central government. Others are paid a salary from chiefdom coffers. Often the actual importance of a particular institution in local governance does not coincide with its legislated role. For instance, chiefdom councils (composed of Tribal Authorities) have specific functions outlined by statute, including the making of chiefdom bylaws.[36] However, in practice, as observed in field research, chiefdom councils seem to have few formal functions beyond the election of Paramount Chiefs and section chiefs.

Roles and responsibilities of section and town chiefs largely mirror those of Paramount Chiefs, although are much less clearly defined or mandated by the central government. By custom, however, these chiefs are considered just as "official" as, although subordinate to, Paramount Chiefs. Town chiefs serve as the main authorities at the town or village level. They play an important role in resolving small disputes. The NHS cited earlier found that 35 percent of disputes and grievances that were reported anywhere outside of the family were reported first to the village chief, the largest percentage for any institution. An additional 2 percent were reported first to the village elders. In small villages, these numbers rose to 51 percent and 3 percent, respectively.[37]

Town chiefs also have the primary responsibility for "strangers"—nonresidents—who are visiting the community. Customary law dictates that strangers must report to the town chief on arrival in a community and that residents must report any strangers whom they have brought into the town. These reports generally are seen as security measures. Town chiefs sometimes also are responsible for collecting tax revenue, which they pass on to section chiefs and the chiefdom treasury clerk, often receiving a rebate equivalent to a percentage of the revenue collected.

Section chiefs, in turn, also resolve cases brought to them but may hear bigger or more important cases—or different types of cases—than their town-level colleagues. (This also depends on the personality of the individual chiefs). For instance, the household survey found that just 17 percent of all cases, but 28 percent of land disputes, were reported first to the section chief. For land disputes, section chiefs were the second-most-used authority after village chiefs.[38] Section chiefs also usually are involved in tax collection and chiefdom decisionmaking.

Other authorities listed in figure 7.1—including women and youth leaders, religious leaders, secret society heads, family or compound heads, and "big men"— generally are not formally mandated, yet play important roles at the local level. (The Ministry of Education, Youth and Sports has been trying to formalize the position of youth leader at the chiefdom, district, and even national level, although a disconnect remains between the higher-level youth councils and local youth leaders.[39]) For instance, researchers found that religious leaders often are involved in decisionmaking and consulted regarding disputes and other grievances, and often are viewed with respect by adherents of the other religion.[40] Sodalities, generally known as secret societies (into which the majority of men and women in rural Sierra Leone are initiated[41]) have been in existence since ancient times and serve both a spiritual and sociopolitical role.[42] Historically, societies sometimes have served as a check on the power of Paramount Chiefs and other authorities, as well as themselves have served as mechanisms of control and authority.[43] However, researchers found signs that societies are declining in prominence and importance in at least some communities.[44]

Women and youth leaders have relatively limited roles, involving primarily mobilizing their respective groups for communal work and resolving some intragroup disputes. Nevertheless, there are some signs that the importance of their roles is increasing (if slowly), particularly the role of youth leaders.[45] Often youth and women leaders are brought into meetings only to speak to visitors—in part, it seems, to satisfy the visitors concerned with gender equity—or when some contribution is required from them. Even when respondents say they are included in decisionmaking, a deeper investigation often reveals that they have been informed rather than consulted or truly involved.[46] In at least some cases, the position of "women's leader" is formally constituted and even filled by election, but in others it is more a matter of a preferred spokesperson. As one 36-year-old female community member from a small village in Moyamba District explained to a researcher, "Women are not organized in that structured manner that you think. Most often when visitors come, the chief calls me and [another woman] to represent the women in the village. I think they call us because they have realized that we are bold, we are presentable, and we can speak in public."[47]

It also is worth mentioning the variety of development committees that operate at a chiefdom or subchiefdom level. Some of these are formally constituted—such as ward development committees (WDCs), created by LGA 2004 but still largely nonfunctional in most locations—but many are ad hoc and linked to particular projects or interventions.[48] The duties of such committees may vary widely, and their composition—even when supposedly selected in a transparent, participatory way— tends to mirror other kinds of authority in the locality.[49]

In addition to these development committees, many communities have one or more people who serve as a sort of development facilitator. This is usually an informal and often self-appointed position, but recognized by authorities and by average people. Thus, community members and even the chiefs themselves may refer a visitor to a particular individual—often someone with greater education or English language skills, or a background of working for a development agency or for the government—to discuss the community's development needs and any planned projects and to serve as a guide and host. (Box 7.1 describes one such facilitator from a remote northern chiefdom.) Another common profile is a head teacher or community health worker who applies for grants and other support for schools or clinics.[50] Some observers criticize such actors as rent-seekers who carve off a slice of development funding for their personal benefit. However, such individuals can perform valuable services for their communities by attracting development projects and helping to fulfill the often significant demands that such projects place on communities (for participation, input, and monitoring). Researchers found that community members and their authorities often see value in these individuals' contributions.[51]

Observations on Sources of Authority in Sierra Leone

"At first government was very far from the people, but with the local council we now feel that government is nearer."

—*45-year-old male farmer and local court*
bailiff in rural Moyamba District

Overall, the most consistent observation from this and other recent research on local governance in rural and peri-urban Sierra Leone is that, despite the tumult of war, the changes of the post-colonial and post-war eras, and the advent of the new local councils, chieftaincy remains the most important system of authority across rural Sierra Leone. Despite the fact that criticism and challenges to chiefs' authority seem to be on the increase,[52] chiefs—particularly the "subchiefs," who serve at section, town, village, or even subvillage levels—often are the primary (if not only) formal authority present and accessible. Moreover, even when alternatives are available, most people still accept the authority of chiefs and look to them to make decisions, resolve disputes, and engage with outside actors such as government representatives or development agencies. There is some variation by context. For example, chiefs may be particularly powerful for "traditional" matters, including land use, but less so for other issues. Nevertheless, chiefs are more trusted across the board, even in how they would administer development funds. For example, the 2007 national household survey cited earlier found that people rated Paramount Chiefs higher than either local councils or central government on measures of trust and responsiveness. Among respondents from the provinces,[53] 65 percent said that their Paramount Chief "listens to what people in this town/neighborhood say or what they need," compared with 43 percent for local councils and 46 percent for central government.[54] Chiefs also scored significantly higher on a measure of how they would spend a large sum of money intended for development[55] and on a measure of trust (46 percent said chiefs can be believed, compared with 34 percent for local councils and 41 percent for central government.)[56]

Box 7.1. Profile of a Chiefdom Development Facilitator

It was on Friday in a predominantly Muslim community at exactly the hour for congregational prayers when the research team entered the chiefdom headquarter town of a very remote northern chiefdom. The vehicle alone gathered attention in a community so far from major transit routes, as did the obvious strangers within. A small crowd soon formed.

Research team members followed their usual process for entering a new community, observing traditional norms by visiting the Paramount Chief first to explain the purpose of their visit. The chief was very old and somewhat feeble, and the team met him on the porch of his house. As they began speaking with him, a middle-aged man interrupted and introduced himself as the chiefdom development facilitator, a voluntary job. He sat himself beside the chief and quickly dominated the interview, answering on the chief's behalf and directing the conversation to what he believed the visitors wished to hear.

The facilitator had formerly lived and worked in Makeni, the capital and largest town of the northern province. The war brought him back to his home community. After the war, he decided not to return to Makeni without the guarantee of a job and opted to stay and, as he said, "help my people." He has only a basic education, but in a chiefdom in which educated persons are few and far between, his qualifications gain him superiority over the others.

In discussions with the research team, he described his role as development facilitator in many ways:

- "I am the project management committee secretary to most projects and often correct contractors when they want to do wrong things."
- "I have overseen a lot of projects."
- "I wrote a letter to NaCSA requesting a school, bridge, health center, toilets etc."
- "We don't have any complaint over project implementation yet. Other areas have weak [project management committees]. That was why they often have problems with their projects."

He also served as the primary guide, host, and contact person for visitors from development agencies. After co-opting the interview with the Paramount Chief, he led researchers to a binder containing information on the chiefdom, including information on the distance and accessibility of all chiefdom sections. The information was extremely useful to the team. He also arranged accommodations for the team and arranged for them to be fed at his own home. Another group of visitors in town to conduct a survey was treated similarly, although perhaps with less attention because their group did not include a foreigner.

Although helpful, the man clearly tried to dominate and control the team's stay. He attempted to control their interview schedule, and even wished to travel around with them on field trips beyond the chiefdom headquarter town. He was clearly uncomfortable when interviews were not conducted in his presence; and when he was present, frequently interrupted to supply answers.

The research team was left with no doubt that although he might be serving the community by facilitating projects, he was also serving his own interests. Before the team left, he collected their phone numbers and told them that he was currently unemployed and would be open to their assistance.

The kin group also remains important in determining and legitimizing authority in Sierra Leone, both within and outside the chieftaincy.[57] Access to some positions—most notably that of Paramount Chief—is limited by law or practice to certain "ruling" or "founding" families.[58] Such requirements may be flexible in the case of lower chiefs—although not for Paramount Chief—and exceptions do exist.[59]

- Members of ruling families often legitimize their position with reference to land. "Our forefathers first came and found this land and they first started building houses here," said a male tribal authority (age 44) from a Moyamba chiefdom.

- "We are authorities because this village was founded by our ancestors. When they passed away, they left it with us to get our living (from grandfather to grandfather) from it. Before their death, they offered sacrifices to God for the development of the village," said another male tribal authority (age 55) from the same chiefdom.

- Others refer to powers conferred by the colonial authority. As one male community member (age 56) from a Moyamba chiefdom said, "The right to leadership position for both town chief and section chief is by ruling families. Their right is gotten from those whose ancestors signed the treaty with the colonial masters."

Even newer, supposedly more democratic positions often are awarded to those with links to ruling families.[60] Past performance of family members—such as fathers or uncles who were previously chiefs—also often are taken into account in selecting individuals to serve in positions of authority, perhaps based on a longstanding idea that positions of power should be inherited.[61] The J4P research team did not often ask people explicitly about their views on the ruling house system, and it may be a worthwhile area for future research. However, in general, it seems that while some people from various walks of life express a desire to make access to leadership positions more open, most people accept and even defend the traditional sources of legitimacy.

Authority in rural (and some peri-urban) areas also is generally concentrated in a particular ethnic group, usually the group considered the *indigenes*—the original inhabitants, or founders—of that particular place. (See box 7.2 for explanation of indigene and its importance in Sierra Leonean society.) This pattern is true even when the indigenes are not in the majority in a particular place, although such cases are probably relatively rare. In some places, the indigene group is the same for the whole chiefdom; in others, different ethnic groups may lay claim to different sections or even villages. This ethnic claim may be explicit and immutable, or may be amenable to exceptions, and the degree of flexibility may vary from place to place and from one position of authority to another.[62] Sometimes, the leaders of a non-indigene ethnic group are considered authorities in their own right. For example, in many chiefdoms, "tribal headmen" are recognized as leaders and representatives of minority non-indigene ethnic groups. In contrast, in one ethnically diverse peri-urban research site in the Western area, each of at least 6 ethnic groups has its own headman, most of whom operate an informal court.[63] However, in nearly all locations, most of the most important positions of chiefdom authority—such as Paramount Chief and chiefdom speaker—are held by members of the indigene group.

Box 7.2. Strangers and Indigenes in Sierra Leone

There are frequent references in the literature to what Richard Fanthorpe refers to as the "extreme localization of criteria of identity and belonging" in rural Sierra Leone (Fanthorpe 2001, 372). "Stranger" status can persist for generations and often is ascribed to or adopted by individuals whose ethnic identity is different from that of an area's original inhabitants (indigenes). Rights and property in rural areas are conferred as both a result and a validation of citizenship. Strangers in a community must frequently form relationships with indigenes through paths such as marriage or the patronage system to gain some benefits of citizenship (Reno 2003). Insufficient family or social connections are a key source of vulnerability and poverty (Richards and others 2004). On the other hand, other factors—such as wealth, political connectedness, or sheer numbers—can change the balance of power between strangers and indigenes.

One illustration of the power and persistence of the stranger and indigene identities is a conflict over access to power in one community in the Western Area Rural District. Decades of in-migration by "stranger" ethnic groups (particularly Temne) has led to a situation in which the indigenes (Sherbro) are in the minority. When elections—first for a local councilor, and then for a village headman—were held, each group put up a candidate. The "stranger" candidate explained that this tension was what sparked his decision to run: "The main reason we decided to contest the election is that the [indigenes] used to refer to us as strangers even though we have spent a very long time here with them. We have been supporting them all along, but they failed to recognize our efforts so we stood for ourselves."

The "stranger" candidates won both elections, which sparked frustration on the part of the indigenes, and tension and outright conflict between the two groups. Invoking tradition and customary law, the indigenes asserted that they owned the land and would not be governed by strangers. The strangers and their allies invoked electoral law and new rules of eligibility that granted the right to run for office to anyone who had been resident in the area for at least five years. Thus, traditional sources of power and legitimacy—ethnic identity and historical claims to the land—came into tension with modern, electoral sources of legitimacy.

—Adapted with permission from Dale 2007

One consequence of this concentration of power among indigenes, and more generally of the strength of indigene-stranger identities, is the marginalization from power and decisionmaking of those considered strangers.[64] Such marginalization is compounded for strangers who also are members of other disempowered groups, such as women, youths, or the disabled.[65]

Areas in which the group considered indigenes are in the numeric minority present an interesting case. In such places, "strangers" often can access power through democratic means—for example, by running for Parliament or local council—particularly because political support tends to follow ethnic lines.[66] The election of strangers can cause tension and conflict if indigenes feel they are being excluded from their rightful position of authority (box 7.2.)

The famously gerontocratic nature of Sierra Leonean society and the generational tensions that have been cited as helping to fuel the civil war[67] are still evident in the structure and exercise of local governance and justice. Young people are expected to respect and obey their elders, while elders are expected to wield authority and decisionmaking power in families, communities, and most other contexts. For instance, two common Krio phrases invoked by respondents to explain why certain people cannot challenge others are *borbor na borbor*[68] ("A young boy is just a young boy") and *u no sae big one na big one*[69] ("One has to realize that an elder is always an elder"). One town chief (male, age 82) from a Moyamba chiefdom told researchers, "It is not right for a child to challenge the town or chiefdom." The "child" he was referring to was 44 years old.[70]

Nonetheless, there are signs from all the sites included in this research that the relationships between elders and youths are changing in important ways—although perhaps more slowly than some might hope. [71] The position of youth leader is more formalized and is seen more positively than it was before the war. Chiefs seem more willing to include youths in chiefdom governance, although the chiefs often fall short of true consultation. In some cases, chiefdom authorities have been convinced that greater inclusion is in their own interests. For instance, in one northern chiefdom, the Paramount Chief and court chairman were convinced by a civil society group that they could avoid criticism that their verdicts were unfair by reserving seats on the court for women and youth representatives.

Youths, in turn, are more likely to speak out and challenge chiefs and other authorities, including over such issues as setting development priorities, managing and using communal resources, and providing communal labor.[72] There are various possible reasons for this greater willingness to challenge. For example, perhaps youths have been more exposed to—and are more likely to embrace—ideas of human rights and good governance. On the other hand, perhaps young men no longer fear challenging their elders because the civil war gave them the opportunity to do so, often violently, and generally without consequence.

Other changes in local justice and governance are evident in many communities. Democratic processes for selecting leaders are widespread. Moreover, although elections are a longstanding practice for many positions (including some traditional posts), there are signs that such practices and the accompanying norms are becoming stronger and more deeply embedded. Many respondents report that exposure to human rights ideas and principles—through "sensitization" by NGOs, news and information heard on the radio, and experiences gleaned during the mobility and upheaval of the war years—have changed the views and behavior of "rulers and the ruled" alike.[73] Additionally, many people, including some who themselves are uneducated, express a desire for the traditional authorities to be educated and to have exposure or connections outside the chiefdom. They feel that the latter would help attract development and protect the community from exploitation. As with democratic procedures, this desire is not necessarily new, but there are signs that it may be increasing. In many cases, the emphasis on education and connections actually reinforces the power of the traditional elites, who are more likely to be well connected and to be able to send their children to school.

Local Councils' Interactions with Other Authority Structures

This section will look more closely at the local councils, and how they interact with the complex network of other authorities described above. Qualitative research findings suggest that local councilors generally have been accepted by communities as legitimate actors, particularly in "bringing development," but are not perceived as authorities equal to the chiefs and others. As mentioned earlier, they also rank lower in quantitative surveys than either chiefdom or central government in perceptions of responsiveness or trust.

However, people do seem to look to the councilors to bring benefits such as schools, roads, health care, and other crucial development needs. Furthermore, in some instances, the councilor is one of the people approached by community members when help is needed. When a group of 9 villages, led by their town chiefs, decided to construct a road to link their villages, the 1 authority they consulted before beginning was the councilor.

They did not approach other authorities—including more senior chiefs, local NGOs, or government agencies—until later in the process, because (by one account) they wanted to "demonstrate our ability" first. When some villages did not turn up for the first day of work, the councilor then got involved, taking action himself to sue the villages in court.

Criticisms of the councils usually focus on the failure of a particular councilor to deliver benefits to the respondent's community, rather than being a more fundamental challenge to the councils' overall legitimacy. This focus is consistent with Sierra Leone's long history of patrimonial governance in which those in power were expected first and foremost to bring concrete and localized benefits to their supporters and home areas. Many people say they do not know their councilor and do not know what he or she or the council as a whole is doing; or do know but find their own councilor ineffective. As one respondent said, "Our [councilor] is not doing much because we haven't seen anything since we elected him into office." This personal concluded that the councils should continue but with the councilors becoming more active. A village development committee chairman (male, age 40) from Bombali District said, "My only problem with the local council goes to our councilor as he is not making moves in bringing development projects in our ward." A paralegal and civil society activist with a local human rights organization (male, age 36) said, "The councilor is not doing anything.... It would have been better we don't have a councilor." However, he added that another councilor from a neighboring ward was "doing well as he has repaired and even constructed a few bridges in his ward," thus showing that his gripe was not with the council per se but with an individual councilor's inaction as defined in terms of local benefits. Bridges, for instance, were seen to benefit only the ward in which they were located rather than the broader area. Several individuals said that they wanted the council to continue even though that they felt they had not benefited to date, because it might benefit them later.

Similarly, praise of councilors is focused on localized deliverables. "The local council is doing well. It has provided tools for the maintenance of roads in this ward," says one community-teacher association chairman (male, age 42) in a Bo District chiefdom.[74] One of the most popular councilors encountered during this research, in Moyamba District, was widely praised for things he had done with his own personal money: buying school uniforms for secondary school students, paying stipends to community teachers, buying uniforms for chiefdom native administration (NA) police officers, sending shovels and a bag of rice to people who were constructing a road to one village, and helping with the construction of a mosque in another. His success as a councilor was dependent more on his own personal wealth and local patronage than on any activity of the council. Such patronage also served him well, reinforcing his role as a "big man" in the community and building a stronger political base for future elections to local council or higher office.

Box 7.3. Getting a Local Council to Deliver

The citizens of one ward in Bombali District had been complaining informally to their councilor for some time that no council projects had come to their area. In particular, they pointed to a broken bridge along one of the main routes out of town that they had wanted the council to repair. According to residents, their community had had the highest rate of payment of local tax in the whole district during the previous year. Having seen no benefit, they started grumbling that they would not pay again the next year.

At some point in 2007, a young man who served as the village development committee chair approached the community elders with an idea: Why not write a letter to the district officials threatening not to pay taxes the next year if the council did not sponsor some sort of project in their ward? The elders agreed, and they wrote to the Paramount Chief, copying the provincial secretary, central chiefdom finance clerk, district council chief administrator, district council chairman, and the resident minister.

Two weeks later, the council came and repaired their bridge. For good measure, the resident minister sent word that he would build a court barrie (a sort of semi-enclosed structure, usually with a roof but no walls, and typically is a public/shared space). It seems that community members have reason to pay their taxes next year.

Quantitative data supports this emphasis on delivering projects. In the NHS survey cited earlier, among respondents who knew of a local council project or knew their councilor's name, councils scored higher (or at least as high) as the central government.[75]

It seems that *consultation is valued much less than delivery.* As one 45-year-old male teacher from a very rural town in Bombali District said, "The councilor often comes to the school and talks to us, but we have never received any benefit from him. I don't think it is necessary to have a councilor."

Nonetheless, clear and open lines of communication between councilors and their constituents are essential, and when they break down, can lead to confusion and suspicion. In one instance in the Western Rural District, a local council project to rehabilitate water supply in several communities was scaled back because of a change in the level of available funding. However, this change was not effectively communicated to the communities, and people felt that the project had been botched or left incomplete. Some began to suspect that the resources had been misused, and at least one community leader suggested that the councilor and town headman had connived to steal the funds.

The relationship between councilors and chiefs—and, more generally, the interaction and engagement between the new local council system and the chieftaincy system—is one of least understood dimensions of local governance. In part, the reason is that the initial design and implementation of the decentralized local government left unanswered many of the questions of how these two systems would interact (box 7.5).[76] In addition, there inevitably would be jostling as new authorities were introduced in a pre-existing governance system to share resources and well as responsibilities.

Box 7.4. Local Councils and Paramount Chiefs: Key Disputes

The Local Government Act of 2004 (LGA) did not fully define the roles and relationships between the chieftaincy and local government systems. As a result, these roles and relationships remain subjects of contestation and conflict. The two systems are not inherently contradictory. District boundaries follow chiefdom boundaries and, except in the urban areas, each chiefdom corresponds to a single local council.1 In theory, roles and responsibilities can be complementary. For instance, councils could be responsible for schools, health clinics, and feeder roads while chiefdoms would manage community-level safety and security and maintain smaller roads and "bush paths." However, for now, confusion and duplication are common.

Two commonly cited sources of conflict between the councilors and the chiefs are revenue collection and the notion of hierarchy and who is "in charge" at a chiefdom level. The latter was a bigger issue when the councils first came into existence, at which point Paramount Chiefs objected to the language that "a local council shall be the highest political authority in the locality" (LGA). Anecdotally, some councilors took this statement to mean that they ranked higher than the Paramount Chiefs, while the chiefs maintained that they were the highest authority in their own chiefdoms. This conflict largely has been resolved by the compromise that, while local councils are the highest political authorities—therefore above any individual Paramount Chief—the chief in each chiefdom ranks above the corresponding councilor or councilors. (This was a general nationwide compromise. In practice, the hierarchies in particular chiefdoms and districts will be context specific and dependent on the individuals involved.)

On the other hand, in many areas, revenue is still a source of tension between councils and chiefs. For instance, the local tax (a head tax levied on all adults) is a primary source of revenue for both chiefdoms and local councils. Responsibility for collecting local tax falls to the chiefdoms, although councils set the rate of tax (typically Le 5,000 per person per annum) as well as the rate of "precept" to be paid by chiefdoms to the councils. This precept is typically 40 percent of total tax receipts. Chiefs complain that this revenue-sharing leaves them with insufficient funds to pay the salaries of chiefdom functionaries, particularly since many other sources of revenue also were removed from the chiefdoms and given to the local councils. Local councils, in turn, complain that they are largely reliant on the good will and largess of chiefs, who may connive with treasury clerks to obscure the amount of revenue collected (and therefore pay less in precept), simply refuse to pay, or delay payment indefinitely. As one councilor in Koinadugu District told researchers after a frank discussion of the tensions between councilors and Paramount Chiefs, "Trying to take money from the Paramount Chiefs is like trying to uproot a tooth from a live snake."

Note: 1 Urban chiefdoms may be covered by both a district council and a town or city council. For example, Kakua chiefdom in Bo District is covered by, and shares tax revenue with, both the Bo City Council and the Bo District Council.

Although talk of chiefdom-council interaction generally emphasizes the conflicts, the Justice for the Poor and Understanding Processes of Change in Local Governance project's (J4P/LG) research findings reveal an unexpected degree of cooperation and collaboration among chiefs and councilors. (Representatives from the government's Decentralization Secretariat also say that conflict and tension between chiefs and councilors have decreased significantly since the councils' inception.[77]) Of course, interaction varies from chiefdom to chiefdom and depends on many factors—including the personalities involved, family connections (or lack thereof), and political affiliations. Nonetheless, it is clear that, in many instances, chiefs and councilors are working closely together and are developing their own informal rules of interaction and shared responsibility, often in the absence of any clear guidance from the central government (box 7.6).

Box 7.5. Paramount Chiefs and Local Councils as Partners: Case from One Chiefdom in the Southern Province

The Paramount Chief is an older woman and has been chief for more than 24 years. She has no formal education and prefers to speak Mende rather than Krio or English (of which she speaks none). She is unusually poor and humble for a Paramount Chief, living in a simple mud house paved with cement. On the research team's first visit to the chiefdom, they found the chief crouched in the dirt courtyard behind her house, surrounded by women and children, stirring food in a large pot. During more extended field work later, the team was struck by how accessible the chief was, not only to them but to others in the community. "[The Madam] is very good to us all and hates to see people taking advantage over others," said one respondent, a male community member who was otherwise quite aggrieved against authorities in the chiefdom.

The local councilor for that ward is a quite wealthy and prominent politician who had served in a ministry in Freetown and, at the time of this research, had family ties to the upper echelons of the ruling Sierra Leone People's Party (SLPP). After being elected councilor for his constituency, he was elected by his fellow councilors to be local council chairman for the district. The chiefdom headquarters is his home village, and he returns frequently—at times weekly—to stay there. His house is located just a few meters from the house of the Paramount Chief and, in contrast to hers, is among the nicest in town, with fresh paint, a zinc roof, and a large thatch-roofed barrie nearby.

Prior to the advent of the local councils, the Paramount Chief of this chiefdom did not play a large role outside of her own chiefdom and often was not included in meetings or other decisions made at the district or higher level. However, since the local council chairman took office, he has frequently invited her to participate in meetings in the district headquarters, and has even offered her a ride in his own car (as she does not own a car and transport from the chiefdom is extremely limited). The two seem to work well together. "The relationship between the councilor and PC is very cordial," said a community health officer (male, age 41). "They visit each other; they meet and discuss matters relating to the chiefdom."

Box 7.6. "Difficulty in Organizing Community Collective Action"

"Sometimes if we want the people to brush the road or construct the bridge, we lie to them that the Paramount Chief is visiting the village at a particular time. That is the only way people will turn up in large numbers. Otherwise it is difficult to get these men to work for the community."

—Ward development committee secretary and community teacher association chairman, Bombali District (male, age 42)

On some level, this close collaboration could be predictable and even inevitable. The councilors themselves come from the same social system that sees the Paramount Chief as the ultimate local authority and that demands deference to him/her and to subchiefs. The councilors are not necessarily any more likely to challenge or reject that system than are other members of the community, particularly other authorities.[78] Some chiefs also may get involved in supporting particular candidates for council elections, in which case these councilors may feel obligated to the chiefs thereafter.

Moreover, many councilors recognize—as does everyone working in rural Sierra Leone—that they will accomplish much more by working with the chiefs than by trying to work against or around them. In fact, the necessity for councilors to work with chiefs seems so obvious that perhaps the more difficult question is why—besides the legal requirement to do so—do the chiefs cooperate with the councilors? This research did not yield a ready answer to this question.

Councilors are heavily reliant on the chiefs in very tangible ways. One is the collection of local tax, which is done by the chiefdoms and then shared with the local councils (box 7.5). The chiefs also have a much greater ability to mobilize labor and enforce cooperation with community projects.[79] In one chiefdom in northern Bombali District, the research team came upon a group of people fixing a rough log bridge. Team members discovered that two of the people involved were local councilors from the neighboring wards. Wanting to fix the bridge but without the power to mobilize labor themselves, they had gone to the section chief and obtained his promise that he would mobilize a group of youths to help with the bridge. The youths never turned up—the councilors believe because the section chief did not fulfill his promise—so the frustrated councilors were left to fix the bridge themselves with the few people they caught passing by.[80]

Although the councilors may have been able to mobilize action without resort to the chiefs—by holding a public meeting, and persuading the community to participate, or by approaching youth leaders directly—they seemed to perceive the chiefs and local courts as their most likely avenue. (Local courts can be used to coerce participation by punishing those who refuse.) When the chief did not help, the councilors found it very difficult to get the bridge repaired.

Another form of reliance relates to the simple fact, mentioned earlier, that it is nearly impossible—and quite often illegal by chiefdom bylaws—to initiate community projects or activities without the permission of the Paramount Chief. This bar is reinforced by the policies of outside agencies that demand proof of local ownership and consultation in the form of the chiefs' involvement. In one chiefdom in Bombali District, researchers spoke to a very frustrated local councilor who had been trying for weeks to get the Paramount Chief to sign off on a small HIV/AIDS project. Funds were available, but to access them, the councilor needed the signatures of key local authorities. The Paramount Chief, a particularly inaccessible man, had not yet agreed to meet to discuss the matter. As a result, the project was on hold and in jeopardy. That the councilor was from one party, the chief was a known supporter of another party, and the chiefdom was deeply divided and embroiled in political disputes probably did not help.

These findings provide only a preliminary, incomplete picture of some of the ways that chiefs and local councilors interact in rural and peri-urban Sierra Leone. The interaction and engagement between these two important groups of authorities would be a rich area for further research, particularly as these relationships continue to evolve and adapt and as further devolution gives greater resources and decisionmaking power to the local councils. It also would be interesting to explore further the extent to which local councils and councilors actually mirror traditional power dynamics—for instance, what proportion of councilors come from traditional ruling elites—as is commonly the case with development committees and other "modern" structures.

Conclusions and Recommendations: Complex, Mixed System of Local Governance Is Here to Stay

This chapter gives a glimpse of the complex and dynamic nature of local justice and governance in rural and peri-urban Sierra Leone. It has shown that local justice and governance in these areas are delivered less by formal, modern state structures—the most "local" of which are the local courts and local councils—than by a complex network of institutions ranging in formality and sources of authority. The chapter also shows that these institutions are constantly evolving and adapting to changing norms and incentives.

Local councils have established a foothold in the local governance system since their reinstatement in 2004, but are just one of many authorities in rural Sierra Leone. Furthermore, the LCs are not divorced from traditional sources of power and authority. They also are not, in fact, very local, and in practice seem to rely on the sub-chiefs (at section and village level) and other traditional actors to fill the resulting governance gap. Councilors also engage extensively and often constructively with chiefs and other local leaders, both as a matter of pragmatism and because, with the majority of Sierra Leoneans, they share an acceptance of and respect for the legitimacy of chiefs.

Chieftaincy remains the most important system of authority across rural Sierra Leone. However, there are signs that the power of chiefs may have decreased since the war, and that people are increasingly willing to challenge chiefs and other local authorities over such issues as communal labor and (less commonly) the use of resources. Traditional authorities are associated with various forms of bias, corruption, and injustice, but so are many modern authorities. Average Sierra Leoneans express greater trust for their chiefs than for either the local councilors or central government officials. At its best, the chieftaincy helps to keep the peace and mobilize collective action, and provides systems for decisionmaking and for the resolution of disputes that are familiar and accessible to average community members. The chieftaincy system and other traditional institutions are also engaging constructively with the new "modern" structures and ideas—most prominently, the local councils, but also with concepts of human rights and democracy, and with civil society groups and various project management and development committees. TAs also are adapting to the changing norms and realities of the post-war era.

Ultimately, it is probably more helpful to see local governance and justice in Sierra Leone as an interdependent network of institutions and individuals with multiple and often overlapping sources of legitimacy than as a clear-cut duality between the "traditional" and the "modern." Just because a development committee is a "modern" creation, with members (supposedly) elected democratically and with representation by women, youth, and other marginalized populations, does not mean that the committee does not also reflect traditional power structures. On the other hand, just because customary law often has been and still can be discriminatory against women, youths, and non-landholding lineages, does not mean it cannot adapt to deliver justice more in line with modern notions of human rights.

Local actors themselves tend to understand and engage with governance and justice institutions in this way, exploiting the relative strengths and weaknesses of each institution. Councils and councilors have recognized that, if they are going to succeed, they need to work with, rather than against, the existing chiefdom governance structures. Chiefs have taken steps—albeit limited and sometimes superficial—to accommodate greater representation and consultation, particularly for youths and women. Individuals and communities frequently "forum shop" to find the system most likely to meet their needs in a given situation.

Outside actors (including Freetown elites) looking to improve local governance in rural and peri-urban Sierra Leone should likewise make efforts to understand and engage with the broad spectrum of systems operating at the local level, and to consider how to build on the strengths of both traditional and modern local governance and justice systems and to minimize their weaknesses. Much of what has been said about traditional forms of justice and governance—that they impose harsh and arbitrary judgments, and that they can be abusive, corrupt, and exclusive, serving the interest of a narrow set of elites while marginalizing the majority of citizens—also has been true of many "modern" systems in Sierra Leone. The important question is how best to eliminate these negative practices, in whichever system or systems are in place.

Rather than offer specific recommendations, the author would like to offer a few questions to provoke consideration and debate about how best to engage with local authority in rural and peri-urban Sierra Leone:

- Is it possible to promote more constructive engagement between chiefs and councils, or even to formalize the often ad hoc relationships between them? As one government participant in the review meeting for this chapter said, "These two systems could be married, with one complementing the other."[81]

- Could the network of formal and informal local authorities be mobilized as a series of checks and balances against one another, to help ensure greater monitoring and accountability all around? For instance, could village headmen, local youth leaders, women leaders, religious leaders, and civil society representatives be given explicit roles in monitoring and publicizing the activities of local councilors, Paramount Chiefs, and others?

- Instead of trying to create new institutions with little local legitimacy, such as village and ward development committees and project management committees—particularly given that such committees tend to mirror local forms of power and authority anyway—could traditional authorities be mobilized to play a similar role? If they were required to adhere to standards for inclusion, transparency, and good governance, the requirement could provide an opportunity to introduce such standards into traditional systems of governance.

- More generally, can some of the requirements of transparency and accountability applied to local councils and to some development projects be applied to the chieftaincy system? For example, could chiefs, like local councils, be mandated to make public their annual budgets and to allow review and comment by civil society groups and by ordinary citizens? Importantly, such mandates must be not only legislated but also enforced.

- Could reforms be introduced to make traditional authority systems more inclusive and representative? Specific changes could include broadening the franchise for chieftaincy elections, imposing term lengths on Paramount

Chiefs and other officials, formalizing the roles of youth and women leaders (and establishing and enforcing standards on how such individuals are selected and who qualifies), or encouraging more public and inclusive methods of decisionmaking, particularly about the use of chiefdom funds. More controversial reforms, such as eliminating the system of ruling houses, may be desirable but less politically palatable.

■ Can interventions achieve greater voice and agency—in both modern and traditional systems—for youths, women, strangers, and other marginalized groups? Research findings show that some changes in this regard are underway but have been limited and often superficial. Can traditional elites be convinced that it is in their own interest to allow, and even facilitate, a greater involvement by these groups? Creativity and persuasion can go a long way in this regard, as can using resources (such as for development projects) as leverage.

The dynamism and complexity of local authority in Sierra Leone could be seen as obstacles to effective delivery of justice and governance, or as opportunities to build a system that combines the local legitimacy of traditional sources of power with the best ideas from new, modern systems. People concerned with developing a lasting, effective form of local governance and justice in Sierra Leone that can deliver services, resolve disputes, and consolidate peace should find ways to engage constructively with both modern and traditional local authorities in rural and peri-urban Sierra Leone, and to build on their best tendencies while minimizing their worst.

Notes

[1] This chapter was written by Ryann Manning, but is based on fieldwork, analysis, and written contributions from the *Justice for the Poor* Sierra Leone research team, particularly Gibrill S. Jalloh, Lyttelton Braima, Hannah Hamida Karim, Edward Tengbeh, and Mahmoud Tarawallie. Other team members, including Geoffrey Pabie Koroma, Millicent Gbenjen, and international researcher John Combey, contributed through their field work and preliminary analysis. *Justice for the Poor* partnered with the Campaign for Good Governance (CGG), particularly Sheku Mambu and Valnora Edwin, in the design and implementation of this research, and later with Timap for Justice for follow-up research. (Both Timap and CGG are civil society organizations.) The author is also grateful for comments and contributions from *Justice for the Poor* team members, World Bank colleagues, external reviewers, and partners in Sierra Leone. The views, opinions, analysis, and recommendations in this report—and most certainly any defects or errors—are those of the author, and do not necessarily reflect the views of the World Bank, CGG, Timap for Justice, or other team members.

[2] Giuseppe Zampaglione, Senior Operations Officer, World Bank, in review comments on this chapter received October 28, 2008.

[3] One hears this not only from academics and civil society groups but also from average Sierra Leoneans. For a summary of the critiques raised during a series of consultative workshops conducted between 1999–2001, see Fanthorpe 2004a. The post-war Truth and Reconciliation Commission also included a long discussion of the history of Paramount Chieftaincy, including the darker sides (Truth and Reconciliation Commission of Sierra Leone 2004). Among the academics and other writers who have documented and discussed the abuses of the chiefs are Richards and others 2004, Archibald and Richards 2002, and Rennie 2006.

[4] Probably the most prominent advocate for this analysis is Paul Richards. See, for instance, Richards 2005, 571–90; and Chauveau and Richards 2008. For the broad strokes of Richards' argument, and the strokes of those who disagree with him, see Sawyer 2008, 389–93, as well as Richards' 2008 response to Sawyer's article. Sawyer argues that chieftaincy may not be as bad as Richards leads us to believe and presents findings of widespread support for chiefs, particularly as agents of local dispute resolution.

[5] This support—often paired with an acknowledgement of the abuses and other problems with traditional authority—is expressed frequently by local and Freetown elites as well as by average Sierra Leoneans, including those living in rural and peri-urban areas. This support emerges in the research explored later in this chapter as well as in other studies. For example, Fanthorpe argues, "For the poor, securing political leaders that remain downwardly accountable is an absolute priority. Many continue to find chiefs preferable to elected politicians and bureaucrats" (Fanthorpe 2005, 45).

[6] Although he does not frame it as a breakdown per se of the chiefdom social order, Fanthorpe argues that large numbers of rural youth were excluded from access to locally defined citizenship, as meted out by chiefdom authorities, and from the privileges—including access to "basic rights to land, living space, and legal protection"—that follow. He argues that "alarming numbers of people have become neither 'citizen' nor 'subject,'" a fact that he believes may help explain why many "underprivileged young Sierra Leoneans" embraced the RUF. (Fanthorpe 2001, 385). Ibrahim Abdullah does not focus on rural power dynamics or chiefs, but he also argues for a characterization of fighters as "lumpen" youth, "largely unemployed and unemployable youths, mostly male, who…are prone to criminal behaviour, petty theft, drugs, drunkenness, and gross indiscipline" (Abdullah 1997, 45–76).

[7] The country's Truth and Reconciliation Commission, for instance, documents the abuses of chiefs and other traditional authorities in both the colonial and post-colonial eras. However, it argues that these abuses resulted from the manipulation and co-optation of chiefs by the colonial authorities and, later, post-colonial political parties. "Chiefs lost sight of their traditional roles and neglected their duties to their subjects," argues the Commission's Final Report. "The Commission calls for the return of Chiefs to their traditional roles and functions… [and] for a national dialogue on the restoration of the Chiefs to their symbolic and traditional roles" (*The Final Report of the Truth and Reconciliation Commission* 2 (3): 59).

[8] Another recent paper tackles similar issues and is useful as a companion to this chapter. See Jackson 2006.

[9] In fact, such complexity can also be found within a single individual, such that the leader of a modern human rights organization is also a traditional chief and secret society member. To make this point in his review comments on this chapter, Guseppe Zampaglione used the example of an interview with the 3 major presidential candidates in the 2007 election during which 2 of the 3— after fluently speaking the language of development and good governance—confirmed that they belonged to secret societies. The third declined to answer the question. (G. Zampaglione, Senior Operations Officer, World Bank, in review comments on this chapter received on October 28, 2008.)

[10] For more information about Justice for the Poor or to download other papers based on this research, please visit http://www.worldbank.org/justiceforthepoor.

[11] "Timap" is a Krio word meaning "stand up." Timap for Justice is a local organization providing community-based paralegal services in a number of chiefdoms in Sierra Leone. Timap receives funding from the World-Bank-administered Japanese Social Development Fund (JSDF), and also partnered with *Justice for the Poor* on research and evaluation.

[12] For more information about the research methodology, please see *Research Methodology: Justice for the Poor and Understanding Processes of Change in Local Governance,* http://www.worldbank.org/ justiceforthepoor.

[13] Figure 7.1 does not include every authority at a community level but only those generally considered more important. At higher levels, it includes only the main justice institutions and the local council; the central government is not disaggregated into its components. It is important to note that figure 7.1 is generic rather than specific. It sketches the authorities common across most Sierra Leonean communities, rather than those present in any one specific location. There is a remarkable degree of consistency in these systems across geographic areas and sociocultural contexts in Sierra Leone. Nevertheless, such systems are inherently context specific and, in a particular place, may differ significantly from the norm.

[14] A recent study surveyed local court clerks in 30 chiefdoms in 4 districts and found that, according to the clerks, the 30 chiefdoms had a total of 56 local courts, of which 50 were operational. The research was sponsored by the Justice Sector Development Programme and designed and conducted in partnership with Justice for the Poor (Koroma 2007, 14).

[15] Local courts are governed by the *Local Courts Act 1963* (Government of Sierra Leone) and subsequent amendments (1965, 1966, 1974, 1975), which include limits on what punishments (fines) courts can assess. In fairness, the limits are based on long-outdated currency values and are highly inappropriate today. The legislation was last amended in 1975, and the monetary jurisdictional limits were last amended in 1965. At that time, the local courts were given jurisdiction "to hear and determine all criminal cases where the maximum punishment which may be imposed does not exceed a fine of two hundred leones" (Section 13, subsection 1, *The Local Courts (Amendment) Act 1965*, GoSL). Two hundred leones today is worth roughly US$0.07 and is not even enough to buy a small loaf of bread. Similarly, a table of allowable terms of imprisonment for nonpayment of fines is comical, if not tragic. A person who defaults on payment of a fine not exceeding 1.0 Le can be imprisoned for up to 7 days, and for non-payment of a fine exceeding 100 Le can be imprisoned for as much as 12 months (Section 26, subsection 1, *The Local Courts (Amendment) Act 1965*, GoSL). The smallest currency unit in use in Sierra Leone today is a 50 Le coin.

[16] The director of Timap for Justice, an NGO providing community-based paralegal services, said that when Timap offered training to a subset of local court officials in 2004, the NGO was told that it was the first training that the officials had received since the early 1980s (S. Koroma 2008).

[17] The Customary Law Office has primary responsibility for supervision of local courts. However, it does not have the power to appoint, remove, or discipline court chairpersons or clerks. The office also is understaffed. Although expanded in recent years, it employs just three customary law officers to cover the entire country. Local court supervisors are more numerous but are based in district headquarter towns and do not have the resources to conduct supervisory court visits.

[18] In part, the reason is that court chairpersons are recommended for their position by Paramount Chiefs. Sometimes the chiefs' influence on cases is systematic. In a Bombali chiefdom, a previous court chairman was alleged to have consulted the Paramount Chief on all cases before ruling. In other cases, the court is alleged in a particular case to have ruled in favor of a party with ties to chiefdom authorities. As one community member (male, age 37) claimed in a debt case in Bo District, "The court supported the [other] fellow because he was related to the Paramount Chief and court chairman."

[19] As one Paramount Chief said at a consultation on the draft Local Courts Act, "…if you take the authority of the local courts away from the Paramount Chiefs, they won't have any power." Consultation in Makeni, Bombali District. June 19, 2006.

[20] Researchers heard allegations of Paramount Chief interference in the courts of all three main provincial research sites (The fourth site, in the Western Area, has neither local courts nor

Paramount Chiefs.) In one case, the Paramount Chief in a Bo District chiefdom allegedly demanded that a case continue even if the parties wished to withdraw, and threatened to shut down the court if it did not continue the case. In another case, the same chief wrote to the court clerk to demand that it forbid a case moving forward, arguing that because all lands in the chiefdom are under the custody of the Paramount Chief, only he or people he selected could hear the case. In a Bombali court, when the chairman (who was said to have consulted the chief on all cases) and court clerk were removed by district-level authorities, the chief allegedly scared off replacement clerks to block the court from operating. Finally, in a Moyamba chiefdom, the Paramount Chief frequently encourages the parties to withdraw cases from the local court and bring them to him to settle "at home." Although this last example was seen positively by some respondents as a way to minimize antagonism and cost for the parties, it also had the potential for the chief to influence the outcome.

[21] Chieftaincies exist throughout the country *except* in the Western Area. As a result of the country's divided colonial system, in which Freetown and its environs (the Western Area) were governed as a colony while the rest of the country was governed indirectly as a protectorate, there are no chiefdoms in the Western Area.

[22] For more information about the qualifications and processes for Paramount Chieftaincy elections, see "Guideliness [sic] for the Election of Paramount Chiefs and Sub Chiefs," received from the Ministry of Local Government and Community Development during preparation for the Chiefdom Governance Reform Task Force, 2006.

[23] A very prominent recent case was the 2006 Biriwa chieftaincy dispute in which the majority Limba population challenged the qualification of the minority Mandingo population (whom they considered "strangers") to field a candidate. The Limbas also complained of biased and inappropriate interference from central government. The Limbas ultimately boycotted the process so a Mandingo was elected Paramount Chief of Biriwa chiefdom for the first time in history. Limba representatives appealed the outcome to the Supreme Court, but their petition was struck down in November 2006.

[24] These include the *Provinces Act (Cap 60) 1933* and the *Chiefdom Councils Act (Cap 61) 1938*. As it stands, the chieftaincy system had its origin in the country's colonial era, although in many areas it builds on a longer tradition. As the British colonial authorities spread their frontiers outward from the colony of Freetown and consolidated their power in the protectorate, they signed treaties with traditional rulers—some of whom had previously gone by the title "king"—and gave them the title of "Paramount Chief," at the same time making them subordinate to the colonial officials. The British also redrew boundaries, at times dividing chiefdoms whose rulers had become too powerful; at other times combining previously independent areas into consolidated chiefdoms, thereby creating chiefdoms with multiple ruling families or even multiple ethnic and cultural traditions. Between 1945 and 1959, the number of chiefdoms was reduced by the colonial authority from 217 to 149. (*Concept Chapter on Chiefdom Governance and Tribal Administration Reform.* Received from the Ministry of Local Government and Community Development during preparation for the Chiefdom Governance Reform Task Force, 2006.)

[25] "The institution of Chieftaincy as established by customary law and usage and its non-abolition by legislation is hereby guaranteed and preserved." *The Constitution of Sierra Leone 1991.* http://www.polhist.hu/alkotmanyok/sierraleone.pdf.

[26] Modified slightly from "Role, Functions, and Responsibilities of Paramount Chiefs and Chiefdom Administration," received from the Ministry of Local Government and Community Development during preparation for the Chiefdom Governance Reform Task Force, 2006.

[27] A civil servant hired and paid by the central government and managed by a district-level central chiefdom finance clerk.

[28] Alie 2007.

[29] Previously, local courts had been chaired by the local Paramount Chief, but this was changed prior to the country's independence.

[30] The survey asked about approximately six specific categories of grievances: disputes over loan or "money business," theft or attempted theft, child support, inheritance, land disputes, and assault. Institutional Reform and Capacity Building Project (IRCBP), *Report on the IRCBP 2007 National Public Services Survey*, May 2008.

[31] An exception is the chief in Moyamba district, mentioned earlier, who is perceived to be highly approachable and also lenient. People often bring cases, even minor cases, directly to her. By one account, they do so because they know the Paramount Chief will not ask them for money.

[32] For example, when members of a Bombali chiefdom wanted to pursue a man they say had stolen their money with false promises of a housing project, they sought the chief's blessing before taking action. Similarly, in another chiefdom, war amputees were promised various services by international organizations. When they found many of these promises unfulfilled, they involved the Paramount Chief in trying to seek redress. Another case in the same chiefdom against a diamond mining company that failed to rehabilitate the mining area or meet other obligations to the community followed a similar path. The Paramount Chief was approached first; but when he failed to attain redress, a paralegal organization got involved.

[33] Usually, a payment of some sort is expected before chiefs (including subchiefs) will hear cases. In the Moyamba research site, several respondents said "You can bring cases to chiefs without money, but they won't take them seriously."

[34] Exact numbers nationwide are hard to come by, but most chiefdoms seem to fall within this range.

[35] For example, the Office of Chiefdom Police is provided for in *The Chiefdom Police Act (Cap 112) 1959*. Subchiefs and headmen are recognized and governed by *The Provinces Act (Cap 60) 1933* and other Acts. Chiefdom councils are governed by *The Chiefdom Councils (Amendment) Act 1964* (GoSL). This is not an exhaustive list; a full review of relevant legislation is beyond the scope of this chapter.

[36] The *Tribal Authorities Act 1938* sets out the main functions of chiefdom councils, which are composed of chiefdom councilors, more commonly known as Tribal Authorities (TAs), each of whom is supposed to represent 20 taxpayers.

[37] IRCBP 2008. A similar survey conducted in 2005 in Bombali and Bonthe Districts asked about a slightly different collection of disputes. That survey found even higher use of village-level officials: 61 percent of minor crimes and disputes reported anywhere outside of the family were reported first to the village headman, and another 25 percent to the village elders (Manning and others 2006).

[38] IRCBP 2008.

[39] This disconnect was described by civil society participants in a discussion meeting about this and other J4P/LG papers held in October 2008. See Appendix B for details.

[40] The most recent government census (2004), found that 77 percent of people were Muslim, 21 percent Christian, and 2 percent other or no religion. Although fewer than 1 percent of respondents reported their religion as "traditional," the majority of Sierra Leoneans combine Christian or Muslim beliefs with various traditional beliefs.

[41] Most literature, as well as conventional wisdom, says that the majority (most say as high as 80 percent–90 percent) of people are initiated into secret societies. In contrast, a recent national household survey found that just 29 percent respondents nationally, rising to 37 percent in villages, identified themselves as members of traditional societies (IRCBP 2008). The cause of this discrepancy is unclear, but there may have been problems with translating the survey, or of people under-reporting to enumerators.

[42] As a 2004 report argues, "In many Chiefdoms, governance issues of critical importance are addressed within the confines of secret societies and not by chiefdom governance structures. These issues are likely to be longstanding disputes dealing with land and/or local political authorities" (DfID 2004, 14). Another 2004 study discusses societies (sodalities) as a form of social capital (P. Richards and others, 2004, 9–11). In a more recent article, R. Fanthorpe argues that Sierra Leone's societies have tended to be strengthened rather than threatened by political modernity. He argues that societies played an important role during the civil war, and in its aftermath were one of the institutions that many people were anxious to reinstate. Using newspaper reports as evidence, he highlights a number of incidents in post-war Sierra Leone that he says illustrate the societies' continued importance, particularly in politics and community-level disputes (Fanthorpe 2007).

[43] Fanthorpe 2007, 9.

[44] For instance, it remains usual (and often mandatory) for candidates for Paramount Chieftaincy to be members of the local society. However, some newer and more educated chiefs seem to have more lukewarm views on the societies. Other individuals whose parents served important roles in the local society have refused on religious or other grounds to take their places. In a peri-urban community in the Western Area, respondents confirmed that societies used to play many of the decisionmaking and dispute-resolution functions outlined above, but argued that the societies had declined significantly as a result of urbanization and Islam. Even in the most remote of the main research sites, Moyamba District—well known for the strength of its cultural practices, including the Sande, Poro, and Wunde societies—there are signs that the local Poro society has significantly decreased in power and influence. For example, the Poro society used to be responsible for cleaning the water wells and setting rules for their use but no longer does so. In another case from the same chiefdom, authorities refused to support the initiation of a local Poro society and later ruled against the society members in a rare public hearing. One respondent argued that the influence of secret societies in that chiefdom had diminished due to the spread of Islam. (Respondent details not available.)

[45] For more information about the changing role and status of youths in Sierra Leone, see R. Manning forthcoming.

[46] For example, a 45-year old female chief in one northern chiefdom said the chief "sometimes" consulted her when he wanted to take decisions and involved her in chiefdom activities. Asked for an example, she cited the case in which the country's president and vice president visited the chiefdom, and she was asked to mobilize female drummers and singers to entertain the visiting dignitaries.

[47] Respondent's age not available.

[48] For example, community-driven projects sponsored by NaCSA (National Commission for Social Action, a World Bank-supported government agency) must be managed by a 10-person project management committee (PMC). In at least one case, a community that already had a NaCSA PMC decided on its own to create a new PMC for a separate project, a school funded by the European Union, even though the EU neither required any such community participation nor allowed any real role for the PMC. Other development agencies often will require that communities form special project committees. For instance, researchers found such committees linked to World Vision, Action Aid, and even local-council-funded projects.

[49] For instance, one respondent alleged that PMC members in a Bo District chiefdom were appointed by the councilor who first initiated the project and that her husband was the PMC chairman. The PMC in one Moyamba research site is particularly striking. The (female) Paramount Chief's nephew is the storekeeper, and her daughter is the PMC treasurer; the PMC secretary is from the other ruling house in the chiefdom and is a nephew of the former Member of Parliament; the PMC chairman is the son of a section chief; and the NaCSA contract was

awarded to the Paramount Chief's son-in-law, husband to the PMC treasurer. Jackson notes the same sorts of dynamics, noting that NGOs have a tendency to work with Village Development Committees (VDCs) which "tend to be dominated by those within the patronage networks rather than outside" (Jackson 2006, 100).

[50] For example, the head teacher in a Bombali chiefdom had successfully applied for funding for both an EU-funded school and a NaCSA-funded clinic. For the former, he said he noticed a billboard in a neighboring town advertising that the school had been built by the EU and then asked around until he found out how to contact the EU office, to which he wrote directly.

[51] The fact that they recognize and permit, if not facilitate, the facilitators' role suggests it is something they value. Moreover, communities that lack such an individual often bemoan the absence, and attribute—perhaps rightly—their own failure to benefit from development projects to the lack of an educated individual (a "book man") to advocate on their behalf.

[52] This was evident from field research, but also has been noted by other observers. See, for instance, Richards and others (2004), 36. "Rural people are now more prepared to challenge authority and seek accountability from government or other service providers."

[53] Respondents from Freetown are excluded because there are no Paramount Chiefs in Freetown.

[54] IRCBP 2008.

[55] IRCBP 2008. Respondents were asked, "If the [Paramount Chief/local council/government in Freetown] was given 500 million Leones to complete a project in this area, do you believe they would spend all the money doing a good job on the project or would they cut [steal] some of the money?" There were five response options: "They would do a great job and spend all the money"; "They would do a good job but cut a little money"; "They would do a bad job and cut most of the money"; "They would just take all the money"; or "Don't know." Responses were scored from 0 to 3. Paramount chiefs scored an average of 1.7, significantly higher than local councils (1.3) and central government (1.4).

[56] IRCBP 2008. The question asked was, "In your opinion, do you believe [.......] or do you have to be careful dealing with them?" Answer options were "Can be believed"; "Have to be careful"; or "Don't know/no opinion."

[57] For a longer discussion of families and chiefs in rural Sierra Leone, see Richards and other 2004.

[58] "Ruling families" are most formalized in the case of Paramount Chiefs. See section below on Paramount Chieftaincy. Ruling families also exist in some places at a town or even section level, although this varies from place to place.

[59] As a deputy town chief (male, age 41) in one Moyamba chiefdom said, "The chieftaincy here is based on inheritance, but if a stranger is serious, active and is able to organize well, the people sometimes make that person chief." In another chiefdom, a man was allowed to stand for section chief despite not being from a ruling house, primarily because for 35 years he had continued to pay local tax in that chiefdom despite living in another province, thus proving his "love" for the chiefdom. After campaigning vigorously, he was elected unanimously by the 36 TAs in his section, earning himself the nickname "Jama" or "Crowd Puller."

[60] As mentioned earlier, project management committees formed to manage specific development projects often mirror other types of authority in the chiefdom and have members from chieftaincy families or with strong ties to those families.

[61] As one Paramount Chief said, the good works of the father convince people to "compensate" the son, although they also take into account the son's character. (Bombali District, June 2006 preliminary field work.)

[62] Exceptions do exist. For instance, in a Bombali chiefdom in May 2006, two women competed for the position of woman chief. The election was by open headcount, and the winner was both younger and a stranger.

[63] Tribal heads interviewed by researchers include those representing the Fullah, Limba, Mende, Sherbro, Susu, and Temne groups. Others also may exist but these were the most prominent.

[64] This marginalization is discussed in greater detail in Richards and others (2004). As they say, "…the rural community is typically divided between leading lineages and the rest, and that the most severe poverty and vulnerability is mainly found among strangers and members of weaker lineages." (p. (c))

[65] As one male respondent in a remote Moyamba chiefdom said, his youth and "stranger" status combined to prevent him from challenging an authority. "I cannot condemn the youth leader because I am a stranger and a small boy," he said. (Age of respondent not available.)

[66] The 2007 national election can be seen as a partial break with that tradition. Although the majority of votes still followed ethnic lines, there were some surprises, particularly in the run-off between the northern and Temne-dominated All People's Congress (APC) party and the southern and Mende-dominated Sierra Leone People's Party (SLPP). After coming in third in the first round, the new PMDC (People's Movement for Democratic Change) party, the founder of which had only recently broken from the SLPP and which therefore had its roots in the Mende-dominated South, threw its support in the run-off behind the APC, which likely contributed to the APC's eventual win.

[67] For one discussion of these tensions, see Richards and others 2004.

[68] A 33-year-old male community member from a Moyamba chiefdom used this expression.

[69] A 38-year-old male youth leader from a Bombali chiefdom used this expression.

[70] This is the "principle of seniority" in anthropology and is used by many societies.

[71] For more information about the changing role and status of youths in Sierra Leone, see Manning forthcoming.

[72] This is evident from field research but also has been noted by others. See, for example, Richards and others 2004, 42.

[73] A large number of respondents attributed change to sensitization. The quoted expression comes from a representative of one such NGO, who said that women's participation had increased dramatically "thanks to…NGOs that have been able to raise awareness of both the rulers and the ruled." (Respondent age and gender not available.)

[74] The respondent went on to accuse local government officials of misusing these tools, and said the councilor had been awarded a construction contract from an international organization to build toilets in the village but had never completed the work. "If that contract was given to a private individual, we would have gone after him to come back and complete it," the respondent said, suggesting that—in this case at least—the involvement of a councilor actually hurt the cause of accountability.

[75] IRCBP 2008, 27.

[76] These ambiguities and the resulting conflicts are discussed in Jackson 2006.

[77] Floyd Davies, Legal Expert, Decentralization Secretariat, J4P/LG discussion meeting, October 28, 2008.

[78] It may be that councilors, by virtue of holding their positions, do feel more able to challenge traditional systems than an average community member. However, there is no reason to believe that this is significantly different than for other authorities, such as religious leaders, society heads, or the informal development brokers and other "big men."

[79] This power to mobilize labor also has been abused in the past and has been cited by some as a contributing factor in the civil war. (See, for example, Richards and others 2004.) Today, it may be a double-edged sword: chiefs mobilizing young men to provide labor may reap the benefits (whether individually or collectively) but may risk breeding resentment that would spark a return to violence.

[80] In another case mentioned earlier, a councilor used the local court to enforce the involvement of several villages that did not show up to work on a road project to which they had previously agreed. However, this project originated with town chiefs rather than the councilor, so the scenario was somewhat different.

[81] Charles Rogers, Deputy Commissioner, National Commission for Social Action (NaCSA), J4P/LG discussion meeting, October 28, 2008.

CHAPTER 8

Reflections and Conclusions on Positives and Problems Resulting from Devolution to Date

Emmanuel Gaima

Begun in 2004, implementation of the National Decentralization Program in Sierra Leone has successfully achieved the stipulated four-year transition phase (June 2004–June 2008). This reform and its reintroduction of (non-indigenous) local governance structures have brought in their wake a number of issues that will require reflection, especially by active participants and stakeholders.

The push that precipitated the decentralization reform came primarily from within the country, with triggers at the level of former President Kabbah. However, given the lack of enthusiasm from some ministers, senior administrative, and professional officers in the bureaucracy, it could be discerned that not all in positions of authority at the time shared the president's vision, commitment, and passion for decentralization. The discrepancies in perception and appreciation had varying effects on the launch of the program and led to a delayed and prolonged start, subsequent slow-downs, and the frequent need to revise implementation plans. The divergent views often placed the IRCBP staff in direct confrontation with government functionaries who normally accused them of applying "undue haste" to the implementation. The MDAs, and to greater extent, even the supervising Ministry of Local Government and Rural Development, often demonstrated their lack of enthusiasm and interest in the implementation by failing to act on pressing matters in a timely manner.

The preparatory work for formulating the IRCBP was facilitated by the National Governance Reform Secretariat (GRS), which played a catalytic and midwifery role. The decision to house the planning and preparatory work in a quasi-civil service entity such the GRS paid its dividend: tasks were carried out professionally in a timely manner and due diligence was observed with results. In all of this, World Bank took a very aggressive posture that culminated in leading the reform, surpassing even in-country donor institutions including DfID, EC, and UNDP. The huge injection of capital, technical assistance, and close implementation support ultimately led to the "passive" acceptance of the World Bank by the other partners as lead supporting agency, and whatever institutional rivalry for prominence had existed was submerged. The World Bank's response to the national requirement for national institutional capacity building support was timely and meaningful. With an initial investment portfolio of US$25 million, the Bank supported the GoSL through a funding window, the Institutional Reform and Capacity Building Project (IRCBP). The IRCBP's overall Project Development Objective (PDO) is to "support the establishment of nineteen functioning local council functioning in a transparent and accountable manner." This funding supported the overall start-up investment in practically everything, from provision of basic office equipment, office working space, and transportation to the bulk of the capacity building and training to financing development projects.

The IRCBP has been recognized nationwide as the program/project that gave effect and meaning to Sierra Leone's national decentralization program. It started off as a wholly World-Bank-funded intervention, but, true to the spirit of coordination and harmonization, other development partners gradually were brought on board. Their entry point came in the form of invitations to participate in the World Bank Implementation Support Missions (ISMs) to review progress of project implementation against progress indicators as well as to review the various approved annual work plans. The leadership that IRCBP has been able to provide to a greater extent than had the country has been due to three facts: (a) most of the native-born professionals are young and desirous of contributing to national development; (b) they have not been part of the country's ailing civil service, which has an unimpressive record of poor performance, and (c) they are relatively well remunerated compared to civil servants in the country. The strong individual and professional profile and personality trait of the first task team leader, sometimes thought to drive "so hard" and often considered to set near impossible targets, has continued to inspire and motivate.

The entire notion of elected local governance seemingly was new to Sierra Leone in 2004 when it was reintroduced after an absence of 32 years (1972–2004). The majority of Sierra Leoneans had had no experience living and working within this system so were unaware of what the reform would entail in practice. The profiles of the majority of the newly elected local councilors not only indicated inadequate education or schooling but also belonged to a generation who had not lived in the era during which Sierra Leone had had a functioning local governance system. This new group of local politicians and the constituents whom they served and serviced needed to stay focused on two processes at once. The first was community development. Second, the politicians needed a mechanism to both inform and assure their constituents that a new dawn had arrived, that a new group of local politicians were now holding and managing the constituents' individual and collective destinies. The World Bank and GoSL project team felt the need to convince the constituents that development was the key aspiration and that the Rapid Results Approach (RRA) provided not only the impetus but also the mechanism by which to stimulate community partnerships through participation. These partnerships would lead to the identification, design, and implementation of a wide range and variety of community development projects.

The RRA was very warmly received by local council leaders and affected citizens. Nevertheless, the enthusiasm had to be periodically re-energized because the RRA soon faced a number of challenges. One was the resistance from elected councilors to bring in "ordinary" and unelected community members and give them strategic roles. The arrogance of power of the elected councilors quickly emerged and, in some cases, slowed much anticipated "quick wins."

The decentralization reform in Africa has faced resistance and bottlenecks that usually have been bureaucratic in nature and were caused mainly by politicians, with active connivance from sector professionals. In the case of Sierra Leone, despite the political commitment at the highest level of the president and vice president, functional devolution commenced very slowly. Since resistance was inherent in the MDAs, the IRCBP, through the Decentralization Secretariat (DecSec), advised the minister responsible for local government to advocate at the level of the Inter-Ministerial Committee (IMC) for the roll-out of functional devolution to start with the three strategic sector ministries. These were the sectors that supported GoSL's human development, growth promotion, and poverty reduction agendas. They included Health and Sanitation, Education, Science and Technology, and Agriculture and Food Security.

There was some amount of cooperation in the health sector so it took the lead in the roll-out. A special session was convened with all district medical officers during their annual professional summit. At that conference, a paper was presented by the director of decentralization on the benefits of heath devolution. The paper analyzed devolution's impact on health care delivery as well as efficiency gains to be made. This paper accelerated devolution in that all-important sector. The Education sector was the least supportive and continually presented the excuse of inadequate data to effect meaningful planning, thus forestalling setting the roll-out date.

The devolution roll-out provided the IRCBP Team the opportunity to realize the lack of a national culture of proper and serious data collection and management. The MDAs collected, and to a greater extent horded, the data, which had to be (illegally) paid for by any entity that requested the information. In the absence of such payments, excuses were made of nonavailability (as was done by the Education Ministry), thereby leading to an imperfect roll-out of functions. There also were evidences of manipulation of technocrats and professionals by the ministers, who were not enthusiastic about devolution. For example, cooperation always was hindered in instances in which such professionals were not convinced of the extent to which their political leadership would give approval.

To ensure that there was harmony among stakeholders on devolution implementation as a goal and an understanding of the roll-out mechanism, using the RRA, the project designed Devolution Roll-out Planning Workshops. These created a forum, facilitated by the IRCBP and acting under the mandate of the Ministries of Finance and Local Government, for the devolving sectors to meet and discuss with the local authorities the roll-out plan as well as the assumption of the devolved functions by local councils. The key product of the numerous roll-out workshops were the Devolution Roll-out Action Plans. They detailed the responsibilities, delivery timeframes, lead persons, and progress milestones/indicators; and provided for mid-point reviews. Next, each action plan was launched in the local authority locale and involved civil society as moderators and advocates for full and effective devolution. Based on the success rating of the first three sectors, this arrangement was used subsequently to roll out functions in other sectors. Initially intended to support local authorities' project management, the RRA was adapted to provide facilitating policy support to jump start and accelerate what would have been a doomed or stalled functional devolution program. In the beginning, the RRA received wide and popular acclamation. However, enthusiasm later dropped, leading to frequent re-energizing through refreshers, known as "clinics." *The notion of community involvement, especially in procurement of goods, works, and services, coupled with the strict monitoring of milestones of progress, proved to be too transparent and nonsupportive of the usual abuse that enabled key stakeholders to enrich themselves..*

Since the inception of the program in Sierra Leone, the Bank has continued to provide financial, technical, and institutional support assistance to GoSL. The requirements of managing World-Bank-funded programs make it mandatory to prepare Annual Work Plan/Programs (AWPs), whereas central MDAs are not subject to such demands regarding their operations. This mismatch generated many implementation challenges, especially related to accomplishing tasks within finite timeframes and to some project activities having to depend on MDAs to release a trigger. MDA staff often accused project staff of rushing them because of the project staff's relatively better incentives. On the other side, MDA staff's resistance to meeting deadlines frustrated contracted project staff, who are subject to performance assessment for key deliverables.

The AWPs were supposed to be considered, reviewed, and approved by a Technical Steering Committee (TSC), which was chaired by professional and administrative heads of the Ministries of Finance and Local Government. However, the committee hardly ever met in a timely manner and invariably delayed approvals. *The institutional overhang from senior public officials and the absence of a culture of delegation of authority to take decisions undermined the activities and operations of the TSC to provide any meaningful technical oversight of IRCBP.* In addition, *the Bank's normal insistence that Ministry of Finance officials sit on all major World-Bank-financed-project organs, such as Sierra Leone's TSC, often subdues mandates of sector ministries and departments of finance, and in Sierra Leone's case, undermined enthusiasm.*

The GoSL is required to process, through the MoF, withdrawal applications for tranche releases of funds into the project's special account to finance project and program implementation. In Sierra Leone, this process was, and still is, faced with excessive bureaucratic delays. The weak performance of the national revenue system also makes it almost impossible for the government to meet its counterpart obligations. This weakness compromised support to the subcomponent on local government infrastructural investment because it often delayed payments to contractors. In addition, there always have been unnecessary delays often created by bureaucratic difficulties. One source is the perception by processing officers that no direct benefits and/or incentives accrue to them, whereas non-civil-service personnel in project implementation units (PIUs) such as the IRCBP reap the benefits of work (processing the withdrawal applications) that they (civil servants) undertake for "free."

The fiscal decentralization component suffered from the unpredictability of transfers to local authorities by MDAs. This unpredictability makes planning and budgeting by the local authorities very difficult despite the huge investment in capacity building for them to execute such tasks. With the increasing and heavy reliance of local government entities on central government transfers, the delays undermined the provision and delivery of frontline services in several documented instances. Over the last years, the Ministry of Finance and Economic Development (MoFED) has failed to mentor the local councils in revenue mobilization.

Simultaneously, considerations of power consolidation made it difficult for the ministry responsible for local government to harmonize the fiscal difficulties between chiefdoms and local councils regarding raising and collecting revenue. It should be noted that despite capacity building and training efforts by the IRCBP and other national and international entities, the inability of local authorities to mobilize adequate own resources is still a huge challenge. *Inadequate own revenue mobilization is perhaps the county's second most serious risk,* following only the unresolved human resource policy issues facing, and ultimately threatening, the future effectiveness of local councils, local governance, and decentralization in Sierra Leone.

In July 2008, the second local government elections in Sierra Leone were conducted, ushering in the second group of mayors, chairs, and councilors of local councils. The preparation was saddled with great controversy, beginning with the delimitation of ward boundaries, the first since 1956. Complaints about the formula used include:

- The new ward boundaries sometimes ignored issues of homogeneity of localities and culture, and may have created wards of significantly differing sizes.
- In areas in which co-located councils exist, placed in district councils facilities that, prior to the 2008 delimitation, had belonged to the neighboring city councils.
- The National Election Commission (NEC) was accused by civil society organizations (CSOs) and opposition parties of failing to organize broad-based consultations to elicit citizens' input in the delimitation exercise.

The political parties also were subject of controversy and crisis. The procedures for assessing and awarding party candidacy were said to be suspect, and most citizens in localities expressed the opinion that party candidacies were sold to people who were little known. It must be stated that, in Sierra Leone, in which political parties are polarized by regions, a candidate's capabilities do not matter. The people are more inclined to vote along partisan lines than on the basis of candidates' merit. The ruling All Peoples Congress (APC) Party returned to office the majority of the local governments in the country,—a total of 10 of 19 local government entities. The main opposition, the Sierra Leone People's Party (SLPP), controls eight returned local councils, and the third and party, the Peoples Movement for Democratic Change (PMDC) controls 1 local government in the Bonthe City Council.

The turnover rate was alarmingly high. However, it should not be hastily assumed that the first group of mayors, chairs, and councilors totally failed to deliver on their electoral mandates. What is certain is that people were much more interested in the 2008 election than the 2004 election. There were much more qualified and better resourced candidates who emerged in the political parties and were able to replace previous office occupants by first overtaking them for party candidacy. Of the aspirants who had lost candidacy at the hands of political party executives and who consequently contested as independents, only a few were able to win their ward elections.

Unlike those of 2004, the outcomes of the 2008 local council elections have shown a marked degree of partisanship and political polarization. There is a sharp North-Western divide in favor of the ruling APC, while South-Eastern (with exception of Kono District in the East) is a stronghold of the opposition SLPP. PMDC lost prominence in districts in which that party had made a strong showing in the 2007 Parliamentary and Presidential elections. This new partisanship is worrisome because it may divert the focus from cooperation and collaboration for the sake of community empowerment and development to an obsession with rivalry and entrenching support at all costs.

There is more partisan behavior within multiparty councils now than in the last four years. This "naked' competition is manifested primarily by the ruling APC and the opposition SLPP. Partisan behavior is shown less by the PMDC. As noted above, prior to the local government elections, the PMDC had been considered the fastest growing political party in Sierra Leone, but its growth has stalled since the elections.

The future trend of how the respective elements and forces will play out is anyone's guess, but one thing is certain. The seeds of local government and decentralization sown in 2004 have germinated and have even greater potential that will blossom and mature in the future. The creation of an enabling environment supportive of sound policies and an ensured, appropriate legal and regulatory framework can produce remarkable dividends in the years ahead.

IRCBP Evaluations Unit: Overview of Surveys

Title	Date of Collection	Geographic Coverage	Unit of Analysis	Sample	Topics
2008 School Survey	Nov 2008	National	School	409 schools, stratified at local council level	Teacher activities, school supplies, school finances, decision making, and supervision
2008 National Public Services	Oct 2008	National	Household and village	6,340 households, nationally representative, clustered by census enumeration area	Access to, cost of, and satisfaction with public services; knowledge of and attitudes toward government; social capital
2008 Decentralization Stakeholder Survey	May/Sept 2008	National	Individual	All paramount chiefs, local councilors, and district ministry officials. candidates, and voters in LC elections. Newly elected local councilors.	Personal background, experiences with decentralization, relationships among stakeholders
2008 PHU (Clinic) Survey	Jan/Feb 2008	National	Clinic	450 clinics, stratified at district level	Infrastructure, staffing, drug stocks, decision making, supervision, observations of consultations, exit interviews, vignettes

Title	Date of Collection	Geographic Coverage	Unit of Analysis	Sample	Topics
2008 PHU (Clinic) Survey	Jan/Feb 2008	National	Clinic	450 clinics, stratified at district level	Infrastructure, staffing, drug stocks, decision making, supervision, observations of consultations, exit interviews, vignettes
2007 National Public Services	May/June 2007	National	Household and village	6,338 households, nationally representative, clustered by census enumeration area	Access to, cost of, and satisfaction with public services; knowledge of and attitudes toward government; social capital
2006 PHU (Clinic) Survey	Oct 2006	National	Clinic	220 clinics, nationally representative	Infrastructure, staffing, drug stocks, decision making, supervision
2005 GoBifo/ENCISS	Nov 2005/ Jan 2006	Bombali and Bonthe Districts	Household and village	2,799 households, 665 key informants, 234 villages; clustered by ward and village	Social capital, trust, participation, access to information, local governance, conflict resolution, war experience, and farming
2005 PHU (Clinic) Survey - SSL	Sept 2005	National	Clinic	100 clinics, nationally representative	Infrastructure, staffing, drug stocks, decision making, supervision
2005 PHU (Clinic) Survey - PETS	Sept 2005	National	Clinic	515 clinics	Infrastructure, staffing, drug stocks, decision making, supervision

Title	Date of Collection	Geographic Coverage	Unit of Analysis	Sample	Topics
2005 School Survey	May/June 2005	National	School (some teacher and class-level data)	292 schools, stratified by school type and local council area	Teacher activities, school supplies, school finances
2005 National Public Services	Feb/March 2005	National	Household	6341 households, nationally representative, clustered by census enumeration area	Access to and satisfaction with public services, knowledge of, and attitudes toward government

References

Abdullah, I. 1997. "Bush Path to Destruction: The Origin and Character of the Revolutionary United Front (RUF/SL)." *African Development* 22 (3/4).

Alie, J.A.D. 2007. Lecture to J4P/SL research team training. Fourah Bay College, University of Sierra Leone. January 23.

Archibald, S., and P. Richards. 2002. "Converts to Human Rights? Popular Debate about War and Justice in Rural Central Sierra Leone." *Africa: Journal of the International African Institute* 72 (3).

Bahl, R. 1999. "Implementation Rules for Fiscal Decentralization." Paper presented at the International Seminar on Land Policy and and Economic Development, Land Reform Training Institute, Taiwan.

Bahl, R., and J. Martinez-Vasquez. 2006. "Sequencing Fiscal Decentralization." World Bank Research Working Paper 3914. Poverty Reduction and Economic Management (PREM), Public Sector Governance Group, World Bank.

Bardhan, P. 2002. "Decentralization of Governance and Development." *Journal of Economic Perspectives* 16 (4): 185–205.

Bardhan, P., and D, Mookherjee. 2000. "Capture and Governance at Local and National Levels." *American Economic Review* 90 (2): 135–39.

_____. 2006. "Decentralization, Corruption and Government Accountability: An Overview." In *International Handbook on the Economics of Corruption*, ed. Susan Rose-Ackerman. Northampton, MA: Edward Elgar.

Blunt, P., and M. Turner. 2005. "Decentralization, Democracy and Development in a Post-Conflict Society: Commune Councils in Cambodia." *Public Administration and Development* 25: 75–87.

Chauveau, J., and P. Richards. 2008. "West African Insurgencies in Agrarian Perspective: Cote d'Ivoire and Sierra Leone Compared." *Journal of Agrarian Change* 4 (8) (October).

Dale, P. 2008. *Access to Justice in Sierra Leone: A Review of the Literature*. World Bank Group. May. http://siteresources.worldbank.org/INTJUSFORPOOR/Resources/ Access2JusticeSierraLeoneLitReview.pdf (09_10_08).

DfID (Department for International Development). 2004. *Identifying Options for Improving Chiefdom and Community Governance in Sierra Leone*. UK.

Fanthorpe, R. 2001. "Neither Citizen nor Subject? 'Lumpen' Agency and the Legacy of Native Administration in Sierra Leone." *African Affairs* 100 (2001): 363–86.

Fanthorpe, R. 2004a. "Chiefdom Governance Reform Programme Public Workshops: An Analysis of the Facilitators' Reports." University of Sussex Anthropology Department. Unpublished. September.

_____. 2004b "Chieftancy and the Politics of Post-War Reconstruction in Sierra Leone." Unpublished.

_____. 2005. "On the Limits of the Liberal Peace: Chiefs and Democratic Decentralization in Post-War Sierra Leone." *African Affairs* 105: 1–23.

_____. 2007. "Sierra Leone: The Influence of the Secret Societies, with Special Reference to Female Genital Mutilation." A Writenet Report. United Nations High Commissioner for Refugees. New York.

Fanthorpe, R., A. Jay, and V.K. Kamara. 2002. "Chiefdom Governance Reform Programme." Formerly "Paramount Chiefs Restoration Programme." DfID. London.

Fox, W.F. 2007. "Fiscal Decentralization in Post-Conflict Countries." USAID Best Practice Paper. Fiscal Reform and Economic Governance Project, USAID, Washington, DC.

GoBiFo. 2005. GoBifo/ENCISS/Decentralization Baseline Survey. http://www.ircbpeval.com/surveys/gbf-2005.html

GoSL (Government of Sierra Leone). 1933. The Provinces Act (Cap 60). Freetown.

_____. 1938a. The Chiefdom Councils Act (Cap 61). Freetown.

_____. 1938b. Role, Functions and Responsibilities of Paramount Chiefs and Chiefdom Administration.

_____. Tribal Authorities Act 1938. Ministry of Local Government and Community Development, Freetown.

_____. The Chiefdom Police Act (Cap 112) 1959. Freetown.

_____. The Local Courts Act 1963. Freetown.

_____. The Chiefdom Councils (Amendment) Act 1964. Freetown.

_____. The Local Courts (Amendment) Act 1965. Freetown.

_____. The Constitution of Sierra Leone 1991. Freetown. http://www.polhist.hu/alkotmanyok/sierraleone.pdf

_____. The Local Government Act 2004a. Freetown.

_____. 2004. National Population and Housing Census. Statistics Sierra Leone (SSL). Freetown.

_____. 2004. "Report of the Public Expenditure Tracking Survey of Financial Year 2002 Selected Expenditures." Ministry of Finance. Freetown.

_____. 2006a. "Devolution Roll-out Plan." Ministry of Agriculture and Food Security (MAFS). Freetown.

_____. 2006b. "Government Budget and Statement of Economic and Financial Policies for the Financial Year, 2007." Delivered by John O. Benjamin, Minister of Finance in the Chamber of Parliament Tower Hill. Freetown. October 27.

_____. 2008. "Local Council Stock-Taking Report." Decentralization Secretariat.

Humphreys, M., and J.M. Weinstein. 2008. "Who Fights? The Determinants of Participation in Civil War." *American Journal of Political Science* 52: 436–55.

IFES (International Federation of Electoral Systems Ltd.). 2004. "Support to the Sierra Leone Local Government Elections 2004." Freetown.

IRCBP (Institutional Reform and Capacity Building Project). 2008. "Report on the IRCBP National Public Services Survey: Public Services, Governance, Dispute Resolution and Social Dynamics." Unpublished.

IMF (International Monetary Fund). 2005. "Rebuilding Fiscal Institutions in Post-Conflict Countries." Fiscal Affairs Department, Washington, DC.

IRCBP (Institutional Reform and Capacity Building Project). 2005a. Capacity Building Strategy to Support Decentralization in Sierra Leone: Discussion Draft.

_____. 2005b. National Public Services survey.

_____. 2007. National Public Services survey.

_____. 2008a. "Guideliness [sic] for the Election of Paramount Chiefs and Sub Chiefs."

_____. 2008b. "Report on the IRCBP 2007 National Public Services Survey." May.

_____. 2004–08. IRCBP Quarterly, Annual, and Mid-Term Evaluation Reports. www.ircbp.sl.

Jackson, P. 2006. "Reshuffling an Old Deck of Cards? The Politics of Local Government Reform in Sierra Leone." African Affairs 106: 95–110.

Kaufmann, D., A. Kraay, and M. Mastruzzi. 2006. "Governance Matters V: Governance Indicators for 1996–2005. World Bank Institute.

Keen, D. 2005. Conflict and Collusion in Sierra Leone. New York: Palgrave.

Koroma, B. 2007. "Local Courts Record Analysis Survey in Sierra Leone." Justice Sector Development Program, GoSL. Freetown.

Koroma, S. 2008. Presentation to the Justice Sector Donor Coordination Group. Freetown. April 2.

Manning, R., P. Dale, and L. Foster. 2006. Crime and Conflict Statistics from the GoBifo/ENCISS/ Decentralization Survey. World Bank Group.

Manning, R. Forthcoming. Challenging Generations: Youths and Elders in Rural and Peri-Urban Sierra Leone. World Bank. http://www.worldbank.org/justiceforthepoor.

National Election Commission of Sierra Leone (NEC). 2005. Statement from the Chief Electoral Commissioner/Chair at the Press Conference. May 20. www.nec-sierraleone.org

Rennie, N. 2006. Silenced Injustices in Moyamba District. Justice Sector

Development Programme Sierra Leone. October. http://www.britishcouncil.org/silence_injustices_in_moyamba_district.pdf (12/16/08).

Reno, W. 1995. Corruption and State Politics in Sierra Leone. Cambridge and New York: Cambridge University Press.

_____. Reno, W. 2003. "Political Networks in a Failing State: The Roots and Future of Violent Conflict in Sierra Leone." Internationale Politik und Gesellschaft 10 (2).

Richards, P. 1996. Fighting for the Rainforest: War, Youth and Resources in Sierra Leone. Oxford: James Currey.

_____. 2005. "To Fight or to Farm? Agrarian Dimensions of the Mano River Conflicts (Liberia and Sierra Leone)." African Affairs 104 (417).

_____. 2008. "A Comment on 'Remove or Reform?'" August. http://afraf.oxfordjournals.org/cgi/eletters/107/428/387 (12/16/2008).

Richards, P., K. Bah, and J. Vincent. 2004. "Social Capital and Survival: Prospects for Community-Driven Development in Post-Conflict Sierra Leone." Social Development Paper 12. Social Development Department, World Bank.

Tangri, R. "Central–Local Politics in Contemporary Sierra Leone," *African Affairs* 77 (1978): 165–73.

_____. 1978. "Local Government Institutions in Sierra Leone." *Journal of Administration Overseas* 17 (1): 17–27; (2): 118–28.

Thompson, B. 2007. "Sierra Leone: Reform or Relapse? Conflict and Governance Reform." Royal Institute of International Affairs. London: Chatham House.

Truth and Reconciliation Commission of Sierra Leone. 2004. "The Final Report of the Truth and Reconciliation Commission of Sierra Leone." http://trcsierraleone.org/drwebsite/publish/index.shtml (1/7/09).

United Nations Development Programme. 1993. *Human Development Report 1993.* New York: Oxford University Press.

Whiteside, K. 2007. "Decentralization Watch: The First Three Years of Decentralization in Sierra Leone." Institutional Reform and Capacity Building Project (IRCBP), Freetown. September. http://www.ircbpeval.com/reports/index.html

Whiteside, K. 2007. The Decentralization Watch Survey. July. www.ircbpeval.com

World Bank. 1998. "The World Bank's Experience with Post-Conflict Reconstruction." Operations Evaluation Department.

_____. 2003. "Sierra Leone: Strategic Options for Public Sector Reform." Report 25110. Africa Region Public Sector Reform Unit.

_____. 2004. "Recent Bank Support for Civil Service Reconstruction in Post-Conflict Countries." In "Findings" #241.

_____. 2006a. Hammad, R., and B. Ammari. "Sierra Leone: The Role of the Rapid Results Approach in Decentralization and Strengthening Local Governance." In "Findings" #261. April. PREM (Poverty Reduction, Economic Management and Social Policy), World Bank. www.worldbank.org/afr/findings/english/find261.htm.

_____. 2006b. "Justice for the Poor and Understanding Processes of Change in Local Governance." Sierra Leone Concept Note. Africa Region Public Sector Reform Unit. December.

_____. 2008. "Decentralization in Client Countries: An Evaluation of World Bank Support 1990–2007." Independent Evaluation Group.

URLs

http://www.worldbank.org/justiceforthepoor.

Eco-Audit

Environmental Benefits Statement

The World Bank is committed to preserving Endangered Forests and natural resources. We print World Bank Working Papers and Country Studies on postconsumer recycled paper, processed chlorine free. The World Bank has formally agreed to follow the recommended standards for paper usage set by Green Press Initiative—a nonprofit program supporting publishers in using fiber that is not sourced from Endangered Forests. For more information, visit www.greenpressinitiative.org.

In 2008, the printing of these books on recycled paper saved the following:

Trees*	Solid Waste	Water	Net Greenhouse Gases	Total Energy
355	16,663	129,550	31,256	247 mil.
*40 feet in height and 6–8 inches in diameter	Pounds	Gallons	Pounds CO_2 Equivalent	BTUs

green press INITIATIVE